Railtown

The publisher gratefully acknowledges the generous support of the Lisa See Endowment Fund in Southern California History and Culture of the University of California Press Foundation.

Railtown

THE FIGHT FOR THE LOS ANGELES
METRO RAIL AND THE FUTURE OF THE CITY

Ethan N. Elkind

UNIVERSITY OF CALIFORNIA PRESS

BERKELEY LOS ANGELES LONDON

University of California Press, one of the most distinguished university presses in the United States, enriches lives around the world by advancing scholarship in the humanities, social sciences, and natural sciences. Its activities are supported by the UC Press Foundation and by philanthropic contributions from individuals and institutions. For more information, visit www.ucpress.edu.

University of California Press
Berkeley and Los Angeles, California

University of California Press, Ltd.
London, England

Library of Congress Cataloging-in-Publication Data

Elkind, Ethan N., 1976–.
  Railtown : the fight for the Los Angeles Metro Rail and the future of the city / Ethan N. Elkind.
      p.   cm.
  Includes bibliographical references and index.
  ISBN 978-0-520-27826-4 (cloth : alk. paper)
  ISBN 978-0-520-27827-1 (pbk. : alk. paper)
      1. Local transit—California—Los Angeles.   2. Urban transportation—California—Los Angeles.   I. Title.
  HE4491.L75E45   2014
  388.4 20979494—dc23   2013017251

Manufactured in the United States of America

23   22   21   20   19   18   17   16   15   14
10   9   8   7   6   5   4   3   2   1

In keeping with a commitment to support environmentally responsible and sustainable printing practices, UC Press has printed this book on Natures Natural, a fiber that contains 30% post-consumer waste and meets the minimum requirements of ANSI/NISO Z39.48-1992 (R 1997) (*Permanence of Paper*).

In memory of my grandfather, Milton N. Nathanson, who rode the Santa Monica Boulevard bus to work every day, and my grandmother, Maria P. Nathanson.

CONTENTS

ILLUSTRATIONS

ACKNOWLEDGMENTS

This book began in the fall of 2004 when, as a second-year law student at UCLA School of Law, I enrolled in a seminar on California legal history. The instructor was professor and former law school dean Susan Westerberg Prager, who designed the course with the somewhat unusual belief that lawyers are well trained to be historians, given their research and writing skills. With Professor Prager's indispensable encouragement, I decided to expand my seminar paper on Los Angeles transit history into this book.

Sean Hecht, executive director of the UCLA Environmental Law Center, provided crucial support for the effort. As a mentor, friend, and selfless advocate for students like me, Sean helped me secure a research grant, committed some of his center's funds, and provided feedback on drafts.

The John Randolph Haynes and Dora Haynes Foundation awarded the grant funds that enabled me to spend part of a year researching, writing, and traveling to archives and interviews. I thank Bill Burke and the foundation board members for their commitment to this story and to supporting social science research.

For the original seminar paper, I had the good fortune to interview former Los Angeles County supervisor Ed Edelman. He was generous with his time, opinions, and referrals, most notably to his chief deputy Bob Geoghegan, who helped bring the story to life through his anecdotes and insights. Residents of Los Angeles are lucky to have had both Bob and Supervisor Edelman as public servants. I was also fortunate to conduct interviews with numerous individuals who were involved in the story as it happened (they are listed in the bibliography). Their expertise and recollections filled important gaps in the history. I hope this story does justice to their efforts.

Various library and archive staff members helped me find source material in sometimes unlikely places. They include UCLA library archivist Chuck Wilson, Jenny Lentz at the UCLA Law Library, and Jeffery Rankin and the superb staff at the UCLA Special Collections Department. Thanks to Supervisor Edelman, I had access to his and Supervisor Kenneth Hahn's papers at the Huntington Library. David Pfeiffer at the National Archives and Records Administration in College Park, Maryland, single-handedly rescued my research trip to that archive by locating key federal papers. Los Angeles Metropolitan Transportation Authority librarian Mathew Barrett regularly provided resources and referrals, while Metro's Denise Villegas, Gayle Anderson, and Michael Lejeune located most of the photos and maps used in the book. In addition, various local transit leaders and experts helped me find material, including Steve Hymon, Gloria Ohland, Martin Wachs, Brian Taylor, Anastasia Loukaitou-Sideris, Ken Alpern, Bart Reed, and Damien Newton.

Many dedicated and smart colleagues in environmental law and policy influenced my thinking on the land use and transportation issues discussed in the book, including Ken Alex, Richard Frank, Terry Watt, Cliff Rechtschaffen, Cara Horowitz, Jonathan Zasloff, Meea Kang, David Mogavero, Geof Syphers, Curt Johansen, Kirstie Moore, and Chris Calfee. Historian Zachary Schrag gave me useful advice about book structure and approach. I also thank my colleagues, past and present, at the Center for Law, Energy and the Environment at Berkeley Law, including Dan Farber, Holly Doremus, Steve Weissman, Mike Kiparsky, Deborah Lambe, Jayni Foley Hein, and Caroline Cheng.

At UC Press, Kim Robinson offered thoughtful input and guidance; Stacy Eisenstark, Jessica Moll, and Elena McAnespie helped with production; and Anne Canright undertook diligent and careful review of the text. Two anonymous reviewers provided comments that sharpened my research and arguments.

Friends along the way made the work easier, particularly Dana and Beverly Palmer, Peter and Amber Schumacher, Peter and Kiersten Kampp, Mark and Shannon Lo, Joshua Dylan Mellars, Kenji Nimura, and Trevor and Kari Shelton, as well as my UCLA Law classmates and instructors. Family friends Stephen and Frances Tobriner and Marjorie and Ted Keeler provided helpful advice also.

I am thankful every day for my family, especially my parents, Peter and Sue Elkind. Their unwavering faith, support, and love made this book—and my career choices—possible. My in-laws Hank and Darlene Breiteneicher, Chris and Laura Lay, and Adam and Arianne Breiteneicher adopted me into their clan and have shown love and loyalty ever since. The Pankins (Stuart, Joy, Andy, and Shannon) provided steady nourishment and love during our time in Los Angeles.

Finally, mere words do not seem sufficient to acknowledge and thank my wife, Jessica. She supported me during many untold hours of work on the book, discussing key points, reviewing drafts, and offering welcome advice, all while ably balancing the responsibilities of family and a career as a historian. And to my three children, Caleb, Maya, and Sadie: I hope this book contributes in some way to improving the world that you and your generation inherit.

ABBREVIATIONS

BART	Bay Area Rapid Transit
BRT	Bus Rapid Transit
BRU	Bus Riders Union
Cal/OSHA	California Division of Occupational Safety and Health
Caltrans	California Department of Transportation
CEQA	California Environmental Quality Act
DOT	U.S. Department of Transportation
EIR/EIS	Environmental Impact Report/Statement (required under CEQA/NEPA)
FAA	Federal Aviation Administration
FTA	Federal Transit Administration
LACMA	Los Angeles County Museum of Art
LACMTA	Los Angeles County Metropolitan Transportation Authority ("Metro")
LACTC	Los Angeles County Transportation Commission
LATAX	Los Angeles Taxpayers Association
LAX	Los Angeles International Airport
L/CSC	Labor/Community Strategy Center
LDF	Legal Defense and Educational Fund of the NAACP
LRTP	Long Range Transportation Plan
Maglev	High Speed Magnetic Levitation train

MARTA	Metropolitan Atlanta Rapid Transit Authority
MOS	Minimum Operable Segment
MTA	*See* LACMTA
NAACP	National Association for the Advancement of Colored People
NEPA	National Environmental Policy Act
NIMBY	Not In My Backyard
NRDC	Natural Resources Defense Council
PMBLCA	Pasadena Metro Blue Line Construction Authority
RTD	*See* SCRTD
SCAG	Southern California Association of Governments
SCRTD	Southern California Rapid Transit District
TRO	Temporary Restraining Order
UCLA	University of California, Los Angeles
UMTA	Urban Mass Transportation Administration
USC	University of Southern California

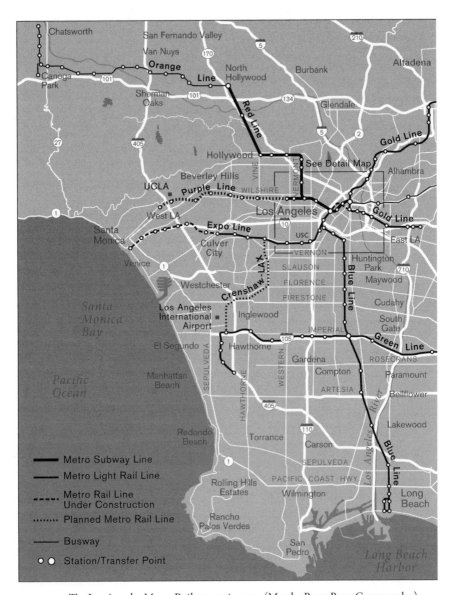

FIGURE 1. The Los Angeles Metro Rail system in 2013. (Map by Pease Press Cartography.)

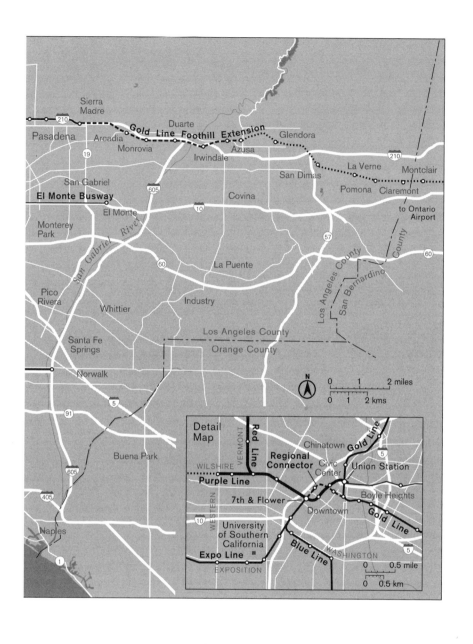

Sierra
Madre

Pasadena

Arcadia

Monrovia

Duarte

Gold Line Foothill Extension

Glendora

Azusa

Irwindale

San Dimas

La Verne

Montclair

San Gabriel

El Monte Busway

El Monte

Covina

Pomona

Claremont

to Ontario
Airport

Monterey
Park

San Gabriel River

La Puente

Pico
Rivera

Whittier

Industry

Los Angeles County

San Bernardino County

Santa Fe
Springs

Los Angeles County

Orange County

Norwalk

Buena Park

Naples

N

0   1   2 miles

0   1   2 kms

Detail
Map

VERMONT

Red Line

Chinatown

Gold Line

Regional
Connector

Civic
Center

Union Station

WILSHIRE

Purple Line

7th & Flower

WESTERN

Downtown

Boyle Heights

Gold Line

University
of Southern
California

Expo Line

Blue Line

WASHINGTON

EXPOSITION

0   0.5 mile

0   0.5 km

The design of this pueblo can be attributed to the whims of its founders as well as to those who later settled there, for they were of the same mind. The only order in the setting of the buildings is disorder, and neither proportion nor design is evident.

JUAN BANDINI, describing Nuestra Señora de
Los Angeles in 1830

Everybody loves the sound of a train in the distance
Everybody thinks it's true

PAUL SIMON, from the song
"Train in the Distance"

Introduction

THE ONCE AND FUTURE RAILTOWN

IN SEPTEMBER 1985, one person controlled the fate of the Los Angeles Metro Rail subway. After more than a decade of planning, numerous political compromises, and millions of dollars' worth of studies, final legislation to fund half of the subway's initial construction costs was pending in Congress. But in a sudden turn of fortune, a powerful liberal congressman from Los Angeles stood ready to vote against it. Henry Waxman was both the local representative and the gatekeeper for wealthy Los Angeles political donors. His opposition would be fatal to a vote in the U.S. House of Representatives.[1]

Up until that year, Waxman had been a nominal supporter of Metro Rail. But he had privately become concerned about gentrification impacts on a historically Jewish community in his district and begun to doubt the overall merits of the system.[2] When a methane gas explosion occurred in March 1985 near the proposed subway route in his district, he used the incident to question the safety of building the line. Stunned rail supporters scrambled to convince him otherwise, citing overwhelming evidence about the safety of tunneling through methane-rich areas. But Waxman was now poised not just to kill funding for the line in his district, but to pull the plug on the entire eighteen-mile subway, regardless of where the methane might be.

Waxman's colleague and friend Representative Julian Dixon moved to intervene. Dixon was a longtime rail supporter who represented a largely African American constituency to the south of Waxman. He hoped to save the subway so it could serve his transit-dependent constituents who wanted access to it. Subway officials huddled in Dixon's office, sketching on a napkin Waxman's methane zone and an alternate route south into Dixon's district.[3] After three days of high-powered lobbying,[4] and just an hour before the floor vote, Waxman relented with a handshake deal. He would allow Metro Rail to survive, but the subway could not enter his district. Congress then approved $429 million for the first phase of construction.[5]

The Waxman compromise, however, threatened to fundamentally undermine the subway's effectiveness. Only one corridor in Los Angeles truly cried out for a subway, based on its population and jobs density, and that was Wilshire Boulevard. Waxman's legislation now banned the subway from serving the most heavily traveled part of Wilshire, with twice as many residents and fives times the number of workers as along Dixon's route, even if new evidence and further study could prove that tunneling would be safe.[6]

Forced to appease one congressman, subway supporters had just bargained away the most effective route for a $3.3 billion investment.

RAIL COMES TO LOS ANGELES

The Waxman-Dixon agreement represented the latest, and possibly the harshest, in a string of political compromises that went into building the Los Angeles Metro Rail system. The ability of one individual like Waxman to distort the subway route at the last minute emblemized the system's history. As Metro Rail proponents quickly learned, building rail in the decentralized democracy of Los Angeles meant appeasing various political fiefdoms, neighborhood groups, and political leaders who too often insisted on mollifying their loudest constituents at the expense of the regional good.

How did Los Angeles, a modern megacity that developed around the car, end up with a rail transit system like Metro Rail? What forces shaped its design and scale? What lessons from its development should influence the future of Metro Rail and other urban rail systems? And what does this story tell other car-oriented cities wishing to develop anew around rail?

At its core, Metro Rail resulted from the determination of optimistic local leaders who viewed rail as the solution to the region's traffic and environmental problems and the missing piece necessary to elevate Los Angeles into a world-class city. These leaders ultimately convinced a diverse, enormous, and traffic-suffering electorate, as well as federal officials, to support a limited rail program.

The resulting multibillion-dollar Metro Rail system is today a permanent feature of Los Angeles. As of 2013, it consists of an 18.6-mile heavy rail subway system (heavy rail trains receive power from electrified third rails) and a 69-mile light rail network (less expensive light rail trains receive power from overhead lines, like streetcars). Metro Rail serves over 350,000 riders daily in the second-largest city in the United States. (Metrolink is the region's long-distance commuter rail system, which is not the subject of this book.) Except for brief periods of dormancy, the system has been in a continuous state of expansion since the early 1990s. Remarkably, all of this rail development occurred in the city that pioneered and glamorized the car-oriented suburban lifestyle, while defining traffic and sprawl for the world.

Despite the successes, missed opportunities and wasted investments have hindered Metro Rail's effectiveness. The enormous scale of Los Angeles, with its sprawling and diffuse political centers, divided decision-making authority over rail and led to sometimes petty regional competition for scarce rail funds. As a result, a few powerful leaders were able to wield disproportionate influence over regional decisions, leading to sometimes crippling concessions on rail routes. Rail supporters had to propose lines that would serve (or avoid) crucial centers of political power in the region, and not necessarily the areas of greatest ridership potential. When it came to determining rail routes, the political map seemed to matter more than the actual map of where people lived and worked.

The negative results played into the hands of rail critics, particularly many urban planning scholars and transportation economists. From the earliest stages of planning, they consistently argued that rail was never a good idea for Los Angeles (or for most car-oriented cities, for that matter). Local critics like urban planning scholar Martin Wachs of the University of California, Los Angeles, and transportation economist Peter Gordon of the University of Southern California viewed rail as wasteful and inefficient for cities like Los Angeles that were sprawling and decentralized and unlikely to change.[7] Rail to them was at best an irrational waste of public resources[8] and at worst an antimarket attempt to force people out of the car-loving, suburban American Dream lifestyle and into cramped East Asian–style living.[9] Instead they recommended low-cost alternatives, such as enhanced, more frequent, and cheaper bus service; one-way streets; congestion pricing (tolls and fees to discourage traffic); bus-only lanes on roads and highways; and deregulated taxi service.[10]

But building a successful and effective rail system in Los Angeles was not necessarily a fatally flawed idea. It just needed to be done right. Over the years, transportation scholars developed a range of formulas, factors, and qualitative approaches to distinguish successful urban rail systems from the failures.[11] Despite the variety of metrics, the general consensus was simple:

the most effective rail systems serve significant concentrations of jobs, retail, services, and housing around the stations and along the corridors they travel. More of this station-area development produces more riders.[12] And more paying riders means reduced public subsidies required to operate the system, with more people benefiting from transit investments.[13] Meanwhile, the station-area development can accommodate projected population growth and housing demand in a more sustainable manner than sprawl.[14]

By these measures, Los Angeles possessed neighborhoods and corridors that could arguably support rail investment. Generally, expensive heavy-rail technology was appropriate for high-density areas like the Wilshire corridor, which represents the most densely populated corridor in the western United States,[15] while light rail service made sense for neighborhoods with significant multifamily housing and job centers, such as the Eastside or West Los Angeles communities. Although not rail, bus rapid transit, with buses built like rail cars and operated in their own lanes or dedicated rights-of-way, worked for multifamily residential communities and job centers, as currently in place in the San Fernando Valley. Finally, with proper planning, local buses, bicycle hubs, bikeways, walkways, and shuttles could radiate from this rail and rapid bus network to reach outlying homes and jobs.

The Los Angeles Metro Rail ended up serving a number of these prime areas successfully. However, residents in some critical parts of the metropolitan region have had to wait while less populated areas with more political power or less organized resistance received rail service. Compounding matters, rail has failed to catalyze private investment around station areas on a number of routes. In some cases, local communities resisted this development, while in others, the route location was so unfriendly to new development that significant public subsidies would be required to spur private investment. These failures have limited Metro Rail's ridership and wasted a significant portion of the investment.

RAIL LEADERS

Early rail leaders were generally aware of the conditions needed to build a successful rail network, but they focused their efforts on the formidable task of simply getting the system started. Former Los Angeles mayor Tom Bradley was at the forefront of these early supporters, and he dedicated much of his twenty-year career as mayor to selling the region on Metro Rail. He worked with allies and elected officials at the federal, state, and local levels as well as representatives from various business and advocacy groups. Starting in earnest in the early 1970s, these leaders waged a determined and often uncoordinated campaign to plan, fund, and oversee construction of Metro Rail.

Rail supporters initially viewed rail as a panacea for the famous traffic, air quality, and sprawl problems of Los Angeles. Like their compatriots in cities such as San Francisco, Washington, D.C., and Atlanta who also pursued modern urban rail projects in the decades following World War II, Bradley and many of his allies were New Deal–style leaders with an overly optimistic confidence in the power of rail. They believed rail would reshape Los Angeles into a more convenient, clean, and economically vibrant place while generating well-paying construction jobs. Supporters from African American and Latino communities believed that rail could knit together neighborhoods segregated by class, race, and ethnicity and provide much-needed access to job centers. Rail would turn Los Angeles into a city more like others around the world, where residents would not have to purchase cars, could walk to services and transit, and could be whisked away on a train to get where they wanted to go. It could, they believed, become a modern railtown.

But rail supporters severely underestimated the difficulty and cost of building their envisioned system. Their desire to persuade the voters skewed their public pronouncements, leading to unrealistic ridership and cost estimates that often proved to be wildly incorrect.[16] They also lacked experience building modern rail transit in Los Angeles, which involved a host of new technologies and laws and regulations. These factors tended to increase costs and delay projects, ultimately reducing the grandiose visions for a comprehensive system to just a few rail lines.

A HISTORY OF RAIL

Rail leaders' advocacy efforts were both helped and hurt by the city's development history. On one hand, modern Los Angeles began as a railtown. When the transcontinental railroad barons connected Los Angeles to the rest of the country in the 1870s and 1880s, real estate developers, as exemplified by Henry Huntington, immediately capitalized on the ensuing population boom.[17] They financed light rail lines (referred to as "streetcars") across the relatively flat landscape to create demand for their far-flung, single-family-home subdivisions. New residents could now live far from the city center in suburban railtowns and take the streetcar to jobs and services.[18] Huntington eventually consolidated these trains into the comprehensive Pacific Electric light rail system, known as the Yellow and Red Cars (fig. 2). To the benefit of modern rail supporters, some of the original rail rights-of-way remained undeveloped, even in the heart of the city.

But as Scott Bottles described in *Los Angeles and the Automobile,* the extensive streetcar system ironically led to the current auto-oriented sprawl, which originally clustered around the spokes of the old streetcar network.[19] This growth occurred haphazardly, driven by real estate interests rather than by good urban planning. "Unlike almost every other city in the world," wrote William Fulton in *The Reluctant Metropolis,* "metropolitan Los Angeles did not grow by radiating from a single center. It appeared when many different centers blurred together."[20]

The automobile quickly came to dominate Los Angeles, making the case for a modern rail line more challenging. While car sales increased in cities all across America at the time,[21] automobiles were particularly popular in this sprawling metropolis built on flat land with pleasant weather. Angelenos adopted the car en masse in the 1920s, which was also a time of enormous population growth.[22] As a result, streetcars began to fall out of favor. Compared to cars, they were slow and less convenient, and their frequent stops and street crossings often created traffic jams.[23] As streetcars began losing money in Los Angeles and other cities around the country for similar reasons,[24] elected officials and the voting public directed funds to support automobile infrastructure instead. In the end, municipalities in Los Angeles and other cities took over the streetcars but never rescued them.[25] The last Red Car, on the route from downtown Los Angeles to Long Beach, stopped service in 1961.

The new car culture encouraged more development across Los Angeles, creating complex and disorganized travel patterns that seemed to disfavor centralized rail service. Downtown Los Angeles hosted a decreasing percentage of the regional jobs as businesses spread out to meet employees where they lived, where land costs were lower and parking and vehicle access easier. By the 1990s, downtown accounted for only 6 percent of the jobs in the region.[26] Commuters in Los Angeles began traveling in different directions from jobs to services to homes, without a strong central business district to serve as a focal point for rapid transit. The car dependency also exacerbated racial inequality in Los Angeles, as low-income African American and Latino residents without cars now had to travel longer distances to dispersed job centers,

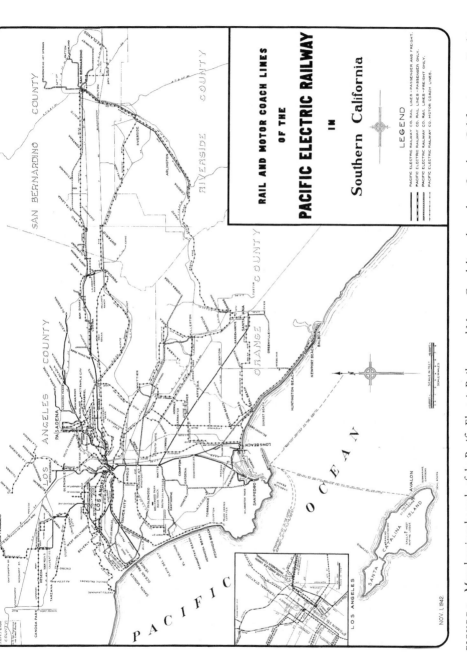

FIGURE 2. Map showing the scale of the Pacific Electric Railway and Motor Coach lines throughout Southern California, 1942. By this point, the system was already in decline. (Courtesy of the Los Angeles County Metropolitan Transportation Authority Research Library and Archive. Reprinted with permission.)

often on slow-moving and crowded buses.[27] In addition, the vast geographic area meant that the distances between urban centers in Los Angeles were immense compared to other major world cities, adding to the expense of providing effective rail service.[28]

As the serious environmental consequences of the new, car-dependent Los Angeles became ever more apparent, however, the public was primed to begin supporting rail transit. Air quality declined precipitously from the 1940s through the 1960s to the worst levels in the country, eventually helping to inspire state legislation and the federal Clean Air Act. Developers rapidly converted open space and agricultural land to new subdivisions, erasing many of the vistas and rural charm that originally drew residents to the area. Some of the worst traffic in the nation became an endless feature of life in Los Angeles.[29] In addition, the dependence on the automobile meant dependence on foreign oil, which left Los Angeles and most of the country vulnerable to gas price spikes caused by instability in the Middle East in the 1970s.

Citing these impacts in making their case to the public, rail leaders began to forge a growing pro-rail coalition. Members included residents nostalgic for the lost Pacific Electric rail system and tired of the smog and traffic, downtown businesses that wanted to attract workers and keep downtown from becoming an economic wasteland,[30] and a growing environmental movement reacting against the pollution and other consequences of the industrial economy. Eventually, construction-related firms and labor unions joined the effort in the hope of developing business opportunities from rail construction.

Rail supporters faced a steep political challenge to convince the local electorate—and subsequently federal decision-makers—that rail was worth funding. Just as development sprawled in Los Angeles, political power sprawled. The byzantine political structure of Los Angeles included eighty-eight cities, an enormous county, and state and federal representatives and agencies. Underlying these entities were communities segregated by class, race, and ethnicity. For example, African American residents south of downtown Los Angeles and Latinos in East Los Angeles tended to support rail transit for the access to jobs and services, given the higher number of "transit dependents" in these areas who did not have access to automobiles. By contrast, a number of leaders in Orthodox Jewish enclaves in Hollywood and the San Fernando Valley objected to rail out of concern that it would disrupt religious lifestyles and communities. Meanwhile, a few influential representatives of wealthy white neighborhoods along proposed routes in the city's

Westside opposed rail out of fear of neighborhood impacts and crime.[31] Without a regional consensus among these various political entities and communities, nothing would get built.

The problem was particularly acute at the county level. Most modern rail projects began via county ballot initiatives to raise funds, usually through a bond issue or new sales tax. For example, both the San Francisco Bay Area and Atlanta successfully passed county funding initiatives for rail during the 1960s and early 1970s. Both of these metropolitan regions covered multiple counties, so when elected leaders in some of the counties decided not to pursue the ballot initiatives,[32] the remaining counties in the urban core continued with successful votes.

But in Los Angeles, rail leaders did not have that option. Los Angeles County is simply enormous. Its four thousand square miles are more than the states of Rhode Island and Delaware combined, with a 2010 population greater than those of forty-two individual U.S. states. In addition to the eighty-eight cities, the county contains vast unincorporated areas within its borders from the Pacific Coast to the west, the semirural high desert to the north, Long Beach to the south, and suburbanized inland valleys to the east. While the City of Los Angeles dominates other county cities in terms of size and power, its amoebalike borders envelop only part of the urbanized areas of Los Angeles (including downtown Los Angeles). In some cases, the City of Los Angeles completely surrounds other independent cities, like Beverly Hills, West Hollywood, and Culver City. Unifying this vast and diverse region would require significant compromises on the route locations and type of transit offered.

Partly as a result of this expansive jurisdiction, early efforts at the county level led to failure. The state legislature created the Southern California Rapid Transit District (SCRTD) in Los Angeles County in 1964 in part to get a subway built down the Wilshire Boulevard corridor from downtown. After four years, agency leaders finally convinced the five county supervisors (known as the "Five Little Kings") to put a sales tax initiative on the ballot. But after a countywide campaign for a new rail system, voters rejected the tax decisively. Rail leaders would have to develop transit plans with broader appeal to earn the support of county voters.

The size of the county was not the only challenge, however. Opposition to urban rail became entrenched nationwide in the post–World War II era, primarily on the part of antigovernment conservatives who resented spending (in their view, wasting) public dollars on urban infrastructure projects that they deemed inefficient and contrary to their values. These critics viewed the suburban lifestyle, with its dependence on cars, cheap gasoline, and abundant land, as the ultimate expression of people's preferences and liberty. Because rail projects primarily benefited urban residents, many skeptics viewed rail investments as part of a larger social engineering effort to force people back into cities.

In Los Angeles, many of these opposition voters lived in the outskirts of the county or in suburban areas that would never receive direct rail service. These regions grew significantly in population during the "white flight" years of the 1960s through 1980s, as white families with schoolchildren fled the City of Los Angeles to avoid the crime and deteriorating academic quality that they feared would result from school desegregation.[33] Many of the urban communities they fled, such as East Los Angeles, became populated by Latinos and African Americans. These suburbanites expressed more local reasons for opposing rail, including fear that rail would bring crime and poverty and lead to the "Manhattanization" of Los Angeles.

Eventually, these homeowners and like-minded residents in wealthier urban areas used their organized associations to fight proposed rail lines. (By contrast, renters tended to be less organized and without the resources to mobilize.) Often referred to derisively by rail supporters as NIMBYs (Not In My Backyard), these residents vocalized sometimes extreme fears about impacts such as increased traffic, parking challenges, blight, gentrification, and criminal elements infiltrating their neighborhoods. Group leaders often dominated public hearings, solicited media attention, and used legal challenges to slow or halt rail lines. Despite their relatively small numbers and sometimes baseless concerns, they used their wealth and political sophistication to wield disproportionate influence over local elected leaders who were all too often willing to accommodate them at the expense of the regional good.

THE UNSTOPPABLE TRAIN

Over time, these rail opponents successfully thwarted a number of proposed lines and extracted concessions on others. But they ultimately were unable to stop Metro Rail completely. In this respect, rail critics in Los Angeles lost the debate: rail now exists in the region and is unlikely to be dismantled, barring economic collapse or massive voter backlash. Voters, particularly in the urban core of Los Angeles, have increasingly affirmed their support for rail, despite periods of negativism. And market trends indicate that a growing segment of homebuyers want more transit-oriented and walkable neighborhoods.[34] The debate in Los Angeles and other cities with burgeoning rail programs is now less about whether or not to build rail but instead how to ensure that transit leaders build rail in the right places and in the most effective manner.

To that end, this book seeks to show the historical context for the decisions and compromises that shaped the development of an urban rail system in car-dominated Los Angeles. It reveals the pressures, personalities, and options facing decision makers at each juncture of Metro Rail and uncovers the sometimes messy and unseemly process of forging consensus in the sprawling political context of Los Angeles. Starting with Tom Bradley's seminal campaign for mayor in 1973 on a platform that promised a new subway, the story follows early efforts to achieve consensus and funding, describes the planning and construction of the early system, details the myriad financial and political setbacks, and concludes with the beginning of a new era of rail expansion starting in 2008. Fighting bruising political battles in sometimes desperate fashion, rail leaders during this period managed to bring rail back to the consummate car city.

ONE

An Eighteen-Month Promise

IN SOME WAYS, THE LOS ANGELES Metro Rail began with a misstatement. At least, that is how Tom Bradley described it. On May 23, 1973, Bradley, a Los Angeles city councilman, was in the midst of a bitter campaign for mayor in a rematch against incumbent Sam Yorty. A week before the election, Bradley called a press conference to emphasize his transportation agenda for the city. In this famous car town, transportation had become a dominant issue. Angelenos were facing higher fuel costs, traffic nightmares, and hazardous smog, and many viewed rail as the solution to these problems.

Bradley shared this belief in the benefits of rail. He made the creation of a subway system his top political priority and became its leading founder. As he had demonstrated throughout his life, he was tenacious and determined to see it happen. After all, Bradley was the son of a Texas sharecropper and the grandson of former slaves. His family had moved to Los Angeles when he was a youth, and this ambitious young African American man became high school class president and an all-city football player. He joined the Los Angeles Police Department in 1940 and studied at night to earn his law degree. In 1963, he was elected to the Los Angeles City Council. Perseverance and overcoming adversity were in his nature.

But giving speeches was not. His career as a police officer had not afforded him many opportunities for public speaking, and early in his political career he would simply stand and read speeches word-for-word. Although he developed more confidence over the years, he often found himself caught between reading and trying to speak from memory as he looked out at the audience.[1] So as reporters in the press conference peppered Bradley with questions, he told them that his number one priority was "to get Los Angeles moving on a rapid transit system," and he criticized the "twelve years of neglect and

FIGURE 3. Los Angeles mayor Tom Bradley toward the beginning of his political career. (Courtesy of the Los Angeles County Metropolitan Transportation Authority Research Library and Archive. Reprinted with permission.)

lackadaisical leadership from Sam Yorty." By contrast, Bradley blurted, he would start construction of a high-speed rapid transit system "within eighteen months" of the day he took office.[2]

He immediately regretted making such an unrealistic promise. The night before the press conference, he later claimed, his aides had presented him with a plan to begin groundbreaking on a subway within eighteen months. Bradley looked at the eighteen-month reference in the policy statement and told his staff to remove it. He knew that the city could not begin work on a project of this magnitude so quickly and called the time frame a "dangerous statement to include." But under the glare of the media lights at the press conference, the eighteen-month time frame "had been so firmly embedded in my mind that it popped out almost spontaneously." In the coming years, as Bradley engaged in an all-consuming effort to achieve political consensus on the route of a new rail transit system for Los Angeles and to secure the billions of dollars in federal, state, and local funds to build it, he found himself plagued by the promise of the deadline. "From that point on," he lamented, "I was never able to get away from it."[3]

THE SPHINX

Bradley beat Yorty in the election of 1973 and became one of the first African American mayors of a major city. He immediately assumed a stature of national significance—one that he would capitalize on in his efforts to bring rail to Los Angeles. With his shy demeanor, he was not a typical politician, and he towered over most people with his tall, athletic frame. His former chief of staff, Ray Remy, noted that his taciturn and aloof demeanor during meetings led people to call him "sphinxlike." He was unfailingly polite to all who knew and worked with him and took a conciliatory approach to leadership that his critics described as cautious. "Tom's very nature as mayor," Remy observed, "was that he tried to find consensus and bring people together. He didn't twist arms but did a lot of 'let's reason together.'"[4]

Bradley had been a booster of public transit from the beginning of his career.[5] He helped spark legislative action in 1971 to amend the state gas tax law to allow its use for public transportation projects[6]—a change that proved crucial to funding the future rail system. In his bid for mayor, Bradley promised voters a world-class rail system for an emerging world-class city. His public advocacy framed rail as a solution for most of the region's ills. A subway would bring the city status, traffic relief, economic prosperity, environmental benefits, and good jobs.[7] He believed that a subway would "make Los Angeles an accessible city" and give it equal stature to other major cities around the world.[8] "Los Angeles is the last of the great cities of the world to secure an underground rapid transit system," he told voters.[9]

To his supporters, this new mayor was a visionary with strong ambition. Supervisor Ed Edelman, who served with Bradley on the city council, described him as someone who "looked ahead to what the area needed and wasn't just interested in looking good. He wanted to accomplish something."[10] He was also a New Deal–style Democrat, and he viewed rail as an economic stimulus tool that would create high-paying construction jobs and stimulate economic activity through station-area real estate development and by leveraging federal funds. As a result, he had strong support from labor leaders. In addition, Bradley believed a subway would benefit residents' quality of life because it "will impact the economy, permit people to move from jobs to homes, reduce the headaches of traffic congestion and it will reduce air pollution."[11]

Bradley was sworn in as mayor by U.S. Supreme Court chief justice Earl Warren, who wrote the *Brown v. Board of Education* decision that ended segregation in the United States. In his inaugural address, Bradley vowed to make transportation his number one priority.[12] He worked immediately to line up funding for rail. But he also publicly backed off the eighteen-month pledge and promised instead that groundbreaking on the subway would happen within four years.[13]

Bradley needed to marshal all sources of funding for rail, from the city, county, state, and especially the federal government. The federal government had been offering significant funding for rail since the early 1960s, when President John F. Kennedy proposed a program of federal investment in building urban mass transit systems. In 1964, a coalition of local governments, downtown business interests, and labor groups pushed Congress to set aside $500 million for capital investments in cities across the country. By 1970, this coalition had grown to include the burgeoning environmental movement, and Congress and a receptive President Nixon increased the funding level five-fold.[14]

The federal offer was generous: if a city could find 20 percent of the funds to build a rail system, the U.S. government would provide the other 80 percent. Local transit agencies would have to apply to the Urban Mass Transportation Administration (UMTA), a division of the U.S. Department of Transportation, which decided the allocation of federal grants on a competitive basis. Federal funding for mass transit was now comparable to that for interstate highways, which received 90 percent of their funding from Washington. However, the era of federal largesse was ultimately brief when it came to investing in the country's urban transit infrastructure.

Bradley immediately tried to assemble a grant package for UMTA. He would need both the 20 percent local match and a plan for a rail route that had broad political support. He worked to secure state gas tax funds for the local match, using Los Angeles County's share of the state gas tax revenue and traveling repeatedly to Sacramento to lobby the state legislature to commit state gas tax funds to the project.[15]

But the gas tax alone would not be enough. So Bradley worked to place before the county voters an initiative to raise the sales tax 1 percent from the then-current 6 percent to fund rail. The state legislature had authorized such a tax in 1964 when it created the Los Angeles County transit agency, called the Southern California Rapid Transit District (RTD).[16] Bradley decided to use his influence on the RTD to get the agency to place a measure on the ballot.

As mentioned in the introduction, RTD leaders had tried this approach before without luck. In 1968, the agency placed a half-cent sales tax measure on the ballot to fund a sixty-two-mile rail system, which voters rejected.[17] Bradley, however, hoped that the wave of political support that elected him would translate into a sales tax victory. Voter approval of a sales tax hike would at once secure the local match and demonstrate to the federal government that the region was committed to rapid transit.

Bradley recognized that winning support from a county as diverse and enormous as Los Angeles would require a "balanced" plan involving roads, buses, and rail. The RTD therefore drafted an initiative that would dedicate half of the sales tax revenue to county buses and the other half to a 145-mile rail transit network.[18] The plan would appeal to county bus riders and rural voters who had no interest in a downtown-oriented rail system. Bradley felt that having the vote within eighteen months of taking office would partially fulfill his eighteen-month campaign promise.[19]

THE CAMPAIGN FOR 1974'S PROPOSITION A

Bradley began campaigning for Proposition A, as the sales tax measure was designated, and forged a coalition of downtown business leaders, civic organizations, and labor groups, as well as some of the leading politicians in the region and state.[20] His strategy was to keep the rail route as vague as possible to avoid creating political controversies, advocating for fixed guideway service (without specifying the technology) in eight broad, heavily traveled corridors.[21] Publicly, he tended to focus as much on the countywide expanded bus service as on the rail plan.

Proposition A supporters unveiled a modest media campaign to earn public support. It included just a few television and radio advertisements and a direct mail campaign. But the media efforts appeared to be hamstrung by the imprecision of the rail plan. Because Bradley had kept the details vague to gain consensus, the overall media message to the public was not specific enough to be effective. The television campaign centered on one sixty-second celebrity spot featuring actor Jack Lemmon standing next to a freeway jammed with cars during rush hour. Lemmon looked into the camera, extolled the benefits of public transportation and how badly Los Angeles needed it, and recited the theme of the advertising campaign for Proposition A: "The time is now."[22]

But rail critics soon began to surface. Most influential among them were transit experts in government and academia whose studies of the economic value of rail led them to believe that rail was a poor investment. Their opinions carried political weight because the media often trumpeted their conclusions to the voters. As one example, Peter Marcuse, a Los Angeles City planning commissioner and a professor of urban planning at UCLA, came out strongly against rail transit in Los Angeles in the spring of 1974, with a detailed critique of the rail plan entitled "Mass Transit for the Few: The Case Against the SCRTD Plan."[23] He criticized the proposal for, among other things, involving a regressive sales tax, promoting sprawl by making it easier for people to live outside the city center and commute by rail to work downtown, and benefiting primarily middle-class riders and wealthy real estate owners. A nervous Norm Emerson, one of Bradley's advisors, described Marcuse's critique as a "potentially damaging piece." Although "many of [Marcuse's] points are valid," Emerson wrote in a memo, he worried that "public consumption [of Marcuse's findings] could be harmful to our efforts."[24]

As the campaign reached its closing days, Mayor Bradley dedicated himself to campaigning throughout the county. He delivered speeches in favor of Proposition A that he tailored to each county region. On the Eastside of Los Angeles, Bradley touted the plan for rail stations that would link to employment centers in downtown Los Angeles and Orange County. For the high-bus-ridership areas of South Central, Watts, and Compton, the mayor spoke of those communities' dependence on transit and how "residents will be able to get to employment, medical and recreational areas much easier than ever before," as well as the new jobs that the rail system would create.[25]

The poor reputation of the RTD, however, started to undercut Bradley's carefully honed political outreach. The RTD experienced a sixty-eight-day bus driver strike in 1974 that crippled the county's transit system, and most Angelenos appeared to blame the RTD. Bradley tried to disassociate the rail plan from the controversy. "Proposition A and the bus strike are two completely separate issues," he told audiences. "One dealt with working conditions, and one deals with solving traffic problems. I hope that you see the difference."[26]

The voters of Los Angeles County did not. In November 1974, they narrowly rejected Proposition A, with 47 percent in favor.[27] It was a stinging loss for Bradley, who had spent much of his first year and a half in office campaigning for the measure. The defeat also jeopardized the local matching funds and sent a signal to UMTA that the region was not yet ready for rail.

The mayor publicly blamed the loss on antitax sentiment and a lack of confidence in the RTD.[28] He argued that Proposition A was the victim of "bad timing," because "people got their [property] tax bills the weekend before the election" and were therefore unwilling to vote to raise taxes.[29] He could just as easily have blamed the enormous size of Los Angeles County, which contained a significant population of voters who lived far from the proposed system. Noting that 57 percent of the people in the city of Los Angeles voted in favor of the plan,[30] Bradley remarked that the proposed rail system "did not go into every neighborhood, and where it did not run in front of somebody's door, they simply were not that enthusiastic about supporting it."[31]

Bradley soon emerged with a new, less ambitious plan. As he later explained, "Since we couldn't get support for the entire system—and it was proposed for about 142 miles . . . we then said, let's take a more modest step. Let's try to develop plans for a starter line, something less than the full system."[32] Bradley hoped to build the rest of the system in successive stages from this starter line.

The problem with Bradley's "modest step" was that a smaller route meant less benefit to the region as a whole. Keeping a political coalition together for a large rail route was much easier than for a small one because many politicians would see rail coming to their districts. If Bradley's starter line were to succeed, he would need the support of the powerful county supervisors. That meant pleasing Baxter Ward.

THE TRANSIT SUMMIT

In 1972, Baxter Ward, a local KABC Channel 7 news anchor, won a coveted seat on the board of supervisors, representing the fifth district, which covered the northwestern part of the county from the San Fernando Valley to the Ventura and Kern County lines.

The board of supervisors was an elite club. In the mid-1970s, just five elected supervisors governed the seven million people living in Los Angeles County. Called the "five little kings" owing to the size of their districts and the relative electoral safety of their seats, they represented more constituents than all but eight U.S. governors and spent twice the money annually as the governments of El Salvador, Nicaragua, Honduras, and Costa Rica combined. They also functioned as both the executive and legislative branches of county government, which meant fewer checks on their authority.[33]

Ward became the critical swing vote on the five-member board, often forming a bloc with fellow supervisors and registered Democrats Ed Edelman and Kenneth Hahn to support rail efforts.[34] By virtue of his powerful position, Ward quickly became an important player in the debate over transit in Los Angeles.

Ward also loved trains. He had fond memories of riding them as a child, and he even had a large model train running in his office.[35] Shortly after joining the board, Ward convinced his fellow supervisors to purchase a historic train to run on existing freight track in the county. Critics ridiculed the plan as "Baxter's Choo-Choo."[36] Because Ward had helped Edelman during his campaign, Edelman felt compelled to vote for the plan as the deciding third vote. "So he bought this cockamamie train," Edelman later recalled, "and it turned out it had all sorts of problems. Eventually it was sold."[37]

Ward's ambitions for rail in Los Angeles differed markedly from Bradley's. Ward wanted a regional rail network to resurrect the defunct Pacific Electric routes and was not interested in Bradley's downtown-centered subway. He proposed using existing rail rights-of-way, such as the ones in use for freight operations and the abandoned Pacific Electric tracks. Ward advocated for a cheaper aboveground rail system that could be built faster and cover more of the county.[38]

Ward and Bradley's competing priorities were on a collision course. In May 1975, President Gerald Ford's secretary of transportation, William Coleman, privately indicated to local officials that a Los Angeles rail project would be "within the ability of UMTA to fund."[39] But Coleman also warned that "Los Angeles should choose a starter line corridor within 60–90 days" or else the federal government would not consider the city when allocating the funds.[40]

The city and county moved quickly to arrange some funds for the local match, with the Los Angeles City Council and the board of supervisors setting aside their respective shares of the Proposition 5 gas tax money (a statewide initiative to dedicate gas tax revenue to mass transit, approved by the voters in June 1974) for the rail line.[41]

Choosing a route would require consensus. The RTD staff sketched a broad corridor from Canoga Park on the west end of the San Fernando Valley, east through downtown Los Angeles, and then south to Long Beach at the southern end of the county. This corridor touched some of the primary power centers in the county but seemingly had little to do with the densest population centers, including most if not all of Wilshire Boulevard. The RTD had literally painted with a broad brush over the county map, "to let the federal government know we're in agreement on a 'broad' corridor," commented RTD general manager Jack Gilstrap at the time.[42]

Hoping this vague corridor would be sufficient for the Department of Transportation, RTD president Byron Cook submitted the plan to Coleman within the ninety-day deadline. He informed Coleman, however, that "specific route alignment, configuration, station locations and transit mode" still needed to be determined by local leaders.[43] Cook's submission qualified Los Angeles to apply for UMTA funding within the year, although local leaders still needed to offer more specificity.

But Ward and Bradley disagreed on the route details.[44] Bradley advocated a downtown- and Hollywood-based route via Wilshire Boulevard that would serve the major population and political centers within the city.[45] Ward proposed a suburban-oriented rail line that would mostly serve commuters coming into downtown from far away. "The bigger the starter line," Ward said, "the better it can serve the county."[46]

The conflict between the two leaders became personal. Ray Remy, Bradley's chief of staff, described the relationship between them as "strained." Bradley had not forgiven Ward for attacking the mayor publicly on his transportation plan. "Baxter fought Tom very vigorously on all of Tom's proposals," Remy noted. "Baxter was constantly trying to get commitments away from the Wilshire line" because "Wilshire was not part of Baxter's district." Remy believed that Ward's background as an investigative reporter gave him a more confrontational approach to politics. "It was such that people got annoyed with him," he observed.[47]

The Bradley-Ward impasse motivated state leaders to intervene in the dispute over the rail route before the UMTA proposal deadline. California governor Jerry Brown sent Donald Burns, secretary of the Business and Transportation Agency, to organize meetings with the key local players to develop consensus. On November 21, 1975, Bradley, Ward, and other rail leaders met in the California Highway Commission Room in Los Angeles to negotiate a starter line route. The organizers dubbed it a "transit summit," and it quickly became a game of political negotiation rather than a merit-based analysis of which rail routes could serve the most people.

At the summit, Ward offered a compromise that would start the first phase of the starter line with a route from Long Beach to Union Station in downtown Los Angeles. The second phase would travel from Union Station through his district in the San Fernando Valley. He was willing to start with Long Beach, even though it was far south of his district, because the starter line advocates needed Long Beach's portion of the state gas tax revenue to fund the line. As a major economic center within the county, Long Beach could potentially contribute an estimated $2.9 million over five years.[48]

Ward argued that his plan would "incorporate Long Beach's money, solve their problem, solve [Mayor Bradley's] problem in South Central Los Angeles and also serve a large portion of the Central Business District to the tunnel." He concluded by stating that his plan "solves our problem for money today" and represented a "compromise of the needs, aspirations."[49]

Mayor Thomas Clark of Long Beach extolled the political benefits of Ward's proposal. Of the twenty-five miles along the route, he argued, "Long Beach has six, Los Angeles has over twelve and the County has almost four. So everyone is basically getting something out of that starter line . . . It's the only line I see that everyone gets something out of politically." Turning to Bradley, Clark said, "I don't know, Tom, if you get enough out of it politically or not, but you have over twelve miles, 48 percent of that's in the City of Los Angeles."[50]

Mayor Bradley was not convinced. "It just leaves me out such a large segment that it's going to be hard to convince our Council on it," he said. "I've been trying to quickly look at the patronage figures for each of these options," he continued. "In our first effort we're going to have to try to do something that represents a successful demonstration. If we ever hope to expand it we want to do a good job on that first phase."[51]

Ultimately, however, Bradley accepted Ward's compromise offer in order to reach a consensus. The leaders unanimously agreed that the first segment of the starter line would stretch from downtown to Long Beach.[52] Burns presented the consensus to Secretary Coleman on December 16, estimating the line to cost over $900 million.[53] Finally, after protracted negotiations with UMTA, by September 1976 the RTD grant application to fund studies on the starter line route was out the door.[54]

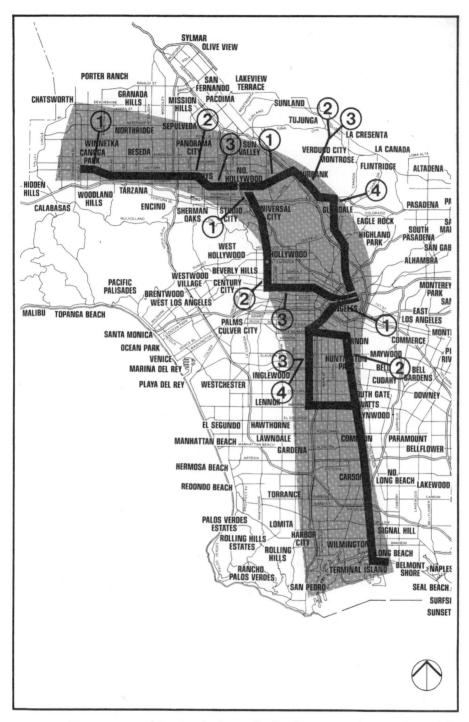

FIGURE 4. The 1975 proposed Los Angeles "starter line" and its permutations, as submitted for review to the U.S. Urban Mass Transportation Administration. (Courtesy of the Los Angeles County Metropolitan Transportation Authority Research Library and Archive. Reprinted with permission.)

Ward did not want to wait for UMTA to decide on the starter line proposal. "It would be tragic," he said, "if we were to allow ourselves to become delayed trying to collect enough money to build a small but gold-plated project. Such a process would be a betrayal to the people we are expected to serve."[55]

In the midst of the RTD's negotiations with UMTA, he announced a plan for the June 1976 ballot: a one cent sales tax increase to finance the development of a 260-mile (later pared down to 232-mile), multibillion-dollar regional rail network. Ward believed that state gas tax funds and federal matching dollars would be insufficient to begin a regional system. His plan envisioned using freeway, flood control channel, and railroad rights-of-way to develop a $7.5 billion light rail network. It would interlock with a future subway starter line and the potential Orange County regional rapid transit system to the south.[56] The rail lines in his proposal covered virtually all of the city of Los Angeles and its neighboring cities.

Harkening to his boyhood days riding the rail, Ward called the project the "Sunset Coast Line." In the proposal, he wrote: "Because the heart still returns to the rails, people still talk about the [Pacific Electric] Big Red Cars. . . . The Sunset Coast Line brings all that talk and nostalgia and hope together." Referring to the air quality problems in the Los Angeles Basin, he observed that "there is not a flicker of feeling for the bus. Their fumes add to our problems with the air." He argued that his plan would solve many problems, from "protecting the natural environment, enhancing the man-made environment, improving the level of movement . . . [and addressing the] uncertainty of energy supply."[57]

The proposal had one serious flaw, however: it was completely unworkable.[58] The cost and revenue figures did not add up, and Ward had neglected to include anyone else in developing the routes or the financing calculations. Even Ward's staffer Jonathan Beaty admitted that the plan was a "conceptual proposal with innumerable problems that have not been addressed."[59]

Despite the many questions surrounding the plan, Bradley and other rail leaders reluctantly announced their support for placing it on the ballot.[60] Facing reelection in another year and needing some kind of victory on transit, he described Ward's plan as another part of the strategy to combat gridlock. His press release stated that the proposed Sunset Coast Line "fits nicely into the balanced concept," and he emphasized the "big transportation

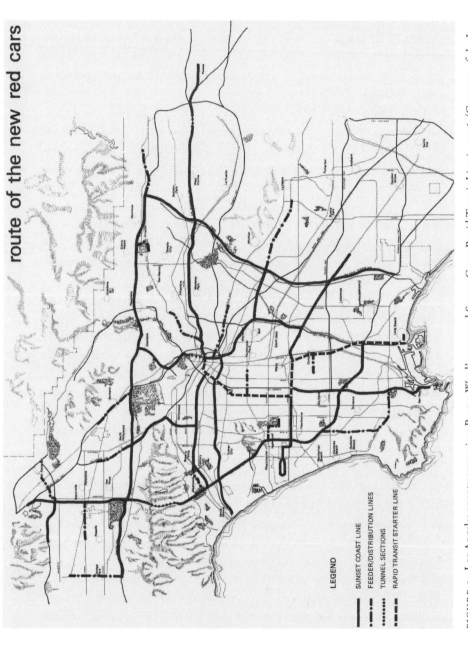

route of the new red cars

LEGEND

SUNSET COAST LINE
FEEDER/DISTRIBUTION LINES
TUNNEL SECTIONS
RAPID TRANSIT STARTER LINE

FIGURE 5. Los Angeles county supervisor Baxter Ward's proposed Sunset Coast Rapid Transit Line in 1976. (Courtesy of the Los Angeles County Metropolitan Transportation Authority Research Library and Archive. Reprinted with permission.)

picture" that he had "advanced over the past three years," including the starter line and the other minor transportation fixes.[61]

Ward's two half-cent propositions became "R" and "T," for Rapid Transit. (He needed two separate propositions to achieve a full cent increase because state legislation only authorized the RTD to issue half-cent measures, and Ward failed to convince the state legislature to allow for consolidation in time for the ballot printing.)[62] Ward mobilized supporters, organizing a coalition that included leading businesses, labor unions, and local elected officials.[63]

Rail opponents also mobilized. They included economic conservatives, academics, and the *Los Angeles Times*. Most of the opposition centered on the expense of the plan as well as its flawed details. Ward's fellow supervisor, Pete Schabarum, led the opposition. Schabarum was an archconservative who did not like tax increases and did not want the government to build large projects like rail. A former college rugby player and halfback for the San Francisco 49ers football team, he went by the nickname "Pistol Pete."[64] One county official described Schabarum as "competitive as hell."[65] He had gained local notoriety for bowling over a fifty-year-old, five-foot-tall grandmother playing catcher during a softball game. Even after she was carted to the hospital, an unrepentant Schabarum said, "The lady was standing flat square in the middle of the plate."[66]

"Pistol Pete" took the offensive against the Sunset Coast Line, which he deemed to be a symptom of wasteful government spending financed by unnecessary taxes. Schabarum lobbied local leaders to oppose it, ridiculing Ward's proposal for having "beautiful renderings" that masked "a New York–like financial crunch" and the possibility of "cost overruns similar to BART," the San Francisco Bay Area rail system that had dramatically exceeded its cost projections.[67] Schabarum, like many other economic conservatives, preferred an all-bus alternative to the transit gridlock in Los Angeles. An all-bus system was "much less costly," and he argued that rail offered "no transportation service advantages" over bus. "California communities, which grew up in an automobile age, apparently cannot easily be served by a rapid transit system modeled after those of eastern communities that developed in a horse-and-buggy age of high population density," he said. "Rail transit is a thing of the past and should be relegated to plywood boards in dens and garages."[68]

Transportation experts in the academic community largely agreed. They almost uniformly disapproved of rail on economic grounds, believing it to be a bad investment because it required heavy subsidies to operate and because buses and other low-cost methods offered far cheaper means of moving people around. Peter Gordon, a libertarian professor in the business and economics department at the University of Southern California (USC), attacked the Sunset Coast Line as part of the "take-over by the public sector of urban transportation facilities" and an "almost reflexive response to the decline of private transit operators." He described rail as an "absurdity" offering "the fewest benefits at the highest costs," asserting that the reality of rail's flaws had not "grasped the imaginations of the fervent advocates of rail transit for Los Angeles." An equivalent investment in highways instead of rail, he argued, would create more jobs and greater stimulation to the economy. "It is rare that society attempts to reverse the decline of an industry that is 'flunking the market test,' and properly so."[69]

A one-day conference of local scholars, held at USC in 1976 to discuss Ward's proposal, produced similar conclusions. Proclaiming that they brought a "close and detached look at the transportation problems of this region," the professors believed they had "something important to communicate to society at large."[70] Robert Ellickson of USC's Law Center alleged that rail advocacy resulted from the backroom lobbying of construction and design industry profit-seekers who could no longer make money from highway construction. According to Ellickson, they joined environmentalists to lobby for rail for profit. Professor Martin Wachs of UCLA claimed that "many Southern Californians are victims of a 'cultural inferiority complex': they believe that they will not have achieved true 'citihood' until they, too, have a subway system." Jack Dyckman of the USC planning department questioned whether Los Angeles had a transportation "problem" in the first place. Commuters, Dyckman argued, "appear well served by the present system."[71]

The negative reviews by academics convinced the *Los Angeles Times* to run a series of damaging articles on Ward's plan just a few weeks before the election. The seven-article series challenged virtually every positive assumption about the impact of Ward's plan. Entitled "Rail Rapid Transit: The Doubts Persist," the series questioned the need for rail transit in Los Angeles and quoted Dyckman, who asserted that Los Angeles "already has a good flexible transportation system—its freeway network." The newspaper discredited the idea that the Pacific Electric cars were worth saving. It quoted UCLA economics professor George Hilton, who argued that the demise of the rail cars was "no cause for regret" and that "efforts to upgrade it would have amounted to a pure waste[,] for ... the operation could have yielded no substantial external benefits." Even in cities with rail transit, such as the San Francisco Bay Area, the paper claimed, traffic had declined by only 2 percent. It finished with a quote from USC urban regional planning professor Harry

Richardson: "To pay billions for half-empty trains and half-empty freeways hardly seems a wise investment."[72]

An exasperated Ward called the series "one hell of a hatchet job."[73] But the negative press influenced the public. On Election Day, June 8, 1976, Los Angeles County voters rejected the Sunset Coast Line by a three-to-two margin (59.3% to 40.6% opposed).[74] Although a poll taken two weeks before the vote showed that a bare 50.2 percent favored it, after the *Times* series that support collapsed.[75]

It was a traumatic defeat for Ward, who proclaimed that rail transit in Los Angeles was "dead."[76] Years later, a newspaper reporter caught up to Ward, then out of public life, to ask him his thoughts on transit in Los Angeles. When the subject of the Sunset Coast Line came up, Ward said, "I had a disaster on my hands," and he called the battle "the single most difficult thing I have ever done in my life." Perhaps imagining the rail cars of his youth on the old Pacific Electric line, he said to the reporter, "If you saw how logical it could have been . . ."[77]

THE FIRST GRANT

Ironically, the defeat of the Sunset Coast Line boosted the prospects for the Starter Line, which emerged as the only proposal left standing. And the presidential election that November brought high hopes for rail leaders in Los Angeles. President-elect Jimmy Carter had developed a close relationship with Tom Bradley and Ed Edelman, and they considered him a key ally in their agenda for Los Angeles.[78]

More good news for rail advocates came in the form of a parting gift from the outgoing secretary of transportation. Just weeks before Carter's inaugural, Secretary Coleman told the RTD that UMTA had officially approved the Los Angeles application for federal dollars to study a starter rail line[79] and was awarding the transportation district $2 million to do the initial engineering and environmental work.[80] He cautioned Los Angeles, though, that the award was not a guarantee that the federal government would approve further funds. He also limited the area of study. "We conclude that further study of fixed guideway alternatives in the Wilshire/La Brea corridor—but only in that corridor—is merited," the secretary wrote to Mayor Bradley.[81]

Rail advocates would need all $2 million of the grant. The process of conducting a rail study was no longer a simple matter, as UMTA was now requiring cities to undergo "alternatives analyses" in which local officials studied various transit alternatives to rail along the proposed routes. The hope was that some local governments would realize that cheaper options, such as light rail or bus-only lanes, would work better. UMTA had adopted this new requirement in September 1976, and Los Angeles was the first city to be subjected to it.[82] The region had missed the window of an easier federal rail process.

The UMTA grant was a milestone for the city and good news for Bradley with his reelection year approaching. He described the award in a press release as "a giant step forward for Los Angeles," arguing that an improved transit system would make Los Angeles "a more attractive place to locate businesses" and would improve energy conservation, air quality, and traffic congestion.[83]

The award was also a victory over Baxter Ward. The Wilshire corridor was the most densely populated part of Los Angeles and the part of the city most suitable to rail. The federal government was now in agreement with Bradley and the RTD that if there were to be rail in Los Angeles, it should serve the areas of density rather than the vast reaches of the county as Ward wanted. But Coleman warned Bradley that the federal government would not want to commit millions of dollars to a Los Angeles system "if a consensus for meeting future transit operating cannot be achieved."[84]

THE PRESIDENT SPEAKS

With expectations running high, opposition suddenly emerged from an unexpected and powerful place. President Carter, it seemed, turned out to be no fan of urban rail. As governor of Georgia, Carter had helped Atlanta finance a new rail transit system called MARTA (Metropolitan Atlanta Rapid Transit Authority). Like Los Angeles, Atlanta suffered from traffic caused by its dispersed, auto-dependent population. Although rail boosters hoped MARTA would spur density through development around the rail stations, the appropriate zoning changes never happened for political reasons.[85] Carter's experience with the system was causing him to think twice about funding new rail programs in auto-oriented cities. In 1977, the president wrote in a leaked memo: "Many rapid transit systems are grossly overdesigned. We should insist on off-street parking, one-way streets, special bus lanes, and surface rail-bus as preferable alternatives to subways. In some urban areas, no construction at all would be required."[86] Carter was beginning to sound worrisome to rail advocates.

Carter's secretary of transportation, Brock Adams, was also dubious about rail in Los Angeles. The generous federal support for rapid transit in the late 1960s and early 1970s had yielded disappointing ridership results, and rising costs had forced UMTA to make cutbacks and direct greater scrutiny on cities like Los Angeles. In April 1977, Adams told reporters that local officials in Los Angeles were "going to have to convince me that rapid transit is feasible" on the Wilshire corridor.[87] He instead expressed strong support for more carpool and bus lanes in the freeway system as a solution to the traffic woes.

In May 1977, the president himself weighed in on the subject during a visit to Los Angeles. He was taping a live interview show on KNXT television when Rick Arroyo, a twenty-five-year-old bus driver from East Los Angeles, asked him about rapid transit in Los Angeles and voiced concern about the "number of cars polluting the atmosphere."[88] Carter answered by referencing his experience as governor of Georgia. He mistakenly compared the population density of Los Angeles to that of Atlanta, claiming that both cities had about 800 people per square mile, compared to Manhattan with roughly 20,000 people per square mile. "You really don't need the highly expensive subway and rail systems as much as some communities do," the president concluded.[89]

Carter's remarks sparked a local uproar. Rail supporters struggled to make sense of them. The president had misrepresented the population density of Los Angeles County, choosing a square-mile population figure that ignored the high-density corridors within the county that rivaled the densities of large East Coast cities. In fact, the Wilshire corridor had the fifth highest population density in the United States and was as dense as much of Manhattan, with over 15,000 people per square mile.[90]

Department of Transportation officials tried to contain the public relations damage done to rail boosters in the nation's second-largest city. Secretary Adams wrote to Bradley, "I want to assure you that this Department has an open mind on the question of funding rapid transit in Los Angeles."[91] But the pattern of comments indicated that the Carter administration was reluctant to spend limited resources on rail in Los Angeles when cheaper alternatives existed.

The remarks from Adams and Carter also exposed a split within UMTA about the desirability of funding rail in Los Angeles. UMTA's regional director for California, Dee Jacobs, favored federal funding of rail along the Wilshire corridor, and he expressed consternation at the public statements of top leaders in the administration. "I'd hate to have the Secretary make too many statements in this vein," he wrote to UMTA's acting administrator. "Since he (nor Secretary Adams) has not received a briefing on the Los Angeles proposal from us, one couldn't expect the President to know that the Wilshire corridor is quite an exception to the conventional thinking that all of the vast, complex LA area is low density sprawl, unsuited for expensive, fixed guideway transit."[92]

Two years later, with the starter line studies almost complete, Secretary Adams voiced similar concerns. On a KNX radio show in March 1979, the secretary declared: "We tried and will continue to look at whether or not you can have a rail system in Los Angeles, but it's very hard to determine where you're going to build it, because the density is very light, and they want to look at the Wilshire Boulevard corridor and we have said you have to be very careful with that." Adams then reiterated his support for putting buses on freeways as a congestion solution. He recommended that Los Angeles try this approach first and "see how well it is working" while still pursuing a rail option. "You have such an elaborate freeway system you may want to go to bus on freeway rather than to rail as your ultimate public transportation system," he told listeners.[93]

The administration was sending mixed signals to Los Angeles. UMTA administrator Richard Page had already publicly sounded notes of encouragement for rail,[94] and Dee Jacobs was a staunch supporter of rail along Wilshire. Jacobs wrote to Page to express frustration with the secretary's "off moment" and urged Page to "brief him on the L.A. situation. Statements like this hurt [Secretary Adams's] credibility. For example, all the political actors in the L.A. area plus most informed people now recognize that the Wilshire Corridor is one of the densest transit corridors in the nation, far exceeding anything we have in Miami, Baltimore, Buffalo and denser than virtually any other rapid transit corridor outside of New York City."[95] The Secretary's comments were delaying UMTA action on the now-completed RTD starter line study.[96]

CONSENSUS AT LAST

While Los Angeles leaders waited for the Carter administration to make a decision, Baxter Ward tried one last time to revive his rail dreams. He placed a nonbinding referendum on the November 1978 ballot with a plan for the "Sunset Coast Limited," a downscaled version of the Sunset Coast Line. The new rail system would cover fifty-seven miles, linking the San Fernando

Valley, El Monte, Los Angeles International Airport (LAX), and Watts with downtown for a cost of $3.8 billion. Describing BART trains as "not exciting," he had the Sunset Coast Ltd. trains designed to have "domes" and to be able to "streak across the place." Once drivers in traffic "see a train going by at 80 mph," he said, "those people will be riding it the next day."[97] The plan won 54 percent of the vote (although only 60 percent of individuals who voted that day actually voted for the measure at all). He hoped the 1978 advisory vote would set the stage for an electoral victory in 1979.[98]

He then returned in 1979 with another 232-mile light rail plan for the November ballot. But Ward had lost credibility. UMTA officials like Dee Jacobs were tired of him, referring to him as "the longstanding problem" who was once again "off doing his own thing, miles from the practical, fundable, reasonable improvements for which political and community consensus has finally been laced together."[99] Even Ward's colleagues on the board of supervisors turned against him—and he needed their vote to place his plan on the ballot. Supervisor Hahn supported Ward, and it came down to Supervisor Edelman to provide the third, decisive vote. Edelman had supported Ward with the purchase of "Baxter's Choo-Choo," but he had had enough. He voted against the plan[100] in order to focus on a Wilshire route, "where you had the density," he argued.[101]

UMTA interpreted the county vote as the beginning of a new era of political consensus in Los Angeles. Ward's competing vision for rail had been eliminated, and the major power centers now supported the starter line as the place to begin. "For years we have challenged the elected officials to get their act together—including political consensus and local financing—as a precursor prerequisite to federal financing," Dee Jacobs wrote to his superiors. "In the last three months they have done that and now are in the process of tossing the ball to us."[102]

WAITING ON THE FEDS

In 1979, President Carter appeared to undergo a change of heart when it came to funding mass transit. With rising energy prices due to the Iranian revolution and hostage crisis, Carter suddenly recognized transit as an important investment in a slumping economy and a critical way to reduce energy consumption. In a speech before the American Public Transportation Association in New York in September 1979, the president said: "Now we recognize the value of mass transit. We stand committed to the rediscovery and revitalization of America's transit systems.... We will build subways, elevated trains, trolleys, people-movers and commuter trains." He promised a "quantum jump" in transportation spending by more than tripling it for the 1980s.[103]

Los Angeles leaders submitted the final paperwork on the starter line in early 1980 with high hopes. RTD staff requested a preliminary engineering grant that would be the final step before beginning construction on the project, which would require yet another UMTA grant. The region had finally secured the state support necessary to guarantee the local match for the starter line, and Department of Transportation officials knew the ball was in their court. "For the first time in its rapid transit development history, Los Angeles will have a local commitment of over $400 million," wrote former Bradley advisor Norm Emerson, who now worked for the Department of Transportation.[104]

But it appeared to be too late. The Department of Transportation claimed that money for rapid transit programs had dried up with the weakening national economy. UMTA presently had roughly $1 billion to spend, but most of those funds were already committed to upgrading existing trains in New York, Chicago, and Boston. Local advocates doubted they would get full funding for the starter line, speculating that the federal government would probably require the RTD to divide the line into smaller, discrete segments to fund over time.[105]

The heyday of UMTA rail grants had ended. While Los Angeles voters were defeating transit sales tax measures and politicians fought over rail plans, UMTA committed to new rail programs in Miami, Atlanta, Buffalo, Detroit, and Baltimore. The only consolation was that most of the competition from other cities was gone. Honolulu was the only major city left that was still asking for rail money.[106]

The Carter administration recognized that transit needed more money. The president therefore proposed a Windfall Tax and Energy Trust Fund via legislation that would place a special tax on oil companies. The administration planned to use the revenues for infrastructure projects like the Los Angeles subway and other transit projects on the Carter wish list.[107] On April 2, 1980, Congress passed a compromise version of the president's windfall tax bill, and Carter immediately signed it into law.[108] Federal funds for systems like the starter line would once again be available. Carter duly promised local officials that UMTA would approve the starter line grant.

Mayor Bradley tried to persuade the president to announce funding for the starter line before he faced voters in his primary race against California governor Jerry Brown and others. But the president resisted, concerned that such an announcement would appear political and therefore discredit the initiative. So a day after the June 1980 primaries (which Carter lost to Senator Edward Kennedy), Bradley and other rail leaders finally announced the news that they had waited years to receive: UMTA had awarded the $12 million preliminary engineering grant for the Wilshire starter subway. UMTA administrator Theodore Lutz described the project as a "careful, highly professional job." The money would pay for engineers to determine the soundness of the route and estimate the construction costs. Officials projected a 1983 or 1984 date to begin breaking ground.[109]

Bradley described himself as "elated" and pointed out that it was the first time in twenty years that there was a consensus on both the route and where the 20 percent local share would come from. When reporters reminded him of his eighteen-month pledge back in 1973, he smiled and said, "A lot of people thought, 'you've got to be loony to think this is going to happen.'"[110]

Local leaders had finally taken a major step forward in the fight to bring the starter line to Los Angeles.

TWO

The New Mulholland

SUPERVISOR KENNETH HAHN WANTED A rail system to serve the whole county, and he wanted it to happen quickly. While Mayor Bradley and other rail boosters waited for the federal government to decide whether or not to fund a starter line, Hahn made plans to finance a complementary system. Like Baxter Ward, Hahn wanted regional rail and felt no particular attachment to an expensive, downtown-oriented subway on the edge of his South Central Los Angeles district. Although he watched three sales tax proposals go down to defeat in twelve years, he was willing to try again with the hope of funding cheaper rail systems to more places.

Hahn was no ideologue like Ward. A savvy, pragmatic politician, he was known for his folksy charm and no-nonsense approach to governing, and he had a close relationship with Mayor Bradley. In 1980, he attempted to accomplish what Bradley, Ward, and other rail leaders had been unable to achieve. His plainspoken determination, against steep odds, would eventually bring rail transit back to Los Angeles.

ATLANTA COMES TO LOS ANGELES

Kenny Hahn had been a fixture of Los Angeles politics since the 1940s, having been elected to the city council at the age of twenty-six and the county board of supervisors at thirty-two. His long tenure in politics meant that he was a witness to the heyday of the Pacific Electric transit system, before automobiles completely took over the county. And because his district contained the low-income and largely African American communities of South Central Los Angeles, including the area scarred by the

Watts riots of 1965, public transit was always a critical issue for his constituents.

Hahn's advocacy reflected his constituents' priorities. He was a civil rights leader and the only elected official to meet with Reverend Martin Luther King Jr. at Los Angeles International Airport (LAX) in 1961, which earned him unwavering loyalty from many of his African American constituents. He was also well known for having helped bring the Dodgers baseball team to Los Angeles from Brooklyn. As John Stodder, a staff member to Supervisor Ed Edelman during the 1980s, recalled, Hahn "was one of the most personable politicians in Los Angeles history. He glad-handed, told stories, spoke from the gut and spread a kind of creative chaos wherever he went."[1]

While Hahn was a fan of rail transit like Baxter Ward, he preferred a "balanced" transit system that included heavy rail, light rail, and improved bus service, especially for his transit-dependent constituency, which had a strong interest in keeping bus fares low and expanding service. But like Ward, the supervisor wanted to see Los Angeles resurrect the Pacific Electric trains. Bradley's eighteen-mile subway alone would not suffice.

Hahn took inspiration from Atlanta, Georgia—ironically, the city that soured Jimmy Carter on rail transit. Voters there had approved a one cent sales tax in 1971, and Hahn began pondering a similar scheme for Los Angeles based on Atlanta's "outstanding model." Hahn liked the balanced nature of the Atlanta sales tax plan, noting that some of the tax revenues "went toward constructing a great new rail system," and the "remaining revenues were used to keep bus fares at 15-cents until 1979."[2] Hahn knew from recent polling that county voters were much more likely to support a sales tax increase if it funded a transportation plan balanced between bus and rail.[3] His assessment was simple: "the Atlanta Plan worked."[4]

Hahn sold the idea to starter line advocates by arguing that an electoral victory would send a signal to the Urban Mass Transportation Administration (UMTA) that Los Angeles voters supported rail. Citing Atlanta, he reported to his transit colleagues in 1980 that the passage of that region's sales tax plan not only generated "important funding for local transit, but it prompted the federal government to come in with matching funds to give form to Atlanta's plans and to stimulate the city's economy along the way."[5] An electoral victory would be a triple win: bus riders would see lower fares; the county could begin construction of a regional light rail system; and the rail dollars would leverage a large federal commitment to build a subway through downtown.

California's state government had created the perfect vehicle for the supervisor to push his sales tax plan. Just a few years earlier, in 1976, the chairman of the Assembly Committee on Transportation, Walter Ingalls, created a new transit bureaucracy in Los Angeles County. As a county supervisor, Kenny Hahn now sat on its board.

Ingalls's plan was remarkable for its audacity. Because he had grown tired of the Southern California Rapid Transit District's (RTD) inability to secure funding to build rapid transit in Los Angeles, Ingalls created a county transportation commission for Los Angeles (as well as separate commissions for Orange, Riverside, and San Bernardino counties to help them avoid the auto-dominated fate of Los Angeles).[6] The county commission would centralize all rail transit planning and project approvals.[7] The RTD would then operate the rail system.[8] As former RTD board member Marv Holen later commented, having two agencies responsible for rail transit "was a true recipe for civic disaster."[9]

Ingalls explained to Governor Jerry Brown that his motivation for the new bureaucracy was to correct the dysfunctional and decentralized system in Los Angeles County, which he blamed for the lack of rapid transit. The area, he said, has been "leaderless for many years in the area of transportation decision-making." The local government structure did "not allow for a strong mayor or a strong county executive," so "Los Angeles has had to continue to rely on an uncoordinated, often competing collection of underfunded bus operators" while "other major urban centers of the nation and world have gone forward with significant mass transit improvements."[10] Ingalls hoped that his new agency would bridge the gap.[11]

Ingalls's legislation gave the county commission the power to place a half-cent sales tax proposition on the ballot to support public transit. Ingalls promptly stripped the RTD of that same sales tax authority that the agency once had.[12]

Frustration with the RTD and the state of transit in Los Angeles propelled Ingalls's bill through the legislative process, and Governor Brown signed it into law in 1976. The Los Angeles County Transportation Commission, or LACTC, went into effect the next year. Ingalls intended for the LACTC to provide a regional perspective on transit planning. Its eleven-member board consisted of the five Los Angeles county supervisors or their alternates, three representatives from the city of Los Angeles (including from the mayor's office), two from the Los Angeles County City Selection

Committee, a member from the Long Beach City Council, and a representative appointed by the governor.[13]

Ingalls planned to introduce legislation to abolish the RTD and centralize all transit planning and operation in the region under the LACTC.[14] But the plan never materialized, and in the meantime, the two agencies coexisted uneasily.

"NOT SOME PIE-IN-THE-SKY PROPOSAL"

By 1980, despite the ballot setbacks in 1968, 1974, and 1976, Hahn was eager to use the LACTC as a vehicle to push a new sales tax plan. As chair of the commission in 1978, he had requested agency staff to "prepare for me the necessary steps to have a MARTA [Atlanta's system] type transportation system for Los Angeles County that is similar to the agency in Atlanta."[15] By the summer of 1979, he invited his fellow supervisors to a luncheon to discuss "an active idea to submit to the people in the November election, a special measure to finance and build a rapid transit system for the entire Los Angeles County."[16] By 1980, Hahn had grown tired of the slow pace and small scale of the starter line. He wanted to get a light rail line up and running on the existing rights-of-way within a few years.

Hahn drafted a sales tax plan that would dedicate 50 percent of the revenue to "rapid transit," defined to include both bus and rail; 25 percent to be returned to local governments on a population basis; and 25 percent to lower bus fares to a flat fifty cents throughout Los Angeles County for a period of five years.[17] The reduced bus fare provision was particularly timely after the RTD announced in January 1980 that it was likely to increase bus fares in March in response to rising inflation.[18] Hahn could now tap into bus rider frustration with the fare hikes. A balanced plan that funded both rail and bus would have a better chance to win the support of bus-riding voters.

The LACTC scheduled an August 1980 vote on his plan, and Hahn lobbied the members feverishly in the run-up to the meeting. LACTC staff tried to build public support by holding hearings to get input as to how the agency should use the sales tax revenues.[19] But the hearings provided opponents with an opportunity to complain and generally produced mixed results. For example, because the corridors that the LACTC selected for rapid transit left out a few cities, officials from those areas objected to the plan. Politicians in *ughhh*

Burbank and Glendale in particular were miffed that their cities were not on the transit list and vowed to oppose the plan.[20]

On the eve of the LACTC vote, Hahn contacted Supervisor "Pistol Pete" Schabarum, who held the critical position of chair of the LACTC at that time. Schabarum was ardently opposed to Hahn's sales tax plan, but Hahn needed at least to dampen his opposition. He wrote to Schabarum that the LACTC vote represents "our last immediate opportunity to provide Los Angeles County with an efficient regional transportation system that will meet the needs of the 1980s and beyond. This opportunity will not come again for at least two more years. We must seize it now." He concluded, "This is not some pie-in-the-sky proposal. Let us at least give the voters a chance to decide for themselves. Tomorrow is the day of decision."[21]

THE RECKONING

On August 20, 1980, the LACTC board gathered for a special meeting to decide whether or not to place Hahn's proposal on the ballot. The existence and shape of the future Metro Rail system would hinge on a single vote on the divided commission.

Hahn faced an uphill battle, and he later described the LACTC vote as "one of the greatest political challenges of my career." The commissioners were generally not excited about yet another transit proposal. Hahn later recalled that his opponents "were frightened by the 1978 taxpayer revolt that resulted in Proposition 13" (California's anti–property tax measure) and "felt the voters simply would not approve a new tax." He also noted that his idea "garnered only lukewarm support from LACTC board members who had already pledged their support to another project," the Wilshire starter line. Hahn's plan did not earmark revenue for that line, and "therefore my measure was viewed as a possible hindrance to the development of the subway system."[22] The fight for scarce transit dollars continued to drive a wedge between rail advocates of different lines.

In addition to his own vote, Hahn needed five commissioners for a six-vote majority on the eleven-member commission. His behind-the-scenes lobbying led him to believe that at least five members might oppose the plan, while potentially four (including himself) were in favor. That meant he desperately needed the support of the last two remaining commissioners, who appeared to be skeptical of the plan. Ironically, they were two of the region's staunchest rail advocates: Ray Remy, Mayor Bradley's alternate; and Bob Geoghegan, Supervisor Ed Edelman's alternate.

Mayor Bradley, an ally and friend of Hahn's, had appointed Remy as his alternate, but the mayor was nonetheless unsure of what position to instruct Remy to take. Bradley thought that voters would probably reject the plan. But even if it did pass, the mayor worried that it would not dedicate enough money to rail to leverage federal funds. Remy recalled in 2006 that during the final days before the vote, "Tom had a variety of concerns about the proposal." The mayor believed that the bus fare subsidies would "suck up all the money," according to Remy, "and we wanted sufficient matching funds from the federal government." Sensing hesitation, Hahn called Bradley's office before the LACTC vote to tell Remy, "This is going to be a close vote."[23] But Hahn had no assurance as to how Remy would ultimately vote.

Unfortunately for Hahn, Supervisor Edelman had instructed his alternate, Bob Geoghegan, to vote against the proposal. Despite being a loyal rail advocate, according to Geoghegan, the supervisor had "really big concerns" with Hahn's proposal to return 25 percent of the revenue to local governments based on population.[24] "To take 25 percent of the money and automatically take it away from where the transit need was greatest and transfer it to where the dollars and ridership needs were the least wasn't optimal," Geoghegan later explained. "That was our reservation going into it."[25] In addition, Geoghegan was aware of the measure's potential unpopularity, ominously noting a KABC-TV "Instapoll" that showed opposition to the sales tax running 57 percent to 28 percent, with 15 percent undecided.[26]

Edelman was also concerned about the expense and length of time that would be required to build a light rail network in Los Angeles. "Prior to Hahn's plan," Geoghegan recalled in 2012, "we had been working on an all-bus proposal, reasoning that buses could work more quickly than rail transportation, which takes up to fifty years to amortize. We could have gotten an all-bus system running much faster. We could have covered the whole county with a lot more buses, and saturated buses in areas where people needed bus transportation the most, where you can't saturate with rail. It would have taken rail years and years to catch up with the immediate advantages of what the bus program could have done." Edelman's draft plan included bus technologies that Los Angeles would not end up deploying until 2000, such as "rapid" articulated buses with synchronized traffic control lights. "But Kenny beat us to the punch and came out with his proposal first," Geoghegan said.[27]

Hahn attempted to win Geoghegan's support immediately before the meeting by sending his chief deputy to lobby him, but Geoghegan informed the deputy about Edelman's position. To make matters worse, Edelman would be unreachable during the meeting. "Ed was over in Camp David, meeting with Jimmy Carter on energy matters," Geoghegan recalled.[28] He was reluctant to call Edelman, who had a strict policy about not being interrupted during meetings.[29]

Hahn's only hope was to persuade Geoghegan and Remy at the meeting for the vote. Hahn opened the gathering with a dramatic speech, meant in part to inspire the two alternates. The speech exemplified Hahn's idealistic vision for an immediate and dramatic solution to the regional transportation problem. He referred to "great men of vision," such as William Mulholland, the famed head of the Los Angeles Department of Water and Power who masterminded the aqueduct that brought water from the Owens Valley in the eastern Sierra Nevada to Los Angeles in 1913.[30] The aqueduct paved the way for the expansion of the city, and Mulholland's somewhat devious exploits later inspired the classic movie *Chinatown*.[31] Just as Mulholland "had enough courage to go up 200 miles north and bring the water to Los Angeles," Hahn wanted the LACTC to take a bold and historic stand in favor of rail transit.[32] Hahn saw himself as the ideological heir to a man who had fixed the water shortage in Los Angeles with a visionary project that laid the foundation for the rapid growth of the city. Hahn's plan would deliver the city from traffic as Mulholland had saved the city from thirst and would form the basis of future urban growth.

With the speech concluded, the plan's opponents voiced their concerns. Wendell Cox, a Bradley appointee and rail advocate, criticized the 50 percent set-aside for "rapid transit" as insufficient to build a viable rail network. He worried that any unused money would simply be redirected for further bus subsidies and not be used to build rail. He felt "that there is virtually no hope of building a rapid transit system under this proposal" and that any reductions in bus fares should come through direct subsidies and not an indirect sales tax plan.[33] Barna Szabo, another opponent on the commission, objected to the timing of the proposal, wanting to wait until as late as November 1982 to put it on the ballot.[34] He had the agreement of Mayor Ed Russ of Gardena, who felt that "we haven't our done our work yet" by building a strong political base of support for the plan. "One more loss at the ballot box," Russ now warned, "could kill this thing forever. It is just foolhardy to move ahead this quickly."[35]

Hahn found allies, including Baxter Ward. Ward wanted the proposal to offer more for rail, but he recognized that Hahn's plan "would at least get a start, granted it would take forever at this rate to build." Ward was more realistic now about the political dynamics, so he supported Hahn's idea.[36] Sam Zimmerman and Russell Rubley also appeared to support the proposal. Zimmerman told the commission that he "came here today prepared to vote against the proposal" because he "saw no ground-swell of people who wanted to work for a tax increase." He had changed his mind, however, perhaps in part because of Hahn's impassioned pleas. "I do have my doubts," he said, but "we can't say it won't pass until we try." Rubley, in contrast, had been enthusiastic about the proposal from the start. "It is better to try and fail than not to have tried at all," he argued. Echoing Hahn, he said, "We certainly need improved transportation in this basin, and that's what we were appointed and elected to do."[37]

With the support of Ward, Zimmerman, and Rubley, Hahn now had secured four votes, including his own. He needed just two more to win approval: Geoghegan's and Remy's. To persuade these fence-sitters, he made a veiled appeal to their sense of duty, given their status as alternates for officials not in attendance. "The law says you are a member when you sit here. You have full rights, freedom, and liberty to speak your own conscience. In the long run you will be glad if you do. And in your hearts you know what you should do." Hahn invoked a Mulhollandesque sense of responsibility to the future, adding: "This decision is important, not only for the seven million people, but the millions of people yet to come to Los Angeles. They deserve our judgment today. The judgment we make today will affect their lives in the year 2000."[38]

Hahn's remarks, and the dynamics of the vote, made an impact on Geoghegan. Edelman's chief deputy tallied the numbers in his head and realized that his might be the deciding vote. Geoghegan decided to take action, and he abruptly left the meeting. "I called upstairs to the office and told Ed's secretary that I wanted to speak to Ed at Camp David, that it was urgent," he later recalled. The secretary interrupted Edelman's meeting with Jimmy Carter. When Edelman picked up the phone, Geoghegan quickly explained the reason. "I said, 'The vote is going on, and it's going to be 6–5 a failure, and you're going to be recorded as a failure,'" Geoghegan remembered telling his boss. "'You've never been against mass rapid transit. It's not the best program in the world, but it is a program that can get through if we vote for it.'" Edelman considered his chief deputy's words. Then he gave Geoghegan approval to vote yes.[39]

Geoghegan quietly returned to the meeting without telling anyone about the conversation. Russ then moved to hold a vote. Ward and Hahn voted first to support the plan, and Rubley and Zimmerman followed suit. Hahn needed two more votes as Remy's turn came.

To Hahn's chagrin, Mayor Bradley's alternate voted no.

Witnessing the turn of events, Geoghegan told himself that "the votes [were] not there" now with Remy's action. The vote came next to Geoghegan. To shocked faces, he voted yes. Five more no votes came in: Russ, Pat Russell, Szabo, Cox, and Schabarum.[40] Schabarum announced that the motion had failed, and with it, Hahn's proposal.

Suddenly Remy spoke up. "I move for reconsideration," he told Schabarum. Schabarum, an ardent opponent of the plan, asked suspiciously, "For what purpose?" Remy replied, "To change my vote." Schabarum, Remy later recalled, "was not a happy camper."[41] In a swift reversal of fortune, Hahn's plan had passed an enormous hurdle. The LACTC had approved placing it on the ballot in November by a bare six-to-five majority vote.

Why did Remy change his vote? He later reported, "Tom's instructions to me were to go ahead and vote no on the proposal, but don't be the final vote against it."[42] Bradley did not want to be on record supporting another losing sales tax proposal, but he did not want to be the deciding vote to stop Hahn either. Remy was counting on Geoghegan's no vote to sink the proposal without Bradley having to make the deciding vote. But after Geoghegan's call to Edelman, the math had changed. Now it was Remy's no vote that would sink the plan.[43]

Bradley's reluctance to support even a scaled-back sales tax plan exemplifies how cautious the mayor had become on transit issues. After the defeats in 1974 and 1976, Bradley wanted to avoid a possibly rail-killing vote. He was also committed to the UMTA process that he hoped would launch the starter line. And a regional rail line was not in his direct interest, particularly when its potential defeat could jeopardize the starter line.

Ultimately, Bradley and Edelman—and their appointees on the commission—came through for Hahn. But they were reluctant allies. Hahn would remain largely alone in this fight.

THE LACTC MODIFIES HAHN'S PROPOSAL

The commission set to work shaping the details of Hahn's proposal. The debate that followed would have an enormous impact on the future of rail in Los Angeles because the LACTC was about to determine the amount of money from the sales tax that would go to rail and bus service, among other categories.

Ward believed that the proposal did not set aside enough money for rail. The LACTC staff projected that the amount of money required to keep the bus fares flat over the five-year period would increase with inflation. The allocation for bus fares would therefore need to increase above 25 percent. To pay for this increase, Hahn's plan required a proportionate reduction in the rapid transit allocation. As a result, by the fifth year of the bus fare reduction, LACTC staff estimated that only between 19 and 23 percent of the annual revenue would be available for rapid transit.[44]

To stop this hemorrhaging from the rapid transit allocation, Ward introduced an amendment to dedicate 50 percent of the tax proceeds specifically to build a rail system, rather than to technology-neutral "rapid transit." But Geoghegan was opposed to the set-aside, arguing that there would be "no money for regional transit" and that the result would be "taking buses off the street and taking service away from the people who need the service right now."[45] Ward responded that anything less than a 50 percent set-aside for rail would "cause the issue to fail." He argued, "You cannot propose to tax people and offer them no more than what they have now. You have to give them something that has appeal."[46]

Ward's once-grand plans for rail now rested on his ability to set aside sufficient sales tax funds to get at least a small rail transit system started. But his proposal went nowhere. Nobody on the commission wanted to set such a large amount of revenues aside solely for rail, and his motion died for lack of a second.[47]

As Ward stewed on the sidelines, a fellow commissioner offered him fateful advice. Wendell Cox, who originally opposed Hahn's plan as not bold enough, shared Ward's hope that sufficient funds could be set aside for rail. Cox was sitting next to Ward, and he privately suggested that Ward try for a minimum 35 percent set-aside for rapid transit instead. "Ward responded that 35 percent was simply not enough," Cox recalled. "I suggested that it was more than nothing." Cox decided to make the motion himself. "[Ward] consented to support my motion," Cox remembered.[48] But Ward insisted that the set-aside be not just for rapid transit in general but that it "implies and states 'rail.'"[49] Ward believed that the term *rapid transit* was too vague. It could mean dedicated rapid busways as easily as it could mean rail, and Ward wanted to make sure the money went to rail.

Cox agreed. He made his motion with the term *rail,* and Ward seconded it.[50] Ward told the commission, "I would prefer 50 percent [for heavy rail]; the ideal would be 60 percent. But I will acknowledge that this still will get us started and this is sufficient to receive the federal subsidy."[51] With the motion for 35 percent for rail introduced and seconded, Hahn indicated that he would accept the motion if it did not interfere with the bus fare reduction plan.[52]

The LACTC then determined the timing of the expenditures, changing the period of bus fare reduction and agreeing to start the minimum 35 percent rail set-aside in the third year (1983).[53] The vote was now seven to four in favor of the modified proposal.[54]

Finally, the LACTC voted on whether to include on the ballot a map of the rail lines likely to be built in the county with the sales tax money. Rick Richmond, the LACTC executive director, had originally drafted a map showing approximately thirteen broad corridors across the county. Richmond explained that the map represented corridors that were "doable in 20 to 25 years," using a mix of busways and rail transit and assuming that 50 percent of the sales tax revenues would go to rail. Now the commissioners had approved 35 percent for rail only, leaving the projections less realistic. However, the commissioners voted six to five in favor of keeping the map. In support, Heinz Heckeroth, representing California as a regional director for the state department of transportation, argued that the commission could use state funds to make up the shortfall for rail.[55] Meanwhile, Baxter Ward argued that the map "shows some kind of plan" and "commits us to something." As he put it to the members, "This is a fair map. It does something for almost everybody."[56]

The plan, with the map, was ready to be presented to the voters. The commissioners had based their funding numbers more on art than on science, and the percentages they chose had an arbitrary quality to them. Despite his unhappiness with the low set-aside for rail, Ward had successfully ensured that at least 35 percent of the funds would go to rail. Hahn's balanced approach had passed the LACTC hurdle. Now he would need to convince the voters.

THE CAMPAIGN FOR A NEW PROPOSITION A

With the election only two months away, Hahn scrambled to assemble a countywide campaign. His sales tax proposal received the ballot title Proposition A like Bradley's ill-fated 1974 attempt. Hahn "took over the campaign, eventually raising just over $36,000." With this shoestring budget,

Hahn recalled, "I took my crusade into the streets, sometimes standing at bus stops, urging riders to vote for the transit tax."[57] He assigned his chief deputy, Nate Holden, the task of distributing Proposition A brochures at bus stops around the county.[58] Meanwhile, his office studied the failures of the 1968, 1974, and 1976 sales tax campaigns in an effort to learn from past mistakes.[59]

Hahn was virtually alone. Local leaders quickly distanced themselves from what they felt was a sure loser. Remy informed the *Los Angeles Times* about the mayor's "lack of enthusiasm" for the plan but indicated that Bradley "probably will support the measure" without being "among the most active campaigners." Supervisor Yvonne Burke was even more direct, telling the *Times* that "I do not believe this [tax] has a chance of winning" and that it would defeat the long-range transit cause.[60]

Undeterred, Hahn reached out to the media, local leaders, and influential businesses and civic organizations. He contacted the top corporations operating in Los Angeles County, such as Chevron, Occidental Petroleum, and Getty Oil.[61] He placed ads in local newspapers with a picture of gridlock below a caption that read, "Los Angeles County desperately needs better transit now."[62] His small budget, however, meant that the campaign would be limited in its ability to run radio and television ads and would be less able to conduct polling to focus the campaign strategy to reach voters.[63]

Nevertheless, Hahn's efforts soon began to bear fruit. The Democratic Party endorsed the plan and included it in its voter guide.[64] He also secured endorsements from the Los Angeles County League of Women Voters, the AFL-CIO, the Los Angeles County Lung Association, and the Los Angeles Taxpayers Association (LATAX), a group consisting of local companies.[65] LATAX in particular was surprisingly supportive. "We normally don't campaign for any kind of tax increase," the group wrote the editor of the *Los Angeles Times*. However, LATAX supported Proposition A "because it is the fairest means of providing the local funding that is so urgently needed to improve public transportation in this region." The group feared more transportation expenses in the future for local businesses if the proposition did *not* pass.[66] Finally, even Mayor Bradley officially endorsed the plan. "Proposition A is an innovative approach to our public transportation problems," he told voters. "I support it."[67]

For his media outreach campaign, Hahn's staff surveyed the major media for editorial support, including radio, television and newspaper.[68] He sent a letter to all publishers and editors in the county in which he cited the success in Atlanta of a similar plan. Referring to the outbreak of war between Iran and Iraq in September 1980, he cautioned that the "hour is late." With the recent gasoline shortages over the past decade, "we have been warned three times of our dangerous dependence on foreign oil." He predicted the "possibility of economic catastrophe" with future gasoline shortages. Again referring to Mulholland, he asked media leaders: "Just think where we'd be if the community leaders of generations before had not planned ahead to bring water from distant places to feed a growing population." Without gas, he warned, Los Angeles "will be a ghost town." He concluded by asking for media help "in getting the facts out."[69]

Hahn was particularly diligent about courting the *Los Angeles Times* editorial staff. In late September he wrote Anthony Day, editor of the editorial page, to solicit his support. "With the *Los Angeles Times'* strong support," he wrote Day, "this measure can pass. Without it, the citizens will be left with continued massive freeway congestion, inadequate bus service, and increasing discontent." After extolling the virtues of Los Angeles, Hahn concluded that "one thing separates the City and County of Los Angeles from true greatness, and that is good public transportation."[70] Hahn even lobbied the chief executive officer of the *Times,* Tom Johnson, writing him that he hoped the paper "will not only vigorously support the measure, but that it will give a great deal of coverage to it like what Atlanta did for its citizens and what we can do for our citizens."[71] Finally, Hahn wrote to the *Times* chairman of the board, Franklin Murphy, who supported Proposition A in a letter to his paper's editor. Hahn was so eager to gain the *Times's* support that he wrote Murphy to thank him for the letter while Murphy was in the hospital recovering from surgery. With 'aw-shucks' charm, Hahn expressed surprise that Murphy needed to write his own editor to get his ideas published. "I just thought a politician named Kenny Hahn had to do that." He joked that the editorial staff probably got a "big chuckle" out of Murphy's tactic.[72]

Hahn's media outreach seemed to work, as a string of key endorsements followed. The *Los Angeles Times* was the most critical, especially given its role in sinking Ward's Sunset Coast Line. The *Times* supported the proposition because of its balanced approach to funding various forms of transit. The editorial approved of the bus fare reduction and the effort to create a rapid transit system in an "era of tenuous energy supplies."[73] The *Los Angeles Herald-Examiner* also endorsed Proposition A in October, citing the "clogged freeways at rush hour" and the pain at the "gas pump meter."[74] *Coast Media* followed suit, arguing that a "countywide rail rapid transit system is critical and essential" while also citing fears of foreign oil dependency and the need to attract federal dollars that the area had been unable to secure for over a decade.[75] The *Valley News* and KFWB news radio joined the endorsement parade as well.[76] Hahn's balanced approach and the fuel shortages were playing important roles in swaying media leaders.

A week before the election, Hahn made his final pitch to the voters of the county. Emphasizing the bus fare reduction component of the plan, he described how the sales tax "represents less than a dime a day for the average person," but if the plan "does not pass, bus fares are expected to go up to 90 cents next year." He also sold the plan as the beginning of a comprehensive solution to the transportation problems of the region. "Los Angeles County is the only major urban area in America that doesn't have a good public transportation system," he noted. "If we fail to pass Proposition A we will be the most foolish." Citing geopolitics and the gasoline insecurity of the time, he told voters that "no one knows when oil imports from the Middle East might be cut off and we will have gas lines or even gas rationing. The war between Iran and Iraq is just one more warning."[77]

ELECTION DAY 1980

On Election Day, November 4, Angelenos in the voting booths considered raising the county sales tax rate from 6 to 6.5 percent. In exchange, Proposition A would "improve and expand existing public transit countywide, reduce fares, construct and operate a rail rapid transit system."[78] The LACTC, with the thirteen-corridor map included, promised that the rail system would serve "at least" the following communities: San Fernando Valley,[79] West Los Angeles, South Central Los Angeles/Long Beach, South Bay/Harbor, the Century Freeway corridor, the Santa Ana Freeway corridor, and the San Gabriel Valley.[80]

The voters responded. In an era of tax revolt, the Los Angeles County electorate finally approved a sales tax increase to finance rail transit. Proposition A secured 54 percent of the vote.[81] Kenny Hahn achieved what Bradley and Ward could not.

Proposition A succeeded primarily because it presented a more modest and balanced approach to the voters. Whereas past initiatives focused solely on rail plans that appealed to about 40 percent of county voters,[82] the bus fare component expanded the coalition. It also seemed like a more sensible transportation solution for an enormous region that could never be serviced

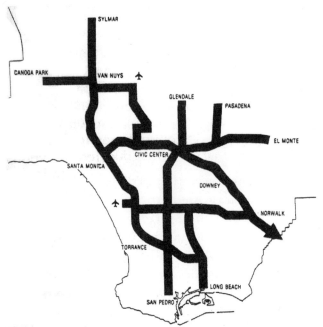

Source: Ballot Proposition A. November 4, 1980

Figure 1·2 Regional Rail Rapid Transit System

FIGURE 6. The original rail rapid transit system map that accompanied the 1980 Proposition A sales tax initiative, as presented to voters in the election material. (Courtesy of the Los Angeles County Metropolitan Transportation Authority Research Library and Archive. Reprinted with permission.)

adequately by rail alone. By balancing Proposition A between rail (35 percent) and bus (40 percent), with the remaining 25 percent to go to the county's cities for "local transit needs," the plan was more likely to appeal to a majority of voters beyond the 40 percent for rail. Its smaller scale may also have swayed voters and critical media leaders who were reluctant to support a massive rail project without trying a pilot approach at first.

Proposition A had an unlikely hero in Baxter Ward. As one of the most outspoken proponents of a massive rail plan for Los Angeles, Ward had ironically made his mark on the future of rail in Los Angeles not through his own lofty transit plans but by insisting that Hahn's more modest proposal fund "rail" and not just "rapid transit." His amendment would guarantee that a rail system would be built in Los Angeles. Ward's support also provided the one-vote margin of victory at the LACTC. Indeed, Hahn later described Ward as the "uncle" of Proposition A for his support and insistence on funding rail transit.[83]

But support for Proposition A would be Ward's last contribution to rail in Los Angeles as a public official. Running for reelection on an anticorruption platform that self-imposed a $50 limit on contributions, Ward was badly outspent by Mike Antonovich, $600,000 to $50,000.[84] On the same day that voters approved Proposition A, they voted Supervisor Ward out of office.

THREE

Bureaucratic Paper Shuffling and Jurisdictional Squabbling

WHERE WOULD THE FIRST MODERN RAIL transit line in Los Angeles go? It was the question that Los Angeles County Transportation Commission (LACTC) rail planners now found themselves in the fortunate position of asking. Budget analysts projected that the Proposition A victory would bring the commission about $225 million in revenue during the 1981–82 fiscal year from the sales tax increase,[1] with roughly $100 million of that amount for rail transit.[2] Rail leaders also expected to leverage even more money from the state and federal government.

The Proposition A victory, coupled with the Urban Mass Transportation Administration's (UMTA) decision to fund subway planning, meant that the LACTC could begin plotting new light rail lines in the county. Meanwhile, the Southern California Rapid Transit District (RTD) mapped out a route and station locations for a heavy rail subway from downtown Los Angeles to the San Fernando Valley via Hollywood.

In both cases, the rail planning process should have involved careful and objective analysis to determine where the most cost-effective rail lines could be located, factoring in likely ridership, existing population and job density, cost, and the potential to develop the land around the station areas to maximize the system's value. While LACTC and RTD staff performed this analysis, the decision-making process was ultimately left to committees of local elected officials, who in turn faced pressure from constituents and state and federal lawmakers who controlled much of the purse strings. As a result, politics, outside circumstances, and the geography of power in the Los Angeles region played an outsized role in influencing where the new rail lines would go.

The passage of Proposition A was a personal triumph for Supervisor Kenneth Hahn, and he sought to bring the spoils of his efforts home to his district. He had raised the money, after all, so the first rail line should go to his district. In those heady days, rail leaders like Hahn believed there would be sufficient funds for a variety of rail lines. And due to the relative poverty of his district, there seemed a certain justice in building the first rail line through the poorest neighborhoods of southern Los Angeles.

With the campaign to persuade the voters over, Hahn's next challenge was to convince his fellow LACTC members to approve a route in his district. With a powerful coalition at his side and pressure to find consensus on the first rail route, Hahn was not afraid to use as much arm-twisting as necessary to ensure that the LACTC voted his way.

Hahn wanted rail on the same corridor that city and county officials had agreed to in the transit summit of 1975, from Long Beach to downtown Los Angeles. Like Baxter Ward before him, Hahn's goal was to resurrect the Pacific Electric Red Car route, and his proposed rail line would occupy the same tracks as the last Red Car line in Los Angeles. Hahn subscribed to the theory that the Red Car lines were successful until car, tire, and oil companies conspired to destroy them after World War II.[3] Despite overwhelming evidence that the trains were in fact money-losers that fell victim to the popularity of the automobile, he viewed the resurrection of the Red Car lines as undoing a wrong done to the region.

Hahn's ultimately unrealistic expectations for a quick planning and construction period stemmed partly from the fact that Los Angeles had no experience building a modern rail line. But he was also inspired by the city of San Diego's recent, successful foray into light rail. Tom Rubin, who consulted for transit agencies at the time, observed, "There hadn't been much rail construction during that period. There had really been only one project in the U.S. that was being built at the time, and that was the original Tijuana Trolley in San Diego."[4] The San Diego line had been built quickly and relatively inexpensively, but it soon proved to be an outlier.

SAN DIEGO FIELD TRIP

While Hahn had based Proposition A on the Atlanta sales tax model, the supervisor now took inspiration from San Diego's Tijuana Trolley, a light rail line that ran from San Diego to the Mexican border. As Rubin explained, the Tijuana Trolley resulted from "a once-in-a-lifetime opportunity" that state senator James Mills from San Diego was able to exploit. Mills engineered the purchase of the railroad right-of-way from a freight company at a bargain price due to tropical storm Kathleen in 1976, which wiped out the freight company's connection to the eastern desert and caused the company to petition to abandon its western rail lines around San Diego. Mills's chosen route, from Tijuana to downtown San Diego, was also a popular transit corridor. "He could have actually made money on it, the demand was so much," Rubin explained. Opened in July 1981, the trolley experienced high ridership and farebox revenues that covered 90 percent of the operating cost. "It was just the absolute right way to do everything," Rubin concluded. "And then of course everybody said, 'That's wonderful. We're going to do the same thing.'"[5]

Hahn was one of those people, and he became an eager student of the trolley, journeying to San Diego three times beginning in 1981 to view the new rail system.[6] He returned to Los Angeles to persuade the public and the LACTC board that the Long Beach line could be another version of the successful Tijuana Trolley.[7] The ease of construction and the low price tag energized Hahn the most. He wrote to the *Los Angeles Times,* "San Diego has shown what can be done with local funding if there is the will," arguing that Los Angeles should employ "San Diego's can-do attitude" to undo the wrong done to the region by the automobile industry, again citing evidence of a conspiracy to torpedo the Red Cars.[8]

To make the case for bringing the Tijuana Trolley model to Long Beach, Hahn began a new campaign aimed at the voting members of the LACTC board. Using the Tijuana example to make a detailed case for the ease of construction and low costs, he told the commissioners that the trolley was built with only $100 million worth of state gas tax funds, including the right-of-way purchase and the rail cars. He cited the simple fare structure and noted that the street cars, manufactured in Germany, were "functional and not luxurious (they are Spartan-like in appearance)," saying that a "person wouldn't want to ride in them for several hours at a time," though they were suitable for one hour or so of commuting.[9]

Hahn expressed belief that Los Angeles could "virtually duplicate" San Diego's trolley within thirty months and implored the LACTC to begin putting out competitive bids as soon as possible, rather than "spending a lot of money for fancy reports for consultants to tell us what to do."[10] He complained that the region had already spent $20 million "hiring experts from around the world to tell us where to put a rapid transit line" without "one mile" of rail construction actually happening.

To support his case, the supervisor assembled a powerful coalition of elected leaders to push for LACTC approval of the line. The geography of the Long Beach route helped because it linked two major employment centers (and the two largest cities in the county) and served the districts of some powerful elected officials, including Congressman Glenn Anderson, who occupied an important seat doling out money from the House Appropriations Committee and was an ally in the campaign to bring federal rapid transit funds to Los Angeles;[11] Assemblyman Bruce Young, chairman of the California Assembly Committee on Transportation; and Supervisor Deane Dana.

Hahn positioned himself as the public face of the LACTC when it came to Proposition A and future rail plans, and he used his high profile to stir public support for the Long Beach route. Shortly after the 1980 election, he took KNBC television reporter Warren Wilson in a Goodyear blimp to see the Red Car right-of-way and tracks that still existed. He told voters that resurrecting this route would be the "quickest, most effective and least expensive way" to develop rail transit in the county. "This will be a bargain for county residents and will help save gasoline and reduce smog in Southern California," he promised.[12]

PRESSURE FROM THE COURTS

A legal attack on Proposition A intensified Hahn's pressure on the LACTC. Two years before the Proposition A vote in 1980, California voters had approved Proposition 13, which required a two-thirds vote for cities, counties, and "special districts" to levy nonproperty or special taxes. Because Proposition A passed by 54 percent and created a nonproperty sales tax, opponents challenged its validity, claiming it required a two-thirds majority to pass, since the LACTC was a "special district."[13] Given the high political stakes, the California Supreme Court stepped in for the lower courts and exercised its original jurisdiction over the case.[14] The Supreme Court, however, was unlikely to issue a ruling for possibly a year or more. As a result, uncertainty hung over Proposition A's fate.

The legal limbo forced the LACTC leadership to try to minimize division and infighting in order to demonstrate to the Supreme Court justices that Proposition A was politically effective and popular. They worried that a hastily chosen route that divided the community might make it politically easier for the justices to invalidate Proposition A (the justices were of course supposed to be immune to political pressure, but rail proponents did not want to take a chance). As a consequence, LACTC board members felt less willing to publicly challenge Hahn and his coalition for fear that it would jeopardize the entire rail program under Proposition A. Bob Geoghegan, Supervisor Edelman's appointee to the LACTC board, wrote that with the legal challenge pending, "it would be wise to continue to keep as broad a consensus regarding transit in the County as possible."[15] The legal dispute already threatened to delay Proposition A's scheduled date of effectiveness of July 1, 1981.

For his part, Hahn was not about to let a few Supreme Court justices invalidate all of his efforts, and he took his case directly to the chief justice. Despite being a party to the case as an LACTC board member, Hahn personally (and probably illegally) lobbied Chief Justice Rose Bird to rule quickly on the Proposition A legal challenge. "I request you to have the case of the LACTC, which is in litigation, be heard as soon as possible by the California Supreme Court," he wrote Bird, informing her that "there are over one million riders a day in Los Angeles County" and the measure "has a plan for better transportation and reduced fares."[16]

GRUMBLINGS

Skeptics of the Long Beach route tried to counter Hahn's efforts. While some critics were opposed to rail in general, some were rail supporters who argued that there were better rail lines that merited funding over the Long Beach route. Many of the elected officials who criticized the proposal had nothing to gain from it electorally, and they instead advocated for lines that served their districts. In the case of the Westside politicians, they had a strong argument that the Long Beach line would not attract as many riders as the Wilshire starter line or even a line to Santa Monica from downtown. They also pointed out that most of the potential riders on the Long Beach corridor were bus riders, so by switching to rail they would not necessarily be reducing automobile use in the region.[17]

In addition to the pressure from the legal challenge, county officials feared they would have to return unused state gas and sales tax funds collected for rail transit if they could not decide on a project. As a result, some local officials felt that the LACTC was rushing to be able to use these funds by making a politically expedient decision on the rail route.[18] As a frustrated Geoghegan wrote at the time, the voters in the San Fernando Valley and throughout the county approved Proposition A because they believed "transit would be provided first where it was justified rather than on the basis of an arbitrary political decision."[19]

An evaluation of alternative transit routes for the LACTC supported some of the skeptics' arguments. In September 1981, the agency commissioned Parsons Brinckerhoff Quade & Douglas, Inc., along with Kaiser Engineers, to study the Long Beach line, asking them to compare it with five other potential transit corridors: San Fernando Valley to downtown, Exposition Boulevard from downtown to Santa Monica, Firestone Boulevard in South Los Angeles, a route linking Union Station and Los Angeles International Airport (LAX), and a Santa Monica Boulevard route from downtown Los Angeles.[20] The firms examined a variety of factors, including patronage potential, local need, and cost efficiency.[21] The Long Beach route lagged in comparison to the other corridors in some key ways. For example, a Long Beach rail line would cost $194 million, whereas a route to Santa Monica from downtown would cost $130 million while serving only slightly fewer riders.[22]

The study prompted criticism of the Long Beach line from planning experts and even some of Hahn's constituents, who preferred a different route to Long Beach than along the old Red Car tracks. Dave Waters, a spokesperson for the National Association for the Advancement of Colored People (NAACP), which constituted a crucial bloc of Hahn's political support, told the *Times* that the "project seems to be politically motivated." A miffed Hahn responded that he had "never even met the man before."[23]

Part of the opposition to Hahn's proposed route came from his insistence that it be built cheaply along existing rail tracks. These tracks were generally located in an industrial and low-density area far to the east of Vermont Avenue, which was a busy transit corridor that formed the backbone of transit-dependent South Central Los Angeles. A rail line down Vermont would have higher ridership and offer better service to the community. The NAACP leadership and some environmental groups objected to the planned route on these grounds.[24]

Hahn was well aware that a heavy rail subway down Vermont Avenue would be superior to a light rail line running parallel along the industrial corridor to the east, but he knew that heavy rail was a political and financial impossibility at that point. Marv Holen, who was chair of the RTD at the time and favored a Vermont Avenue subway, recalled an afternoon meeting with Hahn as the LACTC debated the Long Beach route selection. "I remember him leaning forward," Holen recounted in 2005. "'Marv,' he says, 'it may be better down Vermont, but it will never get done. We can get the line done on the right-of-way, so let's do it there.'" Holen grudgingly accepted Hahn's logic. "Here we are so many years later," Holen acknowledged, "and if not for the [Long Beach] line, there would be nothing there."[25] Hahn's and Holen's assessment was likely correct, especially given the difficulty that starter line advocates had in securing funding for even a small segment of the line from downtown to Hollywood.

WILSHIRE VS. LONG BEACH

An even bigger battle was brewing between Hahn and proponents of the heavy rail starter line subway down Wilshire. Although Mayor Tom Bradley and LACTC appointee Ray Remy had essentially opposed Proposition A from the beginning for fear it would fail, now that the money was available they did not want to see Hahn's regional rail line siphon off the federal money that the Wilshire starter line so desperately needed. The LACTC staff report indicated as much, predicting that the light rail line would compete with the Wilshire subway for funds.[26] Hahn had exacerbated this tension when, within weeks of the Proposition A vote, he met with U.S. secretary of transportation Neil Goldschmidt and RTD president Tom Neusom to discuss the possibility of getting federal funds for his light rail line.[27] Hahn's visit with Goldschmidt drew the ire of Remy, whose subway project could not happen without federal support and who had been carefully lobbying the feds for years. Hahn was now stepping on his turf.[28]

Starter line supporters were unwilling to support the Long Beach route until federal funds were secured for their line first. Supervisor (and subway supporter) Edelman's strategy was to "buy time to use the funds that we have set aside for Wilshire [starter line] as a leverage [sic] for getting Federal monies for the construction of the Wilshire Line."[29] Remy told the *Los Angeles Times* that he would support the Long Beach line only if he received assurance that it would not compete for funding with the starter line.[30] He opposed the study of any particular corridor until the region had an objective analysis that indicated which corridor would be the most efficient and meet the greatest need.[31] Edelman followed suit, writing to the *Times* that, "while we all want rapid transit in Los Angeles as soon as possible, before we make our final commitment to any one line, we owe it to the people in the County to make sure that the line is both feasible and the selection process is fair." He argued, "Each person who supported that tax [Proposition A] hoped that his or her community would be given a fair chance of getting a transit line."[32]

But Hahn refused to back down, and he began to lash out at his critics through the media. He responded to the concerns of people like Remy, who supported heavy rail to the Westside first, by arguing that his route would serve the poor. "In Beverly Hills," he remarked, "everyone has a car and a chauffeur, and they only need [transit] for their maids and gardeners." He was quoted in the *Los Angeles Times* describing the benefits of the Long Beach plan and attempting to intimidate opponents of the line, labeling Remy's concerns "a smokescreen" to protect affluent interests in the downtown and San Fernando Valley regions. "They're playing games there," he charged. "You could build another space shuttle before you build the Wilshire subway. It won't happen in my lifetime."[33]

Hahn's public salvos made an impact. The political situation for the subway and its supporters was perpetually delicate: without a final decision from UMTA on funding for the line, they needed to present a unified front to the federal government. Remy did not want to disturb the fragile starter-line coalition that was crucial to winning federal dollars. According to Edelman's office, in the wake of Hahn's public challenge Remy began to worry that efforts to stop the Long Beach line would backfire on the starter line and possibly hurt Bradley in his run for governor of California that year.[34]

In response to Hahn and the reality of his power on the LACTC, subway advocates changed their tack. Rather than fighting the line, Remy and other starter line advocates instead decided to use the light rail line as further evidence in their case to Washington that Los Angeles was ready for heavy rail as well.[35] Then, to appease the Wilshire line advocates, LACTC leaders lobbied the federal government to consider the sales tax expenditures on the Long Beach line as part of the local match for the Wilshire subway.[36] The compromise benefited both sides and appeared to result in part from Hahn's chest thumping over the Long Beach route.

THE LACTC BOARD VOTES

With the opposition mollified and largely neutralized by Hahn's efforts, the LACTC met to decide the fate of the first rail line to be built on March 24,

1982, almost a year and a half after the Proposition A vote. Supervisors Dana and Hahn, whose districts touched the Long Beach line, gave impassioned speeches extolling its virtues and attempting to address many of the concerns of critics of the route. Hahn expressed hope that the meeting would be a "historic day" to "break through the barrier of transportation in Los Angeles if we had the will to do it."[37]

Following the speeches, the board took a vote. The result was unanimous: the LACTC board decided to bring light rail back to Los Angeles via Long Beach. Despite the reservations that some board members had with the line, they ultimately did not want to cross Hahn and sow disunity at a time when all rail advocates were hoping to demonstrate to the federal government that the region was unified in its desire for rail. Hahn had also assembled a broad and powerful coalition to support the line, and his stature and role in winning the Proposition A vote gave him a moral claim to bringing the first rail line to his district. Richard Stanger, who directed rail development at the LACTC at the time, admitted that the selection was "sort of a reward for Kenny Hahn," but he argued that the route still made sense because "it served a heavily transit dependent area in the county and connected the two largest cities in the county."[38]

The Parsons Brinckerhoff study projected the eventual cost with inflation to be between $192 and $254 million. Although these figures would later prove to be a serious underestimation, based on a less ambitious rail proposal than what the agency eventually built, it also significantly underestimated ridership at 21,000 riders a day. The study's authors predicted that the line could be built in five years.[39] But proponents of other rail routes won some concessions. Based on the report's findings that at least three other corridors were competitive with the Long Beach route, Los Angeles city councilwoman Pat Russell convinced the commission to approve engineering studies, environmental assessments, and right-of-way negotiations for light rail lines on the Firestone Boulevard, Exposition Boulevard, and San Fernando Valley corridors.[40] And Supervisor Edelman commented, "We've not given up hope on the Wilshire line," which he viewed as the county's "main artery of heavy rail."[41]

Then, on April 30, just a month after the LACTC vote, the Supreme Court announced its decision. In a five-to-one ruling, with Rose Bird among the majority, the court concluded that the LACTC was exempt from the Proposition 13 limits because it was not a "special district."[42] The Proposition A victory was therefore constitutional, although the decision would be overturned in 1995 by a more conservative court and then made moot by a 1996 voter initiative, which would impose a two-thirds threshold on all future sales tax measures of this kind.[43]

Hahn was overjoyed, writing another folksy letter to Chief Justice Bird following the decision. "I was visiting China and received a cablegram from my office that the Supreme Court ruled favorably," he told her. "We immediately had a toast."[44] The Supreme Court decision was the final hurdle for Hahn and his fellow Long Beach line advocates. The sales tax increase from Proposition A would now go into effect on July 1, 1982, one year later than scheduled.[45]

Hahn's success demonstrates how a forceful politician, assembling a coalition of powerful elected officials, can bring rail to his district. His stature in the county, his role in bringing Proposition A to victory, and his refusal to let other leaders, including even the state Supreme Court, intimidate him helped him earn consensus on the Long Beach route among the disparate local interests of the sprawling county. As Hahn acknowledged about the region at the time, "In [county] politics there is always the attitude of 'my city' (there are 85 incorporated cities in Los Angeles County and 7 million people) and if they are not personally involved then they do not want to participate even though some of their citizens work downtown and other parts of the county."[46] The Long Beach line overcame this barrier.

The victory energized Hahn as he looked to the next battle: getting the line built. "If we really commit to it," he told the *Times,* Los Angeles could get at least part of the Long Beach line operating in time for the 1984 Olympics.[47]

ON THE ROAD TO NOWHERE

Hahn's ambitions for quick construction were no match for the planning process, however. Two years after the LACTC selected the route, the Long Beach line was experiencing delays and construction had still not begun. LACTC staff could not make a final determination of the route and complete the engineering studies due to the cities of Long Beach and Los Angeles being unable to determine the route of the line through their downtowns. The rest of the line followed the Pacific Electric right-of-way through a low-density corridor and posed less of a planning problem, although there was controversy over whether to separate the rail line from the street level at certain intersections, known as "grade separation." The city of Compton, for example, sued the LACTC to force the line to go either underground or aboveground through its city for safety reasons. With every setback, the estimated cost of the line increased.[48]

The delay exasperated Hahn. He was an old-style politician shaped by the 1950s and 1960s, when government agencies had fewer legal constraints on their ability to impose their will on the populace. New laws and regulations and organized interest groups complicated matters, but so did the varied political terrain of the rail route, which touched multiple cities and various power centers. Nothing could be done without thorough public vetting and broad consensus among the dispersed governing bodies of the transit corridor and their affected constituents along the route. Dissent from a few key politicians or constituent groups could halt the entire project.

Hahn directly lobbied some of they key people holding up the line. He wrote to Long Beach mayor Ernie Kell in September 1984 to express frustration with the inability of Long Beach leaders to determine how the rail line should terminate in their city, thus delaying the entire project. Although he blamed the LACTC for "dragging its feet" and succumbing to "delays and too much indecision," Hahn also felt Long Beach and, by association, Mayor Kell were responsible, too. "Money has been spent, studies have been made, but it all seems to boil down to the usual bureaucratic paper shuffling and jurisdictional squabbling," he told the mayor.[49] Kell responded indignantly. "This is hardly a paper-shuffling exercise," he wrote. "Without a successful first leg of the Light Rail System, the whole project stands to fall apart under criticism of cost and effectiveness."[50]

Hahn's frustration was due to more than just the delay. The cost of the line with all the improvements demanded by local officials along the route was now more than double the original estimate, which had contemplated only a minimalist project.[51] The 1980 estimated cost of $200 million had risen to $500 million by late 1984.[52] Supervisor Edelman even asked his LACTC representative "if it was too late to stop the Los Angeles to Long Beach light rail line" due to the escalating price tag.[53]

GROUNDBREAKING

Finally, in March 1985, the bureaucratic process concluded as the city of Long Beach announced that it had agreed on a downtown route for the rail line.[54]

Two weeks later, the LACTC board approved the final environmental review on the route.[55] With the logjam over, the Blue Line, as it was now called, was about to become a physical reality, five years after voters had approved Proposition A.[56] Despite continuing objections from city leaders in Compton over the route, Hahn had successfully shepherded light rail to his district.[57]

On Halloween Day 1985, the LACTC held a groundbreaking ceremony for its first modern light rail line, paid for completely by local sales tax revenues from Proposition A. Considering that the last Pacific Electric trolley car had finished its run on almost the exact same tracks in 1961, it was a fitting place for Los Angeles to begin a new era of rail service. The route would link downtown Los Angeles to Long Beach at a cost now estimated at $595 million, largely due to a more complicated and expensive route demanded by local officials.

The ceremony was a chance for elected officials to showcase their rail plans. In attendance that day were Mayors Bradley and Kell, as well as Supervisors Edelman, Dana, and Hahn. In his remarks, Mayor Bradley promised that the twenty-one-mile route would serve 35,000 people a day, increasing to 54,000 by the year 2000. "We knew that choosing the first line would be tough," the mayor said, "but with the leadership of the Commission [LACTC] and the support of the communities, we have agreed to start this line." The mayor, who at various points had attempted to stop both Proposition A and the selection of the Long Beach route, concluded: "We all know that Los Angelenos love their cars, but we hope they will fall in love with the convenience and comfort of this light rail project."[58]

The Blue Line had its immediate detractors. Writing in the *Long Beach Press-Telegram,* Jonathan Richmond, a graduate student at MIT, downplayed the benefits of the train. "Light rail has few tangible benefits to offer depressed South-Central Angeles," he wrote. "The work trips of mid-corridor residents . . . are dispersed, with only 9 percent working in downtown Los Angeles." Quoting from a Southern California Association of Governments report on the Blue Line, Richmond argued that the train will "mostly accommodate travelers who would otherwise have taken buses," so the train would likely not result in less traffic or air pollution. Richmond proposed using the money instead for expanded bus service in the region.[59] Peter Gordon, associate professor of urban planning at USC and former ringleader of the anti–Sunset Coast Line academics, was more blunt: "There is just no reason for optimism. It's going to be a ghost train."[60]

But their protests were futile and would ultimately be proved incorrect, as the line would become one of the most highly used in the country.

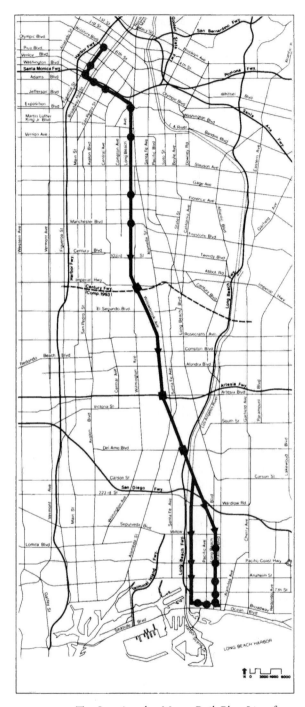

FIGURE 7. The Los Angeles Metro Rail Blue Line from downtown Los Angeles to Long Beach, 1984. (Courtesy of the Los Angeles County Metropolitan Transportation Authority Research Library and Archive. Reprinted with permission.)

Construction was ready to begin to bring rail transit back to Los Angeles, twelve years after Mayor Bradley's "eighteen-month" campaign promise and five years after voters approved Proposition A.

A TAKING

With the Long Beach line selected, LACTC leadership now turned to the question of where to locate the second light rail line in the county. But as they deliberated, a transit opportunity fell into their collective laps, the product of a long-running dispute over the proposed Century Freeway. The legal challenge to that freeway resulted in a settlement favoring transit, and the LACTC board was not willing to let the opportunity pass.

The Century Freeway dispute began in 1965. Ralph and Esther Keith lived then in a typical Southern California neighborhood in Hawthorne.[61] But they came home one day to discover a notice that the California Department of Transportation (Caltrans) would be building a freeway through their property, and they would have to leave. The Century Freeway, as it became known, would be the last major freeway to be built in California. It was originally proposed as a link between eastern Los Angeles County and the coastal area by LAX. The route would plough through largely low-income areas, such as Compton, Watts, Willowbrook, and Hawthorne (the city famous as the birthplace of the Beach Boys).

The Keiths, however, decided to stay in their home and fight the freeway.[62] Five years later, in 1970, the Division of Highways finally had to send an agent to the Keiths' home. Esther Keith locked her front door and refused to let the agent into her house, and thus began the battle over the Century Freeway[63]—a conflict that ultimately led to the creation of the second modern light rail line in Los Angeles.

The Keiths and three other families in the neighborhood found legal assistance from a diverse group of public interest organizations that all had a stake in the freeway plans. The NAACP was concerned about the impact on African American communities along the proposed route, while environmental groups like the Sierra Club and Environmental Defense were in the business of fighting freeways that they viewed as bad environmental policy. These organizations not only had the resources to fight, but they also had new environmental statutes as weapons, particularly the National Environmental Policy Act (NEPA), which provided for community input into environmental impact reports of proposed projects with federal funding.[64]

A ten-year court fight ensued over the freeway's environmental impact statement under NEPA, involving millions of dollars in attorneys fees and intervention from all levels of government, including the cities along the route, the county of Los Angeles, Governor Jerry Brown and his Caltrans chief Adriana Gianturco, and the U.S. Department of Transportation.[65] The parties ultimately reached a settlement in 1981, called a consent decree, that allowed the freeway to proceed as a six-lane highway instead of eight, with a median strip that allowed for the possibility of both rail and carpool lanes.[66] Communities along the way received other concessions as well. Construction began in May 1982.[67]

By that time, Esther Keith had managed to stay in her home, but she was elderly and widowed. Jeff Gates, a photographer who visited with her at this time, observed that the years had taken their toll emotionally. "I think both Ralph and Esther Keith did not know what they were getting into when they decided to protest," he said. "She was sad, and she felt like her life was defined by this situation."[68]

The consent decree meant that Esther Keith had to sell her home to make way for the freeway. She moved a few blocks away but suffered a final irony: although her home was eventually bulldozed, Caltrans's designs for the freeway changed, and the property was never needed. A developer later built homes on the Keiths' empty lot.[69]

LOBBYING FOR RAIL

The 1981 settlement mandated a transit line down the middle of the freeway, but it was up to LACTC leaders to determine its best use. The freeway corridor was identified in the original 1980 Proposition A ballot, so placing rail in the median would fulfill voter expectations. But competing with the Century Freeway line were other transit corridors in more densely populated parts of the city. The Blue Line had been chosen first, largely for political reasons, and now the debate began at the LACTC on the next act.

The Century Freeway corridor was tempting for numerous reasons. Thanks to the consent decree, all the usual obstacles to building a new light rail line were gone: the route was already determined; neighborhood opposition was no longer a factor, since the line would run on the freeway and the protracted court battle had neutralized local opposition; and construction could be relatively quick because it would occur simultaneously with the freeway construction. In addition, the area served by the route was experiencing an economic boom due to the growing aerospace industry in the South Bay, and the route would feature a western terminus near the LAX airport, a major destination for the region. The LACTC members also felt pressure to seize the opportunity to put rail in the median. If the LACTC did not build rail now, the thinking went, it would be a busway, and the chance to put rail there would probably be lost forever.[70] ← reasoning?

As was the case with prior rail selection processes, there was heavy lobbying from local boosters who would benefit from the line. These supporters included members of the South Bay business community, such as the aerospace company Rockwell International and El Segundo-based Computer Sciences Corporation, a software company.[71] Politicians in favor of the route included local mayors;[72] Supervisor Hahn, whose district covered the Century Freeway;[73] and U.S. representative Mervyn Dymally from Compton.[74] Perhaps the most important political advocate for the route was Congressman Glenn Anderson, chairman of the House Public Works and Transportation Committee. Anderson represented much of the Century Freeway area and secured most of the federal funding for it (and it is for him that the freeway was later named). He strongly favored light rail. The Century Freeway "is clearly one of the most attractive rail routes in the County," he wrote to LACTC members. "Of all the potential corridors, the only two ranking higher in both population density and projected daily patronage are the Metro Rail [downtown subway] and the West Los Angeles East-West Line, both of which are significantly more expensive."[75]

Meanwhile, the percentage of Proposition A money available for rail, owing in part to the bus fare subsidy, was steadily shrinking, while construction costs were increasing rapidly. This twofold challenge put pressure on the LACTC to choose a cheap route. Bob Geoghegan, Edelman's representative to the LACTC, advocated securing additional revenue from legislation to create bonds for transit projects. Without that additional cash infusion, he noted, "we'd only be able to build one or two more lines in the foreseeable future."[76]

"WE HAD NO CHOICE"

By June of 1984, Caltrans, the agency responsible for building the freeway, needed a final decision from the LACTC as to which mode of transit the commission would choose. A railway would require different structural engineering on the freeway than a busway, so a decision was necessary to avoid delaying construction.[77] As a result, the LACTC commissioners gathered on June 13 to decide the fate of the median.

At the meeting, member Ted Pierce expressed concern about committing to rail while the Wilshire line's fate was uncertain and the commission was deeply involved in the Blue Line planning. "My only concern is bad timing," he said.[78] Geoghegan agreed but argued passionately that rail was the right decision. He cited an LACTC study led by Richard Stanger showing annual operating cost savings with rail over bus. He also described the impracticality of converting a busway to a railway on the freeway, should the LACTC go with bus first. He wanted the freeway to be built with the best long-term carrying capacity, and that meant a railway. As to arguments that building a rail line would preclude building other, perhaps more deserving, lines identified by Proposition A, Geoghegan rebuffed them. "The staff report that we have indicates that the Century rail line will not reduce in any significant way the opportunity to build any other Prop. A lines," he argued, relying on Stanger's LACTC report that would later be proven incorrect.[79] (Stanger ultimately blamed Caltrans for shifting construction costs unfairly to the LACTC and therefore increasing the final cost.)[80]

The commissioners agreed with Geoghegan. After taking the resolution to a vote, the LACTC unanimously approved building light rail as the best option for the $2 billion freeway.[81] The future Green Line would run down the middle of the freeway and east from the Los Angeles Airport for 17.3 miles to within a few miles of the Los Angeles–Orange County line in Norwalk. Although Caltrans was in charge of building the line, the LACTC voted to fund the $133 million cost with Proposition A funds. At the time, the LACTC predicted that the ridership on the Green Line would exceed 100,000 riders daily and that it would open in 1993.[82]

The political support and potential low cost of building rail on the median appeared to have convinced the commissioners to support rail over a busway. "The rail line had slightly better—but not substantially better—ridership" compared to a busway, Stanger said in 2012. But, he acknowledged, "Most importantly, all 28 cities along the Century Freeway corridor and in the south bay, each one of them, approved resolutions supporting rail conversion in the median. It was the first time all 28 cities agreed to anything, and they all sent resolutions to the LACTC."[83] He also noted that "the cost was relatively inexpensive because Caltrans had to build the busway [in the middle of the freeway] anyway."

LACTC members later claimed to have felt pressured to favor the rail line by the circumstances. "We were going to do it on a priority basis," Geoghegan later explained of the rail-selection process. "But they were about to start construction on the freeway, so the question was whether we build it for carpools or for rail. And if we built it without rail, it becomes prohibitively expensive to ever put it in again. We had no choice."[84] Geoghegan's desire not to miss the "window of opportunity" with the freeway construction forced him into voting for a line that was less than ideal and that was lower on the priority scale than other corridors in the county.

Geoghegan's vote also came from assurances he received from LACTC staff members about future rail plans. He liked the idea of a rail line serving LAX, and LACTC staff promised him that the line would be "to, or near or convenient to, LAX." They told him that a spur line might be built to LAX later.[85]

Ray Remy, Mayor Bradley's representative to the commission, also felt conflicted, but he voted in favor of the line because of the job centers in the corridor. He believed that the area's economic boom would produce high ridership for the line. "Where would you get the majority of patronage for a Green Line? You got it from people who lived in Downey, Norwalk. Not blue collar people, but steelmaker types, working in the aerospace industry. A big chunk of that was in that corridor, in El Segundo, Torrance. It really had a lot of patronage and would take pressure off the Century Freeway."[86] Like Geoghegan, he cited the consent decree's allowance for rail in the median as the context for his vote.

The LACTC approved what would become the Green Line with high hopes: it would help bring rail service to busy LAX; it would have high ridership for the economically booming South Bay; it would link to the Long Beach line; and it would be relatively inexpensive and easy to build. Ultimately, these hopes did not materialize, and the LACTC would probably have been better off building a less expensive busway in order to preserve rail funds for more densely populated corridors with better opportunities for station area development. But the LACTC had now committed itself to a second rail project following the Proposition A victory.

MISSING ITS CONNECTION

The LACTC needed to make a critical—and controversial—decision on the Green Line: at the western terminus of the Century Freeway, would the line veer north to serve LAX or south to serve the aerospace industry? No compromise was possible for this route: serving LAX would take the line irrevocably north, and turning it south would point the route permanently in the direction of the South Bay. The LACTC did not have the funds to build both extensions at the time.[87]

While casual observers wanted the line to serve the airport, the LACTC staff saw greater ridership potential from local employees over air travelers. "At the time, El Segundo had 90,000 jobs," explained Stanger, "and it was projected [in the mid-1980s] to grow to 110,000 jobs in the next ten to twenty years." By comparison, "the airport had 50,000 jobs, but most of them were in the periphery of the airport. The U.S. Post Office had a large center, and there were shipping companies, but they were not in the central terminals. And the periphery is a large area, mainly along [the Imperial Highway bordering the southern runway], where the jobs were all spread out." Air travelers would not make up the difference. "We had done studies of passengers to LAX that would take rail," Stanger continued, "but it wasn't much, maybe five to six thousand a day. Families going to Europe with suitcases are not going to take a rail line anyway."[88]

LACTC leaders agreed with the staff assessment that the line should not prioritize airport service over a larger employment destination. Commissioner Geoghegan generally believed that people tended not to use rail to get to airports because "it's hard to lug your luggage to the airport, and if you're dropped off by a car, you don't need to pay for parking."[89] Remy saw the same problems with airport service. "You don't find many airport travelers who are going to take luggage on a light rail system," he said. "If you're flying on a less expensive ticket, then those people might use it. But those [patronage] numbers are not huge."[90] Rail service to the airport would therefore appeal more to airport employees who needed to commute there regularly but not as much for infrequent air travelers.

The LACTC at the time was chaired by Jacki Bacharach, an at-large commissioner who was elected by a vote of the cities within Los Angeles County, with each city getting one vote. Bacharach represented Rancho Palos Verdes, an upscale South Bay community—a fact not lost on critics when she began advocating for a southern turn to the Green Line. But Bacharach maintained that she was not trying to benefit her home district, despite the southern extension's plan to terminate in Torrance, providing key commuter access for Ranchos Palos Verdes residents. "The people in Palos Verdes don't want any rail and are not demanding it," she said, "so there was no pressure on me."[91]

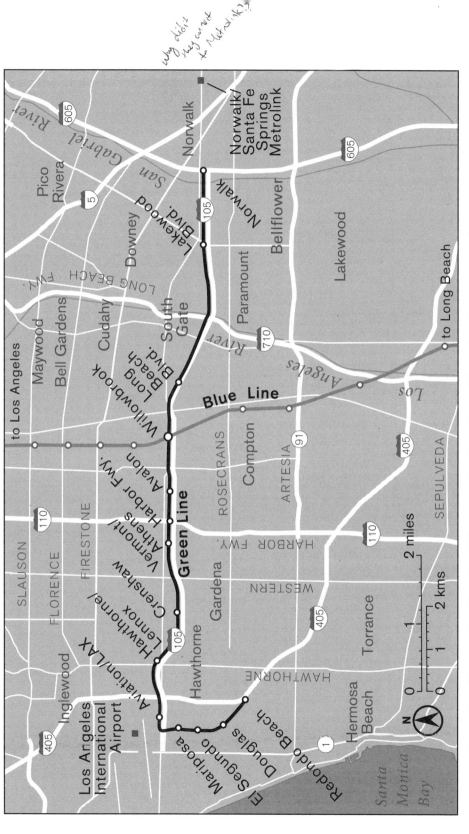

why didn't they connect to Metrolink?

FIGURE 8. The 2013 Green Line route from Norwalk to El Segundo and Manhattan Beach. (Map by Pease Press Cartography.)

Bacharach also had the LACTC studies to support her position based on the greater patronage potential from serving the aerospace industry over LAX. Geoghegan acknowledged that, in retrospect, LACTC staffers like Stanger "couldn't have predicted the crash of the industry there," which occurred with the end of the Cold War in the early 1990s.[92]

Ultimately, Bacharach and her LACTC colleagues decided unanimously that the rail route should head south toward the economic boom areas, with an eventual extension to Torrance and to a possible Blue Line connection in the south.[93] To win the support of members like Geoghegan, the LACTC promised to consider adding a spur line to LAX. Geoghegan also noted that there was "the possibility of a San Diego Freeway line at the time that would connect and possibly go to LAX, so that took away some of the urgency."[94]

Ray Remy also voted in favor of the southern terminus configuration, but he later admitted, "It was stupid not to go to airport." However, Remy felt that the Century Freeway consent decree was done in part "to serve the aerospace industry, El Segundo, and there was not a significant benefit going north to airport."[95] LACTC arguments, as well as the possibility of a northern spur line to Santa Monica from the airport, convinced Remy to approve the Green Line plan.

LACTC staff had envisioned the Green Line as the foundation for various light rail extensions, including south to Torrance, east to Orange County, and north to LAX and Westchester.[96] But as the money for these extensions dwindled, the existing line would have to suffice by itself, and an airport connection would prove elusive.

THE CENTERS

While LACTC leaders were learning about the political realities of trying to plan the first Proposition A light rail lines in the early 1980s, RTD staff had already encountered these challenges in planning the starter line. The RTD began the process in the late 1970s, using the Ford administration's UMTA funding grant to begin determining the starter line route. As with the LACTC experience, politics and external circumstances played a significant role in the decision-making process and often overrode objective analysis of ridership and land development potential. Plotting a subway through the politically decentralized landscape of Los Angeles meant ceding control to numerous fiefdoms of federal, state, and local politicians who had their own interests when it came to planning subway stations that often did not match the best means of maximizing the rail investment.

In developing a subway route, RTD staff took inspiration from the innovative planner of the city of Los Angeles, Calvin Hamilton, who had drafted a vision in the early 1970s for how rail could intersect with future high-density "centers" planned throughout Los Angeles. Although RTD planners tried to direct the subway to Hamilton's centers, by the time the process ended, coordinated land use and rail planning had died a gory death.

Hamilton embodied smart and visionary planning, and his concept for how rail could complement and enhance land use was in some ways ahead of its time. World War II helped teach him what made a city great, as he spent his time during the war as a guide for radio operators in South America. In the process, he observed the critical attributes that made certain cities around the world so successful. After the war, the Indianapolis native went to Harvard to get his degree in urban planning, and he eventually became the Los Angeles city planning director in 1964, in which capacity he could put his theories into practice.

When Hamilton arrived in Los Angeles, the size and enormity of the region bewildered him. He chartered helicopter trips over the city just to get his bearings. Then one year after his arrival, the state began requiring cities and counties to draft "general plans," legal documents that would present a local master plan for future development. Hamilton and his crew in the City Planning Department began conducting outreach with residents to draft the city's first general plan.

In that process, Hamilton learned firsthand that in Los Angeles "the car is king" and that most Angelenos considered single-family homes with a barbecue and a pool the ultimate symbols of a good life.[97] But he also learned that the picture was more complex than most casual observers of L.A. life assumed. He recalled that Angelenos of the 1960s "also indicated that there needed to be more of a variety of housing that would meet their needs at very different points." Single-family houses were certainly the ideal for families, but most people Hamilton talked to recognized that young couples, for example, might prefer to begin their lives together in an apartment in denser neighborhoods not far from the single-family suburbs of their youth.[98]

Years of outreach finally produced a general plan from the City Planning Department in January 1970. In 1974, the City Council formally adopted what became known as the "Centers Plan."[99] Hamilton envisioned a future for greater Los Angeles that would contain forty-eight high-density centers

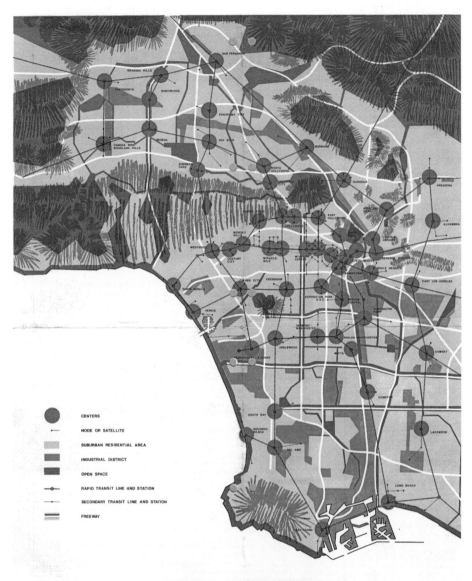

CONCEPT • LOS ANGELES

FIGURE 9. The Los Angeles County "Centers Concept" in 1974, in which rail transit connected high-density centers across the region, indicated here by the circles. (Courtesy of the Los Angeles County Metropolitan Transportation Authority Research Library and Archive. Reprinted with permission.)

throughout the region, each one containing a concentration of jobs, housing, and retail. Twenty-nine of these centers would be within the city's boundaries, and they would all be linked by heavy rail transit.[100] Theaters, restaurants, department stores, and grocery stores would coexist with high-rise office and apartment buildings, all located above high-speed subway stations. Beyond each center, the plan preserved the low-density Los Angeles neighborhoods of single-family homes. Buses would ferry residents of these neighborhoods to the center.

The Centers Plan attempted to concentrate future growth in walkable, urban communities that contained all of the necessities for living, while allowing neighborhoods that preferred a low-density character to avoid development. Because each center would be linked by rapid transit, travel throughout the region would be fast and efficient, and the increased density within the city meant less development pressure on outlying areas, as well as less traffic and smog. The Centers Plan was Hamilton's attempt to balance the decentralized nature of the Los Angeles lifestyle with a desire for increased mobility and compact, car-free urban neighborhoods.

THE BATTLE OVER WOUNDED KNEE

Political realities quickly tested Hamilton's vision. Pressure from Mayor Bradley and the city of Los Angeles forced the RTD to cut short the subway's route along the high-density Wilshire corridor in order to service the San Fernando Valley to the north. "The Valley constituency is extremely important in Los Angeles," observed Marv Holen, chair of the RTD at the time. Holen and others at the RTD wanted the subway to travel all the way down Wilshire, forming a "backbone" to supplement the bus system. But Holen noted that "anyone who wants to be mayor has got to carry the Valley."[101] And that meant supporting a rail line that served the Valley as well as Westside constituents.

Despite its generally suburban character and lack of population density sufficient for rail, the San Fernando Valley represented over half the landmass of the city of Los Angeles and much of its money and voters. Mayor Bradley knew that Valley constituents needed to have a stake in the subway system, and he even proposed a two-way start on subway construction from both the Valley and the downtown terminus to reassure Valley residents that they would have a station.[102]

If the Valley had to have a subway, Holen preferred that the line travel most of the way down the densely populated portion of Wilshire Boulevard to Westwood Boulevard near UCLA and then veer north under the Santa Monica Mountains to Van Nuys in the Valley. But state senator David Roberti, the powerful official who represented Hollywood in Sacramento, and the Hollywood Chamber of Commerce did not like that plan. That route would bypass Hollywood completely, and the Hollywood Chamber of Commerce felt it needed better rail access to attract investment and revitalize their dilapidated community. As Mike Woo, former councilman to the area and Roberti aide, recalled, "Community leaders recognized that getting rail transit could be a very strong impetus for real estate development."[103]

The chamber found a willing advocate at the right time in Roberti. Roberti was majority leader of the state senate and member of the senate finance committee, and he was ready to defend the interests of the chamber. "I represented the area and I wanted to have a relationship with the business community," Roberti later acknowledged, adding that the chamber "definitely would have had an influence on me."[104] But Roberti also had philosophical reasons for wanting the subway to serve downtown Hollywood. A rail station in central Hollywood would give better access to low-income riders than if it continued along Wilshire through wealthy communities. "If it was going to go west," Woo remarked, "he wanted to ensure that people who weren't rich would have access to the system."[105]

Roberti also harbored doubts about the wisdom of the starter line in the first place. "His attitude was that if it was going to happen, he really would prefer that it benefit his district," Woo said. "But there was also more a part of him that was questioning whether this was really the right decision for L.A."[106] Given Roberti's ambivalence about the value of the line in the first place, he was not afraid to jeopardize funding for it to get his demands for a station met. "I believe the money should go for buses, anyway," he told the *Los Angeles Times*.[107]

Roberti's influence on the RTD, coupled with political pressure to serve the Valley with the small starter line, forced planners to choose a subway route through Hollywood and out to the Valley at North Hollywood. After conducting the federally mandated alternatives analysis on the route, the RTD board of directors voted on October 12, 1978, to approve an eighteen-mile rail rapid transit line that extended from Union Station through downtown Los Angeles and west along Wilshire Boulevard to Fairfax. At Fairfax, the subway would turn to the right and head north through Hollywood, under the Santa Monica Mountains, and out to North Hollywood. It included seventeen stations and came with an estimated price tag of $1.12 billion.

Despite the premature turn to the Valley, Holen and other Wilshire advocates had at least managed to get the Wilshire segment of the subway west to Fairfax. As a result, the starter line would serve the "Miracle Mile" district that stretched along Wilshire from La Brea to Fairfax. This area included some of the region's top attractions, including the Los Angeles County Museum of Art and the Page Museum at the La Brea Tar Pits, as well as Hamilton's proposed centers at Fairfax and La Brea. Many of the museum leaders were strongly supportive of a subway, believing rail would increase the number of visitors, and Holen had a personal affinity for cultural institutions and an appreciation for history and art.[108]

This route, with the turn at Fairfax, became known as the "wounded knee" alignment because of the shape it took on a map, with the "knee" being the right turn at Fairfax. After traveling north along Fairfax, the subway took another right to the east at Santa Monica Boulevard, heading backwards before going north under the mountains again. On a map, the route looked like a human leg forced to the ground by an injury. The "wounded" part of the nickname would become sadly prophetic.[109] But the route laid the foundation for what would become the heavy rail system in Los Angeles.

ROBERTI BENDS THE KNEE

Roberti, however, was still not satisfied with the station locations in the RTD plan. After traveling north on Fairfax, the subway would stop in Hollywood at the intersection of Selma and Las Palmas, near the major intersection of Hollywood and Highland. From there it would continue to the Hollywood Bowl (later redirected to serve Hollywood and Highland) and out to the San Fernando Valley, bypassing the core of downtown Hollywood and the famous intersection of Hollywood and Vine and also missing an opportunity to serve one of Hamilton's centers.[110]

Roberti used pending state legislation that would set aside state gas tax funds for the starter line as leverage. The RTD was counting on the state to help fund the eighteen-mile starter line's $2 billion cost. The agency needed a 20 percent local match of $400 million, and with the LACTC pledging $100 million, the RTD was relying on Sacramento to contribute the remaining

$300 million from state gas tax revenues collected in Los Angeles County. "I was majority leader [of the state senate] at that time," Roberti later stated, "and we were trying to leverage that."[111]

Roberti blocked passage of the bill, AB 1429, in order to introduce amendments that would guarantee a station in Hollywood and that would give the LACTC oversight over RTD decisions on the route. Mayor Bradley opposed Roberti's amendments, but he was concerned that the legislature might defeat the bill without Roberti's support. If AB 1429 died, it would end Bradley's hopes to apply for federal funding in 1980. To make matters worse, another state senator began demanding a station change. Senator Diane Watson, who represented the area south of Roberti, started clamoring for a station at Wilshire and Crenshaw to serve her predominantly transit-dependent constituents along Crenshaw Boulevard to the south.[112]

Local officials negotiated with Roberti through the LACTC.[113] They agreed to Roberti's demands to have the LACTC review all RTD decisions on the matter (a compromise that the RTD deeply resented)[114] and gave Roberti two new stations, at the intersections of La Brea and Santa Monica Boulevard and Sunset and Cahuenga. This second stop would place the subway near the famous intersection of Hollywood Boulevard and Vine Street in central Hollywood.[115] With Roberti finally appeased, the RTD voted in September 1979 to reaffirm its choice for the Wilshire route via Hollywood, as part of its ultimate proposal to UMTA.[116] Roberti had gotten his wish.

THE END OF THE CENTERS

With the subway route mangled by politics, the final blow to Calvin Hamilton's dreams of orderly development occurred in 1986. That year, the electorate had grown tired of progrowth policies in Los Angeles and the perception that local government would simply do the bidding of real estate developers. Residents began revolting against high-rise development in their communities and the politicians who benefited from it. The city of Los Angeles had never implemented Hamilton's centers concept through zoning. Hamilton blamed the cozy relationships that developers had with council members and Mayor Bradley. "When we were dealing with zoning or community plans, there were often business people who wanted to add to the size of their commercial development or build a new one, or realtors who wanted

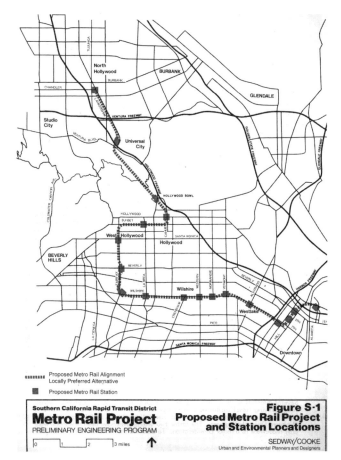

Southern California Rapid Transit District
Metro Rail Project
PRELIMINARY ENGINEERING PROGRAM

Figure S-1
Proposed Metro Rail Project and Station Locations

SEDWAY/COOKE
Urban and Environmental Planners and Designers

0   1   2   3 miles

FIGURE 10. The proposed Los Angeles Metro Rail subway line from downtown, through Hollywood, and ending in North Hollywood in the San Fernando Valley, as submitted in 1983 to the U.S. Urban Mass Transportation Administration by the Southern California Rapid Transit District. The route was dubbed the "wounded knee" alignment due to its shape. (Courtesy of the Los Angeles County Metropolitan Transportation Authority Research Library and Archive. Reprinted with permission.)

to increase the size of their apartments or whatever," Hamilton said. "So they would definitely tell the councilperson that if the councilperson supported what they wanted, they would help provide funds for the next time the councilperson wanted to go for the next election. And they did the same thing in many cases for the mayor."[117]

Savvy politicians picked up the antidevelopment mood. Councilmen Marvin Braude and Zev Yaroslavsky, representing Westside districts increasingly frustrated by development and worsening traffic, introduced Proposition U to limit growth.[118] Yaroslavsky recalled the problem up to that point: "It was a one size fits all approach," he said, "with high-rises being built next to single-family homes... casting permanent shadows" on the homes. "So one day Marvin and I had a sandwich in his office," Yaroslavsky remembered, "and we said, 'We gotta do something.'" They were tired of "fighting every lobbyist who comes in and lobbies the city council and the mayor," so they decided to "pole-vault over all of this craziness" and go to the people with a ballot initiative.[119]

Voters overwhelmingly approved Proposition U with 69 percent of the vote, one of the many statewide antigrowth (or "slow growth") initiatives that year that limited opportunities for transit-oriented development in urban areas. Proposition U cut commercial development in half throughout the city of Los Angeles. Excepted were downtown, Hollywood, and the Wilshire corridor, which therefore preserved some of the density along the subway route. The initiative hastened the demise of the Centers Plan, and the city planning department finally killed the plan through rezoning in 1989.[120]

Despite the rise of antigrowth sentiment in the late 1980s in response to an urban building boom, remnants of the Centers Plan can still be seen today in Los Angeles. The plan resulted in a few high-rise centers at the Warner Center, Universal City, Westwood, Long Beach, and Century City. But only a handful of these centers are connected by rail transit, as Hamilton had once envisioned.

Ultimately, Hamilton's ordered and coherent vision for the region failed for the same reason that comprehensive and objective rail planning never happened. The dispersed political power centers of the county and the exigencies of outside circumstances made it virtually impossible for leaders to implement grand visions.

FOUR

Henry Waxman's Hot Air

THE EXPLOSION THAT FOREVER CHANGED the course of Metro Rail
had its roots in a turn-of-the-century dairy farm. In 1901, Arthur Fremont
Gilmore owned a 256-acre farm near West 3rd Street and Fairfax Avenue, at
a time when the Fairfax district in Los Angeles consisted mostly of bean
fields and cattle pens. He set out to dig a water well on his property, but in
true *Beverly Hillbillies* fashion, Gilmore accidentally struck oil.[1] His discovery prompted an oil exploration boom, and his property later became part of
the Salt Lake Oil Field with over four hundred oil wells.[2] This field, located
on land that would eventually become part of the Wilshire corridor and the
most desired route for the Los Angeles subway, was suddenly the most valuable land in California.[3]

By the 1920s, clever capitalists had largely drained the fields and then
abandoned them. But the state had no laws governing cleanup operations and
the proper capping of wells.[4] Deep pockets of methane gas, a byproduct of oil,
were now rising to the surface from improperly capped wells, joining methane formed from decaying plant and animal matter.[5]

As Angelenos covered the abandoned oil fields with streets, houses, and
businesses, the cement formed a cap that prevented the gas from percolating
through the soil and evaporating. Meanwhile, locals drained the underground aquifers for drinking water, which gave the gas room to expand. In
1976, when scientists determined the water was unhealthy, the city stopped
using the wells. Unusually wet winters over the next decade replenished the
aquifers and pushed the methane to the surface.

One methane pocket was located approximately forty feet below a Ross
Dress-for-Less department store on Fairfax Avenue. The gas seeped between
the floor slab and foundation walls of the store into a basement room that

lacked ventilation.[6] Annexed to the room was the store's employee lounge, and at 4:47 P.M. on March 24, 1985, a worker punched the time clock there. Then all hell broke loose.[7]

Sixty-two-year-old Rose Sanchez was buying a robe for her mother at the Ross cash register when suddenly the earth began to shake. "For a moment we thought it was an earthquake," she said.[8] Then the explosion hit, and it sent the walls flying. Flaming clothes hangers swirled overhead. Chris Moore, a security guard who lived a block from the store, felt the blast in his apartment. "Windows and everything was shaking. I looked outside and I could see debris two or three hundred feet up in the air."[9]

Smaller explosions quickly followed the initial blast, and inside the store Sanchez and several other customers huddled together on the floor. "Suddenly we could see the sky through a large hole in the roof and air came rushing in, creating something like a tornado," Sanchez said. "It looked like it was raining fire. It was like a cyclone. Gusting air, screams, ashes, black objects flying around. It was horrible. Everything was on fire."[10]

The explosion had blown the ceiling up into the air, but now it began to fall back to the ground. Fortunately, a gust of wind caught the roof before it could land on the customers. With fire raining down, they decided to escape to the street. They grabbed pieces of clothing and placed them over their heads to protect themselves from the rain of fire. As they ran to the parking lot, another explosion knocked them to the ground. "We saw the earth crack and flames shooting out," Sanchez said.[11]

Outside, the explosion had ruined the automobiles in the parking lot, cracking the car windows and blistering the paint. The shock wave smashed windows as far as three blocks away and damaged a nearby beauty shop, bank, cafeteria, fish market, variety store, and paint store.[12] Twenty-one people were ultimately sent to the hospital, including some with severe burns.[13]

The disaster shocked Los Angeles. The front page photo of the *Los Angeles Times* the next day resembled a scene of biblical destruction worthy of a Hieronymus Bosch painting.[14] Fairfax residents asked themselves which buildings in the area would be next.

Although businesses in the area reopened four days later,[15] the effects of the explosion on Los Angeles rail transit would last for decades. Henry Waxman, the area's powerful congressman, would use the threat of another explosion to stop a subway he never much cared for in order to protect neighborhoods in his district from gentrification and disruption caused by rail.

FIGURE 11. Aftermath of the Fairfax explosion at the Ross Dress-for-Less store, March 25, 1985. (Photo by Dean Musgrove. Courtesy of the Los Angeles Public Library Photo Collection. Reprinted with permission.)

WAXMAN VS. THE VOLCANO

Following the explosion, Representative Waxman expressed concern that a similar methane gas disaster could occur in the subway tunnels. Waxman was not just an ordinary congressman. He represented some of the wealthiest and most politically liberal constituents in the country. His district on the Westside of Los Angeles included Fairfax, Beverly Hills, Hancock Park, and Westwood, as well as most of the Wilshire corridor where subway advocates hoped to bring the line. He used his access to this fundraising base for the Democratic Party to create a political empire. After Waxman helped his close friend and college classmate Howard Berman get elected to Congress from a neighboring district,[16] local politicians began to fear the "Berman-Waxman Machine," which also included political operative Michael Berman, Howard's brother.[17] A politician who showed disloyalty to the group might find his or her access to wealthy patrons on the Westside cut off, as well as a primary challenger funded by Berman-Waxman supporters.

Leaders of the Southern California Rapid Transit District (RTD) needed Waxman's support for the starter subway line, now officially called Metro Rail. They counted on Congress to authorize $427 million to guarantee completion of the first subway segment.[18] But congressional leaders would not authorize those funds if the representative of the subway's district opposed the project, particularly given Waxman's position as gatekeeper to wealthy Los Angeles political donors. "The notion of vote-counting against Henry Waxman was not something we saw as a good business model for Metro Rail," commented Bevan Dufty, one of the congressional staff negotiators for the system.[19] The Fairfax explosion appeared to be changing Waxman's mind about the value of rail to Los Angeles precisely when the RTD needed his backing the most.

Waxman described himself as a "strong supporter of the original Metro Rail route" during the time leading up to the explosion. But he acknowledged that as a federal representative who tended to campaign on national issues, he "didn't pay much attention" to an issue that was primarily a local matter. "I knew we needed an innovative transportation network," he recalled in 2009. "I was just a supporter, though. Transportation had not been one of my issues legislatively."[20]

Some of Waxman's contemporaries, however, believed his initial support was only tepid. "I don't think he was ever particularly intrigued with the subway system," Ray Remy, Mayor Tom Bradley's former chief of staff, observed.[21] Zev Yaroslavsky, then a Los Angeles city councilman who represented the Fairfax district, also felt that Waxman "was generally skeptical about the subway to begin with."[22]

Waxman admitted that his limited dealings with subway advocates did not leave him impressed with the concept of a subway for Los Angeles or with the politically gerrymandered route designated for the starter line. "When I was brought into the picture and looked at the route, it didn't make a lot of sense to me," he later said. "It just seemed to me it had a lot of territory to cover to get people out of their cars, and this was a very expensive system." Waxman also disapproved of how politics had determined the route. "I asked them, 'Why this route? What about that route?'" he recalled. "They said, 'Well, some important state senator wanted this because of this important constituency and he wanted us to have Metro Rail go through this particular area.' And there was concern about the Valley being left out. So they wanted to go to the Valley, and they wanted to go down Wilshire."[23] The entire project seemed to lack coherence in Waxman's eyes.

Not trusting the RTD's arguments, Waxman relied on an unusual source for counsel. "I remember talking to a reporter at the *L.A. Times*," Waxman recalled, "and I said, 'You've covered this issue a long time; does this make

FIGURE 12. Southern California Rapid Transit District general manager John Dyer *(left)* presents a model subway station to Representative Henry Waxman *(center)* on May 23, 1983. (Courtesy of the Los Angeles County Metropolitan Transportation Authority Research Library and Archive. Reprinted with permission.)

sense to you?' He said no. That weighed heavily on me. Here was somebody who knew about it, and I didn't know a lot about it."[24]

Waxman's lack of commitment to the subway may have been exacerbated by his reportedly weak relationship with Mayor Bradley, the subway's principal advocate. As Remy explained, Waxman's political machine, which included Yaroslavsky and state senator David Roberti, "had a different organizational outlook. They did not in any way want to be directed by the mayor. It was not a warm and fuzzy relationship."[25] With no political or personal ties to Metro Rail, Waxman likely felt less obligated to support it.

HANCOCK PARK, CRENSHAW, AND FAIRFAX

Compounding matters for subway supporters, many of Waxman's most influential constituents opposed the subway, making his support even less likely. In particular, vocal residents of Beverly Hills, Hancock Park, and Fairfax had opposed the subway for various reasons, but mainly out of concern that the rail system would change the character of their neighborhoods by bringing in commuters, traffic, and gentrification. Many Angelenos in other parts of the city suspected that these predominantly white communities feared the influx of minorities.

Homeowner associations in Beverly Hills mobilized to protest Metro Rail, fearing its potential impact on their communities, and the methane explosion gave them a new argument against the project. Diana Plotkin, vice president of the Beverly Wilshire Homeowners Association, testified at a subway hearing that residents in her community were "deeply concerned" about the possibility of another explosion. "Whose idea was it to build a Metro Rail through an oil field?" she asked.[26] But her fears were not just about methane: "If Metro Rail is built," she said at a Los Angeles Planning Commission meeting, "the problems that we would suffer would be tremendous," citing heavier traffic and parking shortages.[27]

For their part, Hancock Park residents had already fought and lost a bitter battle against a proposed Metro Rail station at the intersection of Wilshire and Crenshaw, galvanizing some in that community against the system. Hancock Park was a wealthy, semirural pocket of mostly white owners of single-family homes, including some of the most influential Angelenos.[28] Together with city planners like Cal Hamilton, Hancock Park residents had devised the "Park Mile Plan," which created a two-story height limit on any building along the otherwise densely developed Wilshire Boulevard in their neighborhood. As celebrity resident and RTD board member George Takei related, "We didn't want retail on [the Hancock Park portion of] Wilshire Boulevard. We wanted to preserve the character of Hancock Park as well as the south side of Wilshire" near the neighborhood.[29]

As a result of the land use restrictions, the original Wilshire subway route did not include a station in the Hancock Park area. The decision, however, angered residents along Crenshaw Boulevard to the south, which ended at a "T" on Wilshire in the middle of Hancock Park. Crenshaw Boulevard traveled through some of the most transit-dependent, economically challenged, and African American neighborhoods in Los Angeles, and residents of the corridor wanted a subway station at Wilshire and Crenshaw to provide convenient subway access for bus riders. In response, Hancock Park residents threatened to sue the RTD if the agency placed a station at Crenshaw.[30]

The dispute brought racial politics and community opposition into play for the first time in the subway's history. Crenshaw advocates accused

Hancock Park residents of racism for not wanting "those people" to come to their neighborhood on the subway. "Many supporters of Metro Rail thought it was largely a reaction to having poor people, gang members, and criminals coming out the subway into their neighborhoods," former city councilman and Roberti aide Mike Woo said.[31] Takei acknowledged hearing racist fears privately from neighborhood residents. "Some of the sentiment was 'We don't want that kind of people who use the subway,'" he said. Not wanting his neighborhood's reputation to suffer if the racism of some residents became public, Takei opposed the Crenshaw station to avoid "public hear-ings" and the subway system being "tarnished with that kind of issue."[32]

While racism contributed to the Crenshaw controversy, community opposition to the subway was within the norm of homeowner politics for many reasons besides race. Almost without fail, homeowners tended to oppose large projects in their community, whether they involved subways, hospitals, schools, or high-rise buildings, out of fear that they would bring additional traffic, noise, and development. The subway represented the ultimate bogey-man, combining all those worries. Community opposition to the subway "is not because someone's black or Hispanic," Roberti mused. "It's because they don't want thousands of commuters, whoever they happen to be."[33]

But the conflict became more intense in a city scarred by racial division and violence. The media helped stoke the tensions. In an August 15, 1982, column, for example, Bill Boyarsky of the *Los Angeles Times* mentioned the racial implications of choosing or not choosing a station at Crenshaw, specifically referring to local politicians who believed racial animus played a factor in the station decision-making.[34] Los Angeles city planners took offense and criticized Boyarsky for not mentioning how the station conflicted with the "Centers Concept" (the planning department's blueprint for growth that projected new, high-density development around transit stations) and land use plans for the area.[35] But the racial tensions placed enormous pressure on local officials to defuse the conflict. Supervisor Kenneth Hahn's staff worried that the matter would "develop into a serious community controversy."[36]

Ultimately, the RTD board relented, and its final Environmental Impact Statement (EIS) for the subway included the Crenshaw station. Hancock Park residents had lost the battle, and many remained embittered and opposed to the subway as a result.

While Hancock Park and Beverly Hills opposition may have influenced Waxman (he denied it), resistance from the Fairfax community almost certainly did. Fairfax was home to an enclave of Jewish homeowners and renters, many of them elderly who had settled there after World War II. According to the United States Census of 2000, the Fairfax district had a population of over 12,000 individuals in an area of approximately 1.2 square miles.[37] Yaroslavsky, who represented the neighborhood in the city council, explained: "Congressman Waxman was concerned, and I think legitimately, even before the explosion, about what the impact of the subway would be on the Fairfax area and its residents, the character of the area, the demographics of the area in terms of older people versus younger people, older people and seniors who lived in rent-controlled apartments who were on fixed incomes versus gentrification."[38] Ray Remy saw the same dynamic from the mayor's office, observing that Waxman worried about increased home values that would negatively impact his "elderly and Jewish" constituents.[39]

Yaroslavsky, who was Jewish, also noted the cultural significance of the predominantly Jewish Fairfax neighborhood to Waxman, who was also Jewish. "Henry and I were both elected seven years apart," Yaroslavsky said. "And we were elected essentially by the same constituency of old Jewish mothers who are important to us both culturally and politically," he added with a laugh.[40] Waxman and Yaroslavsky's cultural ties to Fairfax may have made them more sensitive to potential disruptions to the community.

Waxman did not deny wanting to protect Fairfax from gentrification caused by the subway. "I didn't like the idea of it going up Fairfax particularly, because of the disruption of that community," he later said. "But that was the route they had already decided on, and my role was to support getting federal funds for this area."[41]

Metro Rail planners and advocates were aware of the opposition to the subway in the Fairfax community, particularly from businesses and residents along the main thoroughfare who were concerned about construction impacts.[42] However, they hoped that they could overcome the antisubway sentiment and prevail on a route that they believed was in the best interest for the region. By traveling farther west down Wilshire to Fairfax, the subway would attract more riders. But they underestimated the importance of the neighborhood to Waxman.

Once the methane explosion occurred, Waxman was no longer so sure he wanted to support the system. As Yaroslavsky later explained, "That was the straw that broke the camel's back."[43]

Following the explosion, Waxman fixated on the dangers of tunneling through a methane field. He convened a congressional hearing in Los Angeles for engineers and others to testify about the safety of such tunneling. The RTD lined up a panel of experts to support their contention that the subway drilling would pose no threats. At the hearing, engineers overwhelmingly spoke of the safety of drilling through methane gas deposits. Byron M. Ishkanian, principal engineer for mining and tunneling of the state Division of Occupational Safety and Health (Cal/OSHA), gave what Waxman described as "very strong testimony" supporting the safety of tunneling techniques in that area under current construction guidelines.[44]

Meanwhile, the city of Los Angeles appointed an engineer named Ronald J. Lofy to testify as a consultant. Lofy had been on-site immediately after the explosion and had dealt with methane gas complications on other projects in the Fairfax area.[45] Although Lofy believed that the tunneling and train operation could be performed safely, Waxman seized on Lofy's comment that, although there would be relatively little danger once a subway tunnel was in place, "I do not know if any of the present-day conventional tunneling equipment and safety procedures would be able to cope with (an) unexpected chance breakthrough" into a large pocket of methane. After the hearing, Waxman told reporters that the RTD "may not be able to establish that this is the safest route. In that case, I think they're not going to be able to succeed in going forward."[46]

RTD officials scrambled to convince Waxman otherwise. Ishkanian followed his testimony with a letter to Waxman, writing: "Without appearing to be an advocate of the Metro Rail project, I nonetheless feel that it is feasible and much less dangerous to excavate and build than many other projects constructed in the Los Angeles Basin since 1972."[47] Richard Proctor, executive secretary for the RTD Board of Geotechnical Consultants, likewise sent a letter to Waxman: "It is my opinion that the L.A. Metro Rail subway can be safely completed and operated if the appropriate Cal OSHA requirements are met. . . . Indeed, the subway atmosphere may be safer than the basements of some existing structures."[48]

Waxman's allies at the state and local levels began their own investigations. State senator Roberti launched the state's investigation into the explosion. Roberti was a close associate of Waxman, as the congressman had launched Roberti's career by appointing him chair of the Los Angeles County

Young Democrats when Waxman was chair of the statewide body. Roberti also represented Fairfax and did not care for the proposed Fairfax subway extension for reasons similar to Waxman's. "It would pretty much destroy an ethnic community that was long established in Los Angeles," Roberti explained. "If your constituents don't want thousands of commuters coming in, there's not a politician in the world who is not going to respond to that, okay?" Roberti believed that Waxman felt the same pressure from his Westside constituents and chose not to ignore them, even if the project might be for the greater regional good. "They didn't want thousands of commuters, and an office holder responds to that. God knows I did."[49]

Councilmen John Ferraro, who represented Hancock Park and took the neighborhood's side in the battle against the Crenshaw station, and Yaroslavsky, both beneficiaries of the Waxman-Berman Machine, helped launch a city task force to study the methane dangers. Within three months of the explosion, the task force released its findings that deemed the area around Wilshire and Fairfax to be a "high potential methane risk zone."[50]

John Dyer, general manager of the RTD, wrote to Waxman in a last-ditch attempt to reassure him. "We are convinced that Metro Rail can be safely constructed and operated," he said. "Let me be clear, we will not tunnel through any area where a reasonable doubt exists among experts . . . as to the safety of the Project's construction or operation."[51]

But Waxman had made up his mind. Following the release of the studies, he announced that he would oppose federal funding for Metro Rail if the system were to pass through the Fairfax area along Wilshire. "I consider it irresponsible to support a Metro Rail system that would tunnel through areas of potential . . . explosion," he stated. "I'm not willing to take the risk of lives being lost. . . . I want safety to be the paramount issue."[52]

He agreed to support the larger subway project only under the condition that the RTD not tunnel in the methane risk zone identified by the city task force report. "At that point," Waxman later said, "I started getting concerned about the whole system. They were going to tunnel through a high methane gas zone. The whole route included a lot of methane. We didn't know clearly at that point whether that made a lot of sense."[53]

The RTD response to Waxman's threat did not assuage him. "I said, 'This thing doesn't seem to be thought out,'" he remembered telling RTD leaders. "And every time I raised that issue with some of the people from L.A., they were pushing me hard to support it. 'Don't block the system,' they said. 'Don't block the system because we're going to get federal funds. And we've got to get those federal funds.' I said, 'What if you have a system that doesn't work, or it's dangerous? What if it doesn't have the ridership and it's not going to succeed?' They said, 'We think it's good enough, and we don't want to redo it. We don't want to rethink it because federal dollars are at stake.'"[54]

LOSING ONE WITH THE GIPPER

RTD leaders were understandably concerned that Waxman's position would undermine federal support for the entire Metro Rail system. Since the 1980 election of Ronald Reagan (on the same day that Los Angeles voters approved Proposition A, the sales tax measure that jump-started local rail transit), local leaders had to contend with a president and an administration that had an ideological antipathy to public works projects like urban rail transit. The conservative activists who rode to power on Reagan's coattails wanted to roll back domestic spending and shut down federal support for urban transit, and the Los Angeles proposal was a prime target.

Upon assuming office, Reagan issued a "no new rail starts" executive order that halted funding for any urban rail system that had not begun construction. His administration then decreased the original Urban Mass Transportation Administration (UMTA) bargain of 80 percent federal matching funds for local projects. RTD officials had hoped for 75 percent,[55] but Houston city leaders, who were also competing for federal money for their $2.35 billion proposed rail project, requested a 50 percent federal share.[56] In response, RTD leaders decreased their request to 62 percent.[57] Los Angeles had clearly missed the window in the 1970s when the federal government had offered a strong funding commitment for local transit.

At this point, the Los Angeles congressional delegation (including Waxman) was generally friendly to the rail project, and Congress was still dominated by representatives who wanted to fund large infrastructure projects for their constituents. When Houston voters rejected a bond measure to fund their rail system in 1983, Congress offered Los Angeles $117.2 million to finance advance design work and begin construction.[58] A reluctant President Reagan signed the earmark into law in August,[59] and local officials hoped for a June 1985 groundbreaking.[60]

UMTA still had not made a long-term commitment to fund the project, however. As a result, the RTD chopped the subway route into smaller fundable segments. The original 18 miles now became an 8.8-mile "Minimum

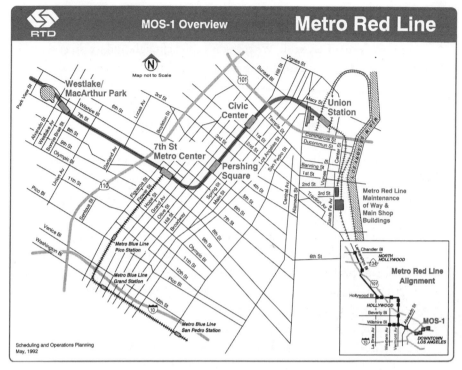

FIGURE 13. Southern California Rapid Transit District map depicting the stations of the first four-mile minimum operating segment (MOS-1) of the Los Angeles Metro Rail subway, as well as an inlay of MOS-1 in relation to the rest of the line, May 1992. (Courtesy of the Los Angeles County Metropolitan Transportation Authority Research Library and Archive. Reprinted with permission.)

Operable Segment," or MOS, from downtown to Hollywood. But UMTA leaders were reluctant to commit funds for even the 8.8 miles. Instead, they offered to fund the subway from downtown to Alvarado or possibly Vermont.[61] These first four miles of the line included only five stations from Union Station, the city's main railroad terminal, to Wilshire Boulevard and Alvarado Street. This alternative was designated the truly Minimum Operable Segment, or MOS-1.[62]

This small starting segment represented a departure from how other cities' regional rail systems began. For example, in 1969 Congress authorized $2.5 billion for a planned 98-mile rail system in Washington, D.C., that started with construction on a 47-mile segment.[63] Leaders in the San Francisco Bay Area planned the Bay Area Rapid Transit (BART) system to cover 71.5 miles, with a 28-mile first phase.[64] While the minimum segment in

Los Angeles may have benefited federal funders who wanted to cut annual costs and obligations, it created a political challenge for local leaders. The small size led to parochial objections from leaders in other parts of the region who were frustrated that rail was not coming to their constituents right away. And the segment engendered criticism of the hefty price tag that was disproportionate to the initial ridership. After all, the ultimate ridership benefits would not come until the regional system materialized. As Dufty commented, "4.4. miles wasn't that exciting. Not when it's for people to go from Union Station to Macarthur Park."[65] It was akin to building the first telephone when there was nobody yet to call.

UMTA approved the project in November 1984, agreeing to pay $555 million of the 4.4-mile project's estimated cost of $721 million.[66] But the tiny route pleased no one and threatened to splinter the rail coalition of downtown business leaders, San Fernando Valley constituents, and state and local politicians. Frustrated San Fernando Valley officials tried to force the subway to come to their district immediately. State senator Alan Robbins from Van Nuys proposed a bill that would require subway work on the North Hollywood station to begin within a year of downtown subway construction and 15 percent of all nonfederal Metro Rail funds to be spent on Valley projects each year.[67] Meanwhile, the downtown business lobby became upset with RTD leaders' negative response to the Reagan administration for its antisubway policies. The pro-Reagan business leaders threatened to drop out of the federal lobbying efforts altogether. "Metro Rail is probably a lost cause as it is," wrote Supervisor Ed Edelman's chief of staff Bob Geoghegan at the time, "but if we lost Republican and business support by attacking Reagan, I don't think there will be any hope at all."[68]

Reagan's landslide reelection in November 1984 only emboldened his opposition to the subway. With the price of the subway to the Valley now estimated at $3.4 billion,[69] the project became a political target for the Reagan administration. UMTA head Ralph Stanley chided the region in February 1985: "Los Angeles has got to recognize that there is not unlimited federal funding for both highway and mass transit projects."[70] Meanwhile, Reagan's budget director, David Stockman, threatened to erase Metro Rail from the federal budget entirely, citing the massive budget deficits.[71] He called the subway "foolish for us, as federal taxpayers, who are bankrupt, to get into."[72] As the administration pressed Congress to reign in subway funds, Los Angeles city councilman Zev Yaroslavsky stated the obvious: "Metro Rail is clearly in critical condition."[73]

The delicate federal situation made the RTD unwilling to cede to Waxman's demands to reroute the subway away from Wilshire. RTD leaders feared that any change in the route would undermine existing support and provide opponents with ammunition to destroy it. In response, Waxman intended to offer an amendment to the congressional funding legislation that would withhold all funding for the subway.[74]

Waxman found a willing Republican ally in local congresswoman Bobbi Fiedler, a conservative who rode to power in 1980 on Reagan's coattails and the backlash against school integration efforts. Shortly after coming to office, Fiedler had successfully helped torpedo Bradley's beloved downtown people mover automated rail project, a proposed 2.9-mile, fully automated and electrically powered elevated rail system that would have carried travelers from Union Station to the downtown convention center. Although the Carter administration had committed funds for planning, the newly elected Reagan wanted to kill the project.[75] Fiedler added a legislative amendment to strip it of federal funds, which would have covered 80 percent of its cost. (Visitors to downtown Los Angeles can still see empty spaces in buildings where the people mover would have gone.) Her victory emboldened her to take on Metro Rail and city leadership.[76] At one point, she even engaged in a verbal sparring match with Los Angeles deputy mayor Tom Houston, telling Houston that the subway was "catering to the downtown business interests," while Houston called her a "liar."[77]

The Waxman and Fiedler duo were now ready to launch a bipartisan death assault on Metro Rail. The House Subcommittee on Transportation had approved $130 million in funding for the 4.4-mile MOS-1,[78] with an unprecedented directive to the recalcitrant Reagan administration to guarantee $427 million total funding for this segment.[79] The bill would now go to the House floor, where Waxman and Fiedler lay in wait.

RTD officials knew they needed to do something to stop Waxman. "This was high profile," commented James Seeley, chief lobbyist for the city of Los Angeles in Washington, D.C. "And the fact that Waxman had [Fiedler] to side with him, and within his district, would give him some clout and might be able to keep the project from happening."[80] Metro Rail supporters sent a team of influential lobbyists to Washington to meet with Waxman, including Mickey Cantor, future chair of Bill Clinton's 1992 campaign for president and secretary of commerce under President Clinton in the late 1990s.[81] Democratic congressmen Julian Dixon and Glenn Anderson, both key allies of Tom Bradley's and strong supporters of Metro Rail, also lobbied Waxman directly.[82]

Congressman Dixon was a close friend of both the mayor and Waxman, whose machine had helped elect Dixon.[83] Dixon's involvement in the negotiations became critical. He represented the area immediately south of Waxman's district, with a predominantly African American constituency and outside the methane zone identified by the city's task force report. Although it, too, contained methane gas deposits, the task force report never studied Dixon's district. His constituents generally supported Metro Rail and were prepared to reap the benefits of the subway if Waxman's constituents did not want it.[84] RTD leaders hoped Dixon could broker a compromise with Waxman.

Only an hour before the floor vote, after three days of lobbying, Dixon persuaded Waxman to allow Metro Rail to veer south through Dixon's district and thus avoid Waxman's district to the north. The compromise also included an alternate route north to the Valley to avoid Fairfax. When Waxman journeyed to the House floor to tell Congresswoman Fiedler of his change of heart, her face reportedly turned white with shock.[85]

Waxman and Dixon's amendment passed the House, along with the appropriation of $429 million for MOS-1.[86] California's two senators, Democrat Alan Cranston and Republican Pete Wilson, shepherded the compromise plan to success in the Senate.[87] After a contentious conference committee,[88] President Reagan signed the bill as part of an enormous federal spending bill just a few days before Christmas 1985.[89]

Despite signing the bill, Reagan later called the subway an example of "a ton of fat in this trillion-dollar government," singling it out in a weekly radio address. "I'm talking about government spending over $2 billion for a Los Angeles mass transit system," Reagan complained, "about as much as government could collect in revenue from all the individual income taxes paid in the state of Mississippi this year."[90] Reagan tried to direct UMTA to negotiate a bad contract with the RTD for the funds. A high-ranking official in the U.S. Department of Transportation said, "If you are asking if we will take every opportunity not to spend the money on the project in Los Angeles, the answer is yes."[91]

Undeterred, Bradley called the signing a "wonderful holiday gift." Acknowledging the opposition that had consumed his effort to build the subway, he said: "If we had a dollar for every time somebody said Metro Rail was dead, we could have built this system."[92]

UMTA finally committed to spending $402 million of the money that Congress had appropriated. The federal commitment would total $605 million of the overall $1.25 billion price tag for the 4.4-mile MOS-1. The remaining $203 million in federal funds would have to be secured from new congressional appropriations in the coming years.[93]

After all these years, local officials finally had money to begin construction of the Los Angeles subway.

UNDERSTANDING WAXMAN

The Waxman-Dixon compromise had kept the subway alive, but it was wounded. Waxman's opposition meant that the subway would not be able to travel down the densely populated Wilshire corridor.[94] Wilshire Boulevard, which stretched sixteen miles from the downtown business district to the ocean in Santa Monica, arguably constituted the most transit-friendly corridor in the western United States. In the postwar years, development mushroomed with dozens of modern high-rise office buildings, luxury hotels, and residential apartment towers, albeit punctuated by a low-density pocket at Hancock Park and in some parts immediately surrounded by neighborhoods of single-family homes. The corridor was also home to major civic institutions like the Los Angeles County Museum of Art and the University of California, Los Angeles. Bus ridership alone on Wilshire was among the highest in the United States, with combined ridership in excess of 100,000 riders per day by 2006.

As Supervisor Edelman commented in 2004, "Unfortunately, [the subway] should have gone along Wilshire Boulevard all the way to the ocean." Edelman did not believe methane was a legitimate reason to stop the subway, and he blamed Waxman and his constituents. "People there didn't want folks to come out of the subway into their neighborhood. Pathetic," he said. "Methane is not limited to one area," Edelman continued. "We have it all over. That was used as a pretext to stop the thing."[95] Supporting Edelman's argument, Bob Geoghegan cited a construction engineer who pointed out that "we put storm drains down through there all the time, multistory skyscrapers all over town." Ironically, Geoghegan observed, "Methane gas is higher outside of the exclusion zone" through which Waxman wanted no tunneling.[96]

Waxman responded to these criticisms by arguing that safety had always been his primary concern, citing his public support for Metro Rail up until

FIGURE 14. The Wilshire corridor follows the namesake boulevard through Los Angeles in this March 2006 photo. Westwood Village and part of UCLA are in the foreground, with Century City in the center to the right of Wilshire. Downtown skyscrapers are visible on the horizon following a row of buildings along the boulevard. (© 2013 Ron Niebrugge /wildnatureimages.com. Reprinted with permission.)

the Fairfax explosion. "How many of us would take an airline trip which had been identified as extremely hazardous, when we could merely avoid the flight and take a different one?" he argued. "It's no different in this instance."[97]

But Waxman's argument that tunneling was unsafe always rested on weak evidence. Engineers overwhelmingly supported the safety of tunneling through these pockets. Even Waxman's ally Zev Yaroslavsky conceded the point. "I never believed, and none of our building experts ever believed, that there was an issue of safety," he said in 2005 of the methane issue. "You need to vent it, you need to take precautions, but it's totally mitigable."[98] The inability of these engineers to convince Waxman during those hearings indicates that the congressman's hardened position was not solely about methane. His disdain for the subway project in general, and particularly for its chosen route via Fairfax, made him unwilling to entertain evidence to the contrary.

Ultimately, the factual weakness of his position, coupled with strong constituent desire to expand rail to the Westside, left him subject to criticism and suspicion by many rail transit advocates. They charged that his position was phony and motivated by a desire to protect his "Not in My Backyard" (NIMBY) constituents. For example, in 2005 writer Eric Berkowitz called him "the obstructionist" who pandered to the "fears of his well-heeled constituency" in the *Los Angeles Weekly*.[99] And that same year, author D.J. Waldie wrote an op-ed for the *Los Angeles Times* arguing that "Anglo homeowner fears of 'those people' coming to their neighborhood" was the reason for the subway ban."[100]

But Waxman remained resolute, always arguing for safety. "Basically he is straight now as he was then," said James Seeley, the Washington, D.C., lobbyist, in 2008. "He has always been tough on health aspects, like clean air. Probably he wanted to be a doctor but became a politician instead." Seeley summed up Waxman's position: "He didn't need a whole lot of rationale, and he didn't move once he got set in his ways. That was it."[101]

REROUTING THE SUBWAY

The Waxman ban forced the RTD to find a new route from downtown Los Angeles to Hollywood that did not involve Fairfax. Before the ban, subway officials planned to reach Hollywood via the Wilshire route, with a northward jog directly underneath Fairfax. State senator Roberti had an alternative route in mind: Vermont Avenue. After the methane explosion, Roberti helped restrict the use of state funds for the subway in the methane zone as Waxman did with federal funds, and he used the subway explosion to force a route change to Vermont. "I took advantage of that [the methane explosion] when I was in a position of leadership," he said, "for that period of time when the activity was at the state level, which wasn't that long."[102] Roberti's efforts had Waxman's blessing: the route was part of Julian Dixon's handshake agreement with Waxman to save the system.[103]

Roberti was born and raised along the Vermont corridor in Hollywood, and he saw Vermont as a good location for the subway. "There was generally fairly decent support ... for that line up Vermont," he noted. He recalled riding the Pacific Electric Yellow Cars along Vermont as a child and observed that the corridor had developed around that transit route. "So it made sense in my mind that you could recreate what were the conditions that built the place up in the first place," he said.[104]

The Vermont corridor was a politically inviting place to locate rail. It contained large health and educational centers that the subway could service, including hospitals and Los Angeles City College. But more important, the corridor was far less residential than Fairfax. "If a rail line goes through an

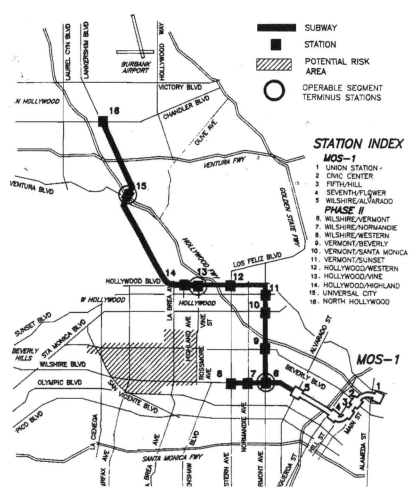

SCRTD METRO RAIL
LOCALLY PREFERRED ALTERNATIVE
WILSHIRE/VERMONT/HOLLYWOOD BLVD. SUBWAY
LPA ADOPTED BY SCRTD BOARD OF DIRECTORS JULY 14, 1988

SUBWAY

STATION

POTENTIAL RISK
AREA

OPERABLE SEGMENT
TERMINUS STATIONS

STATION INDEX
MOS-1
1 UNION STATION
2 CIVIC CENTER
3 FIFTH/HILL
4 SEVENTH/FLOWER
5 WILSHIRE/ALVARADO
PHASE II
6. WILSHIRE/VERMONT
7. WILSHIRE/NORMANDIE
8. WILSHIRE/WESTERN
9. VERMONT/BEVERLY
10. VERMONT/SANTA MONICA
11. VERMONT/SUNSET
12. HOLLYWOOD/WESTERN
13. HOLLYWOOD/VINE
14. HOLLYWOOD/HIGHLAND
15. UNIVERSAL CITY
16. NORTH HOLLYWOOD

FIGURE 15. Final Los Angeles Metro Rail subway route avoiding the Waxman methane zone (shaded), formally adopted in 1988. The new route traveled north to Hollywood along Vermont Avenue and then underground to the San Fernando Valley, with a small stub line down Wilshire Boulevard in anticipation of a future extension. (Courtesy of the Los Angeles County Metropolitan Transportation Authority Research Library and Archive. Reprinted with permission.)

area that is fifty percent residential, you have no chance of getting it built," argued Richard Stanger, rail development director for the LACTC. "It's irrational, but that's the way it is. If it's five percent residential, you have a pretty good chance of getting it approved with the environmental review process. And Vermont was a much less residential corridor and was more of a hospital and business corridor."[105] With large institutions that wanted rail service and a smaller concentration of homeowners who might mount opposition, the Vermont corridor was a breath of fresh air for embattled subway planners.

The Vermont route had RTD supporters from the days when the RTD was originally deciding on a northward route from Wilshire along Vermont, Western, or Fairfax. George Takei, the RTD board member and Hancock Park resident, believed Vermont "made the most sense" because Vermont would serve more popular destinations along the route, such as the hospital complex and community college, than Western or Fairfax. But Takei also had an eye on future subway plans. "We'd have to expand eventually, and Vermont made the most sense going south because we had USC [University of Southern California] and the sports and recreational opportunities of Exposition Park. And that route would serve transit dependents."[106] A rail line along Vermont was also cheaper than Fairfax because it represented a shorter and more direct path to the Valley from downtown Los Angeles.

Roberti pressured the RTD to choose Vermont, using the state investigation into the methane zones and its effect on state funds as leverage. "It was a hammer whereby we could get the route up Vermont," he described of his methane report. "And so we used it."[107] With a less hostile community along the corridor, the Vermont compromise quickly became the path of least resistance for the RTD.

The new route would take the subway north from Wilshire at Vermont, with stations at Beverly, Santa Monica, and Sunset boulevards. It then turned west and continued along Hollywood Boulevard with stops at Western, Vine, and Highland. Finally, the subway would journey under the Santa Monica Mountains to a terminus in North Hollywood.

GROUNDBREAKING

On July 11, 1986, UMTA finally announced the signing of a contract with the RTD to begin funding the construction of the Metro Rail MOS-1. An

FIGURE 16. The Metro Rail subway groundbreaking on September 29, 1986. Second from left to second from right: RTD board member Nick Patsaouras, Los Angeles county supervisor Kenneth Hahn, Los Angeles mayor Tom Bradley, and Hahn chief deputy Nate Holden. (Courtesy of the Los Angeles County Metropolitan Transportation Authority Research Library and Archive. Reprinted with permission.)

elaborate signing ceremony took place the next month.[108] Mayor Bradley told the assembled guests, "I couldn't be happier if the Dodgers, Raiders, and Lakers all won world championships this year." After thanking the federal congressional coalition that made the appropriation happen, he reminded everyone of the continued need for funds: "I am confident that the same coalition will prevail in Congress to secure the remaining $203 million over the next two years, and the federal support needed to take Metro Rail past the 4.4-mile starter line."[109]

Bradley's words emphasized a harsh reality. The RTD had no guarantee for funding beyond the MOS-1 segment, so Congress would need to appropriate more money in the coming years to ensure that the line would become more than just a stranded minisubway of 4.4 miles at a cost of over a billion dollars.

In September, the RTD held the official groundbreaking ceremony. Amid political, business, and labor leaders, Mayor Bradley beamed as he addressed the crowd of roughly 1,200 guests. The start of construction was a "tribute to tenacity," he said, "in the face of what many said couldn't be done and shouldn't be done." Plans called for completion of the segment by 1992.[110]

Bradley and other subway advocates had survived possibly their biggest challenge to date from a lawmaker in their own party, who used the peculiar geology of Fairfax and a tragic explosion to oppose the system. Although the subway would survive Waxman's assault, his legislation meant that Metro Rail would barely serve the Wilshire corridor—the one route in Los Angeles County that merited rail over all others.

But Bradley could still claim victory. Thirteen years after winning office, the mayor finally broke ground on his promised subway.

FIVE

Tunnel Stiffs, Fires, and Sinkholes

"HISTORY REMEMBERS THE BIG SHOTS," Art Lemos told the *Los Angeles Times* on September 28, 1986, as he and his construction crew from the Los Angeles Department of Water and Power began the actual groundbreaking for the Metro Rail subway. At the corner of 5th and Hill streets in downtown Los Angeles, Lemos's crew set about jackhammering the pavement in order to install underground utility pipes that would run through the future subway tunnel. His crew would be the first of roughly two thousand construction workers who would physically implement the grand transit vision of elected officials and the voters. "We're the pioneers," Lemos remarked.[1]

The task of these builders and their overseers would be one of the most challenging of any large public construction project. The sheer size of the Metro Rail project, combined with the amount of public money at stake, the high profile and image of Los Angeles as an auto-dependent city, and a coming economic downturn, would place this project under a national microscope. Investigative reporters would trumpet construction mishaps to the voters and to members of Congress. Politicians would demagogue agency mismanagement of the project. And the public would become frustrated by the perception of agency incompetence and cost overruns. Even the light rail projects, though smaller and less expensive, would suffer delays and cost overruns. In the end, the rocky construction process weakened support for Metro Rail and the idea of rail transit in Los Angeles more generally.

But first came the construction crews and their equipment.

Subway tunneling technology dates as far back as 1824, when English inventor Marc Brunel wanted to build a vehicular tunnel under the Thames River in London. Like Los Angeles in the next century, London was suffering from gridlock, albeit of a different sort. There were too many carts on the London Bridge, and merchants found that their produce was wilting in the sun before they could bring it to market. In order to build a tunnel to relieve the congestion, however, Brunel had to keep the oozing river mud from filling the tunnel as fast as workers could dig it.[2]

Brunel developed a device called a "tunnel shield," which revolutionized tunnel-digging. The tunnel shield was a large, cast-iron, rectangular frame that tunnel diggers lowered into the tunnel shaft. Workers stood inside the frame, protected from cave-ins around them. Through the front opening of this shield, facing the direction in which they wanted to tunnel, they removed dirt with picks and shovels. Workers then carted the dirt aboveground. Behind them, outside of the shield, other workers would line the exposed tunnel walls with bricks. As the bricks went up in the back, workers pushed the tunnel shield forward into the newly excavated space in front with screw jacks that braced against the brick behind it. The whole contraption moved forward like a great caterpillar, eating through the dirt and depositing a brick wall to line the new tunnel.

Brunel's idea revolutionized soft-ground tunneling, and his London tunnel became the world's first under a body of water. But the work was excruciating—diggers traveled just 400 yards in eighteen years.[3] Foreshadowing modern tunneling difficulties, the Thames tunnel also suffered numerous mishaps. "Every morning, I say, 'Another day of danger over,'" Brunel wrote. His tunnel collapsed on a few occasions, filling with water and killing six workers. At one point, his company suspended work on the project for several years due to lack of financing. Brunel himself became something of a laughingstock among the English at the time, who satirized his work (and his French roots) in a popular poem:

> Good Monsieur Brunel
> Let misanthropy tell
> That your work, half complete, is begun ill;
> Heed them not, bore away
> Through gravel and clay,
> Nor doubt the success of your Tunnel.

That very mishap,
When the Thames forced a gap,
And made it fit haunt for an otter,
Has proved that your scheme
Is no catchpenny dream;—
They can't say "'twill never hold water."[4]

The ridicule of Brunel was unsurprising given the high-profile nature of his project in the center of a major world capital and the accidents that ensued. Los Angeles rail leaders could have learned from Brunel's fate: like him, they were attempting to build a massive subway project in the heart of a world capital. In many ways, the agencies in charge of rail would become as much a laughingstock to their contemporaries as Brunel was to the English. But Brunel could claim a measure of victory over these long-deceased naysayers: subway trains in London still use his tunnel today.[5]

TUNNEL STIFFS

To build the Metro Rail tunnel under the busy streets and seismically active mountains of Los Angeles, construction crews relied on an improved version of Brunel's tunnel shield technology. Instead of oozing mud, the boring machine needed to drill through rock composed of sand, silt, and clay. This material originally washed into the ocean from rivers that flowed 5 to 10 million years ago. As the debris settled on the ocean floor, sediment gradually compressed it, along with fossils of sea life, and seismic activity lifted it to dry land. (Boring samples near 5th and Hill and 1st and Hill had produced seashells, fish bones, and sea urchin spines embedded in the rock.)[6] Although the soft earth would not require blasting, engineers worried about the tunnel crumbling. As a result, workers would have to build supports for the tunnel immediately after digging.[7]

In reality, engineers had no way of knowing exactly what tunnel workers would encounter underground. To minimize the uncertainty, engineers rigorously tested boring samples from throughout the route of the tunnel, shearing them, baking them, compressing them, and pushing them until they learned about their composition. "There are bound to be surprises," noted Robert Vogel, curator of civil engineering at the Smithsonian Institution. "Tunneling is unlike building a bridge or a building, where you're building in the air; it's all there, and there are no mysteries. To a certain extent, [with tunneling] you're working blind."[8]

The tunneling process started in the spring of 1987. Like all tunneling projects, the Los Angeles Metro Rail attracted a peculiar type of laborer. On the East Coast, they were known as "sandhogs," but in California the tunnel workers were called "tunnel stiffs." They developed a reputation as hard-living risk takers, eager to make extra money doing dangerous work. "You finally get to where you don't pay much attention," admitted veteran tunnel stiff Audrain Weatherl. "You drive your car a little faster and jump off of higher cliffs than do people who've been living in a real world." The risk of tunnel collapse and flooding were just two of the occupational hazards faced by these laborers. "A lot of people think these tunnel stiffs are crazy," Weatherl said. "Maybe we are."[9]

The first portion of the tunneling started at Wilshire Boulevard and Alvarado Street, at the western end of the first subway segment in downtown Los Angeles, known as MOS-1 (minimum operable segment). Workers there excavated a rectangular shaft several stories deep. At the floor of the shaft, they assembled the circular tunneling machine based on Brunel's technology. The machine would bore through the dirt and rocks, heading east to Flower Street in the downtown financial district.[10] The shield cost millions of dollars and took months to build. "It's not like walking into a dealership and buying a Chevrolet," James Monsees, a chief tunnel engineer on the project, told the *Los Angeles Times*. "No two tunnels are exactly the same," he explained, so every tunnel shield had to be uniquely designed and constructed for the particular soil conditions.[11]

On the surface at Wilshire and Alvarado, workers stabilized the soil above the tunnel to prevent collapses and subsidence, particularly for buildings with footings just 25 to 30 feet above the tunnel. They drilled 60- to 70-foot deep holes in an umbrella pattern over the path of the tunnel and then injected a mix of sand, water, and cement into the holes, called "grout." Injected under pressure via pipes, the grout gradually enlarged like a sponge taking on water, forcing the surrounding soil to become more compact and stable. Because the grout work had to be done from the surface in an urban environment, the Southern California Rapid Transit District (RTD) obtained temporary easements to allow workers to shoot grout from building basements and alleyways along the route. Workers then monitored the stability of the soil with settlement instruments.[12]

With the groutwork completed, the tunneling began. Using a backhoe-type shovel, the tunnel shield carved out a 17.5-foot-diameter circular hole through the soil, wide enough to fit a train car, between 50 and 60 feet below

FIGURE 17. The subway tunnel boring machine in downtown Los Angeles, November 19, 1987. (Courtesy of the Los Angeles County Metropolitan Transportation Authority Research Library and Archive. Reprinted with permission.)

the surface. At this depth, the tunnel could pass below the footings of tall buildings downtown. But the tunnel was also shallow enough to ensure that the future stations would not be too deep. The deeper the station, after all, the more expensive the excavation would be. And the path of the tunnel could not vary much in depth or else the train ride would not be smooth and efficient.[13]

As the shield removed soil, called "muck," tunnel stiffs transferred it out of the tunnel shield on a conveyor belt that dumped it into a "muck train." The train carried the muck out of the tunnel, where city-approved dump trucks hauled the muck down certain city streets at specific times to a storage location on the Eastside of Los Angeles near Alameda Street. A mountain of dirt began to accumulate there, lasting for more than a year;[14] eventually, "muckers" gave it to dirt brokers to sell to landfills and other places that needed loose soil.[15] Some landfills were so desperate for clean soil to bury their trash that they paid to haul it away.[16]

To support the newly exposed tunnel walls, tunnel stiffs assembled segments of the tunnel's circular lining inside the shield. Like Brunel's bricklayers, Metro Rail tunnel stiffs had two options for lining the walls: either they could place precast concrete liners as they dug, or they could line the tunnel with steel ribs and timbers, adding concrete lining later. Most contractors favored the "ribs-and-timbers method," which made the tunnel look like the inside of a barrel, and the cheaper price tag of this method made it the preferred option for Metro Rail's first segment.[17]

Metro Rail tunnel stiffs had to address two factors unique to Los Angeles: methane gas and earthquakes. To prevent the invisible, odorless, and highly explosive methane gas from infiltrating the tunnel during construction, workers called "sniffers" used sensing devices to detect the gas while tunnel stiffs kept the environment well ventilated. To prevent methane from entering the tunnels after construction, workers wrapped the tunnel and station walls with high-density polyethylene. This liner became sandwiched by another layer of precast concrete that would form the inner tunnel walls visible to passengers on the train.[18]

Meanwhile, engineers kept the entire tunnel lining flexible to withstand earthquakes. As Monsees explained, "When an earthquake wave comes through, the ground actually goes through a wave motion," and the tunnel starts "snaking" as it follows the "earth wave." It goes into an "ovaling mode, where an original circle gets bent into an oval," Monsees added. "The whole goal is to build [the tunnel] in such a way that it can follow these ground movements . . . and return right back to its shape."[19]

Working three shifts around the clock, tunnel stiffs were expected to make 50 feet of progress on the tunnel each day.[20]

THE STATIONS

To construct the stations, workers began at street level, excavating an enormous pit where the station would be. Once the pit reached the depth of the bottom of the station, workers built steel supports and constructed an underground structure with the roof at street level. They called it a "station box," and it resembled a multistory building on its side.[21] They placed wood decking on top so that cars could continue to drive on the street above the station box. Workers performed further excavation from the side, forming ramps that would eventually become the stairs and escalators of the station.[22] Eventually, the steel supports got buried in concrete as the station took shape.

In the first phase of subway construction, the tunneling machines bored to the station boxes. Then workers had to disassemble the machine, carry it across the station box that was under construction, and then reassemble it to begin digging a new tunnel on the other side. The expense and delay of this process, however, motivated engineers on later phases to have the tunneling machines bore first, with workers digging the station boxes around the excavated tunnels afterward. This reform saved money and time.[23]

RTD staff weighed two options for subway station design: create identical stations, like the cookie-cutter stations of the Washington, D.C., Metro, or use different artistic and aesthetic features for each station while leaving them functionally the same. The RTD opted for the latter. As subway engineer Ed McSpedon explained, "L.A. is such a diverse place and the neighborhoods are so different, it really opened up some opportunities to kind of have some fun with some of these stations. They could reflect the creativity here and the artistic nature of the place, as well as tie into the sense of place."[24] The different aesthetics meant higher maintenance costs without uniform replacement parts. But the different station appearances would make it easier for riders to identify their stop.

The contest to design the stations attracted some of the most reputable architects in Los Angeles, including Frank Gehry and Maxwell Starkman, designer of the Los Angeles Museum of Tolerance. "Everyone was competing hot and heavy for these jobs," McSpedon recalled.[25] Subway planners also hired eighty local artists to design sculptures and paintings for the stations, particularly for the later stages of the subway around Hollywood.[26] The architects often traveled to other subway stations around the country to take photographs and become inspired. For example, the design theme for the never-built Fairfax station included references and motifs based on the Eastern European Jewish community there. McSpedon observed that the station architecture always attempted "to reflect the context in which the station was going to be built and the communities around there and what was significant."[27]

GREEN LINE GOING, BLUE LINE BLUES

While subway construction had just begun in 1987, the Los Angeles County Transportation Commission (LACTC) had already been busy building the two light rail lines, officially known as the Blue Line, to Long Beach, and the Green Line, along the Century Freeway. The LACTC construction process, however, soon became bogged down in cost overruns, construction mishaps, and delays—ultimately serving as a preview of what subway workers could expect on the starter subway line.

Ed McSpedon worked on both systems in a leadership capacity and saw the difficulties firsthand. McSpedon had come west from New York to work on Metro Rail. A structural engineer, he jumped at the opportunity for exciting work with the new Los Angeles rail system. Construction had been in his family, and he valued workplace safety above all else. His father, a construction worker, was killed in a construction accident when McSpedon was a sophomore in college, leaving behind Ed, his mother, and four younger siblings. After a stint working on the designs for the doomed Fairfax station for the RTD, he rose to positions supervising the Long Beach Blue Line and the Century Freeway Green Line for the LACTC.

Compared to the other lines, the Green Line construction process happened with relative ease. Because most of the route followed the Century Freeway median, construction did not involve intersections, freight lines, tunneling, cities demanding aerial sections, and other complicating factors associated with building rail through an urban environment.

Caltrans was already constructing the Century Freeway when the Green Line builders started work. The original plan for the freeway included a busway, but with the LACTC decision to build rail in the median, a whole new infrastructure was required. "Trains need power, so we had to make sure there were power substations off to the side of the freeway," explained McSpedon, who oversaw Green Line construction. "But power needed to get to the median, so we had to make sure Caltrans put duct banks and cables to provide power to the middle."[28]

The freeway construction made the rail construction easier because some of the work was similar. "The rail tracks needed some kind of roadbed underneath," McSpedon said. "So as long as they were out doing the road, they could use the same contractors to do subsurface work and lay foundations for catenary poles, stations, and things. A lot of the things we wanted the freeway contractors could do while they were out there. It was much more economical to have them do the work while they were there. So we got the freeway built ready for rail."[29]

At 3:13 P.M. on October 14, 1993, the Century Freeway opened for the first automobiles, completing a thirty-year planning and construction period.[30] However, rail construction in the median of the freeway continued. When the freeway had been closed, rail workers could store materials and equipment on the lanes. But the opening of the freeway created difficulty for workers who needed to get themselves and their equipment in and out of the median.[31]

The freeway itself had become something of a showcase for the country, given its prominent location in Southern California and incorporation of public transit in the middle. Even before it opened, President George H. W. Bush had used it as a campaign stop during the fall of 1992 to highlight construction projects, labor union work, and the aerospace industry during the economic downturn. While the president ate fried chicken and cookies surrounded by construction workers, California governor Pete Wilson, and hundreds of members of the media, he chatted with the workers on topics ranging from Iraqi dictator Saddam Hussein to golf.[32]

Compared to the Green Line construction process, the Blue Line had become a bit of a boondoggle. Even though the route followed the tracks of the last Red Car trains and modern freight rail cars, the job was more complicated than anyone seemed to have anticipated. "It was a five-year job," McSpedon recalled of the line that Supervisor Hahn had originally hoped to build in two years before the 1984 Olympics. "But it was way more than a full-time job: twenty-two miles, five municipalities, endless stakeholders, utilities, and railroads."[33] By the time the Blue Line was completed, its costs had soared.

The Blue Line building process started with an underground section stretching from the site of the heavy-rail subway station at 7th Street in downtown Los Angeles, where the Blue Line would intersect with the subway, to 11th Street along Flower Street. Rather than tunnel underneath Flower, workers excavated the tunnel from the street and placed plywood above the ensuing trench for cars to use. This method was called "cut and cover" and resembled the construction practices of the subway stations.

Out of the tunnel, the tracks headed south at street level along Washington Boulevard to Long Beach Avenue. Workers needed to build the light rail tracks along the tracks reserved for freight trains. "We were in the railroad right-of-way, sharing it with Standard Pacific and Union Pacific," McSpedon said. "We had to move their railroad tracks over to one side to create room for us." Lengthy negotiations ensued with the railroads. "It was 'Who pays for what?' We had to keep them operating while we were relocating them," he recalled.[34]

Building the rail lines was not as simple as just laying new track. The new light rail lines required complicated wiring below the tracks. As McSpedon described, "We had to build the tracks up from the bottom, and we had to run a lot of cable. We had signal cable, power cable, and communication cable. We also had to move the utilities and redo all the grade crossings." The cables required power stations along the route. "Every mile or so we had to put in a power station," McSpedon explained. "That has to go somewhere off of the line, so we really got into the neighborhoods and had to do some property acquisition. And these were some of the poorest, and in some cases some of the most dangerous, parts of the city."[35]

The LACTC also had to retool all the intersection crossings. "With the old Red Cars, when drivers would cross the streets with the trains on them, when they got to the tracks there would be a big hump," McSpedon said. "We lowered all that, which had reduced traffic speeds, so the traffic now runs better."[36] But the hump removal meant that LACTC construction crews had to shave sixteen miles of the right-of-way flat, adding costs and time.[37]

In addition to the technical challenges that drove up costs, city leaders along the route protested how the line traveled through their communities. Many local residents did not want trains traveling at street level near busy intersections; they worried about traffic jams and pedestrian safety. As a result, the LACTC had to build a number of aerial sections to elevate the tracks, which increased costs significantly. Cities also extracted concessions from the LACTC over infrastructure costs. When the LACTC removed the sewer, traffic lights, electric utilities, and other city-owned infrastructure from the construction path, standard contract language required the LACTC to "replace" the infrastructure. If the replacement was superior to the original, the LACTC could deem it a "betterment," for which the city would have to contribute. Conflicts arose when cities claimed that LACTC "betterments" were merely replacements and refused to pay. James Okazaki, working for the City of Los Angeles Department of Transportation, noted: "There were continuous disputes about whether changing up six-inch sewers to ten-inch sewers is a 'replacement' or a 'betterment.' Every intersection they went through, there were improvements. And a lot of those areas hadn't been worked on in a long time. That's why costs went up."[38]

Finally, as the construction neared Long Beach, a new controversy erupted from business owners along Long Beach Boulevard, who would share street space with the tracks. "There were a lot of automobile dealers there," McSpedon said, "and they were really opposed to the project. They thought people buying cars didn't come by train, so the line had no value to them. They didn't want the disruption." The city of Long Beach intervened to oppose the route, and the eventual settlement resulted in a downtown Long

Beach loop instead of a dead-end rail terminus. Long Beach leaders hoped the loop would rejuvenate the area. "As it turned out," McSpedon said, "the auto dealers packed up and moved anyway. It was crazy."[39]

The Blue Line construction process also had its share of mishaps. In one incident, workers carelessly left their keys in a bulldozer before leaving for the weekend. Curious neighborhood kids jumped in, turned the engine on, and got it in gear. As the bulldozer started moving, they panicked and jumped out. The driverless bulldozer then demolished a church in its path. No one was injured, but the LACTC had to provide tents for that Sunday's services and compensate for the damage. In another incident, a 400-ton rail bridge collapsed one morning onto a pickup truck that was stopped below at a light. The fallen bridge crushed the front and back of the truck but miraculously left Alejandro Hernandez and his uncle Marcos Pacheco Ramirez unharmed but in shock. The truck's cab occupied the space in between the bridge's two beams.[40] Tragically, one worker was killed on Washington Boulevard when the crane he was operating accidentally hit an overhead power line.[41]

Meanwhile, costs continued to mount as the freight railroads extracted expensive improvements to their tracks in exchange for letting the LACTC build the rail line there. Cities along the route forced pricey additions and route changes, and when the agency tried to purchase land for park-and-ride lots, the cities that owned the land "didn't give away the space easily," McSpedon observed. "They had a lot of leverage."[42] Richard Stanger, rail development director at the LACTC, observed of the effort to extract concessions from the rail program: "You get to a point where everyone's money is no one's money. So you begin to think, 'I'll just use a little more money because really it's not my money.'"[43]

The end result was that the line cost almost twice as much as anyone anticipated when the project was approved. "When Kenny Hahn originally proposed the line, it didn't include upgrading all the crossings and the downtown station," Okazaki noted. "It was just a back-of-the-napkin, $5 million-per-mile kind of thing."[44] The cost overruns meant less money for other rail projects and eventually contributed to the LACTC's subsequent debt.

THE REBIRTH OF RAIL

In July 1990, the first rail line since 1961 opened in Los Angeles, on the same path as the last Pacific Electric train. The Blue Line was ready for the public, at a cost of $877 million—$270 million more than projected at groundbreaking five years earlier. At least 25,000 people jammed the trains for free opening-day rides from Long Beach to downtown. Nick Patsouras, president of the RTD, said in English and Spanish in his opening remarks: "I feel like dancing," noting that "a lot of the skeptics said this would never happen. The skeptics were wrong. The trains are back. This is the beginning of a transit renaissance."[45]

The arrival of light rail sparked a wave of public nostalgia for the Pacific Electric Red and Yellow Cars and of excitement about having rail transit back in Los Angeles. All of the local television stations aired stories on the opening, which featured excerpts from the political speeches, shots of the large crowd, and mentions of the historic nature of having rail transit in Los Angeles after twenty-nine years without it. Although the media coverage was largely positive, at least one station reported on the fears of some local residents about riding the trains through some of the lower-income and largely African American neighborhoods on the route.[46] In anticipation of this concern, LACTC executive director Neil Peterson devoted a significant amount of resources to security on the line. "My peers thought I was nuts," he said. "But from day one, no one touched that line."[47]

The occasion belonged to Supervisor Hahn. He had fought for Proposition A, the sales tax measure that funded the system, and he had convinced LACTC board members to choose the Long Beach line over other routes. The system that he hoped to open in time for the 1984 Summer Olympics was now finally running, almost ten years after voters had approved Proposition A.

"It was a hard fight, but we won," he said at the ceremony. And then in an echo of his 1980 speech to the LACTC board that persuaded them to authorize Proposition A for the ballot, he paraphrased William Mulholland, who had presided over a similar occasion in 1913 when he opened the Owens Valley Aqueduct that brought water and a new era to Los Angeles: "The Blue Line is here," the supervisor said. "Now use it."[48]

TRIAL BY TUNNEL FIRE

Ironically, at the same time the Blue Line opened, the subway experienced its first serious construction accident. In the tunnel under the Hollywood Freeway near Union Station, tunnel stiffs were placing four feet of wood timbers between each steel rib for the first layer of the tunnel wall. They often welded metal brackets onto the steel ribs to hang wires and lighting equipment. Early on Friday, July 13, 1990, workers, eager to get home after a long day, finished their work in that section of tunnel and hurriedly removed the brackets with welding torches. They covered the wood and steel with polyethylene liner but without following the normal procedure of spraying water on the timber and ribs first. They vacated the tunnel.[49]

The welding torch had left molten embers from the steel brackets. These embers were still hot when the workers mounted the liner and were now trapped between the polyethylene and wood. While polyethylene could ignite easily but burn out quickly, timber was difficult to ignite but would burn for a long time. The subway timber was particularly flammable because workers had treated it with chemicals to prevent rot. The molten slag now caused heat that ignited the plastic membrane, and it burned hot enough to ignite the timbers. The fire department later determined by the height of the flames that the fire had burned intensely due to the fuel from the timber.[50]

The next day was a Saturday and the date of the Blue Line opening. Ed McSpedon had just been appointed to oversee the subway construction following his Blue Line duties. His family was in town from the East Coast to celebrate, and he received word of the fire during preparations for the Blue Line festivities. He arrived at the site to find not just a construction accident but a public relations disaster. "It was July, and it was very hot, a cooking day. I noticed a lot of media there and a hundred fire engines. The media were all out on an island in the blazing sun, and they were unhappy they couldn't see anything—the guy in charge had refused to let media near the site. We quickly worked out an arrangement for a pool camera, so we took someone down there to film and then daisy-chained the video for the other networks."[51]

The fire had gutted an entire 750-foot section of the tunnel directly below the Hollywood Freeway.[52] They had no choice but to close the freeway. "We're out of the subway construction business," McSpedon told his team that day. "Now we're in the freeway reconstruction business." The media wanted to know what would happen on Monday when commuters needed to use the freeway. McSpedon worked with Caltrans to devise a plan to shore up the tunnel, and he told the public not to take the freeway on Monday. He predicted that at most they would have a lane or two and the shoulder open. When Monday came, McSpedon kept the media informed throughout the day about the progress on the tunnel. "We tried to be a little conservative," he remembered, "and turn the story around to the progress being made."[53]

FIGURE 18. Smoke from the subway tunnel fire escapes from various points under the closed Hollywood Freeway near downtown Los Angeles, July 13, 1990. (Photo by Larry Bessel. Published in the *Los Angeles Times*, July 14, 1990. Reprinted with permission.)

The freeway eventually reopened completely a few days later, and the subway regained the lost time on the construction schedule. The final cost of the fire was $2.2 million, but the real damage was the diminished public confidence in the subway construction process.[54]

Rail officials held a press conference to explain what went wrong. Going forward, they decided to forgo wood and steel in the tunnels and use more expensive concrete liners for future tunneling. Despite the greater expense, their priority was to avoid suffering this kind of accident again. Defending the construction crews, McSpedon argued, "These workers are hardworking guys and were under time pressure. They wanted to get home, and there was pressure from management. And the engineer has to try to make it as foolproof as possible."[55]

The construction mishap played into a media narrative about RTD incompetence. Almost from the beginning, the RTD appeared to struggle managing the subway construction. In early 1987, the *Los Angeles Times* reported that internal RTD battles and mismanagement were causing potentially costly problems with contract management.[56] The allegations included reports of soaring administrative costs, lax control over travel and entertainment expenses by board members and executives, and the possible payment of hundreds of thousands of dollars in phony insurance claims.[57] Then in 1988, federal consultants reported to the Urban Mass Transportation Administration (UMTA) that all but two construction contracts had fallen behind schedule and that the project suffered from contract mismanagement and delays related to poor planning. Contractors began blaming the RTD for slowing down the process with stalled paperwork processing, and the disputes were beginning to cost money and time. The *Los Angeles Times* quoted a former RTD employee who, having been fired by the agency, alleged that the RTD was "grossly unfamiliar with the whole [contract management] structure." Meanwhile, unforeseen construction difficulties, such as the discovery of hazardous gas near Union Station, had slowed down construction, particularly near Hill Street downtown. "Hill Street's become the land of the unknown," admitted William Rhine, the RTD official then overseeing construction.[58]

The difficulties prompted local leaders to force a change in management. Agency leaders chose McSpedon to oversee the subway. Coming from light rail, where the motivation was to build as "economically as we could," McSpedon now had to deal with a subway project that "was big, big money." Referring to the LACTC, he said: "We thought we were a little more efficient and managed contracts better." Now with the subway, he observed firsthand the fallout from the disgruntled subway contractors. "Honestly, the contractors were not happy and didn't feel like they were being treated well," McSpedon said. "They were not getting good information and there were legal disputes. I did outreach to contractors and told them that we were going to change things and be a better partner client. But otherwise the litigation costs and claims were huge stuff piling up. There were a lot of unresolved issues, and I had to deal with all of that."[59]

The tunnel fire added to the negative coverage. The media pounced on the story, providing front-page accounts and nightly news coverage. "When the tunnel you're building underneath a major freeway, a highway in Hollywood, catches on fire and shuts down an eight-lane freeway in the heart of Los Angeles, that's going to create a problem for the agency involved and the commuters," said *Los Angeles Times* investigative reporter Jeff Rabin, who covered subway construction at the time.[60]

The subway fire signaled the beginning of more intense media scrutiny of the subway. The owners of the *Los Angeles Times* devoted resources to cover the rail construction process, believing they would uncover important stories for the public. "The reason the subway got so much scrutiny," Rabin explained, "was that it was being built in the second largest city in the country, the entertainment capital of the world, one block from one of the best newspapers, the *Los Angeles Times,* which had resources to devote two people full-time to monitor the agency building it and to do the kind of reporting that wouldn't normally get done in major American cities."[61]

The reporters assigned to the beat relished their roles exposing public sector incompetence and, in their view, malfeasance. Rabin, for example, came of age during the 1960s and 1970s and decided to become an investigative journalist while watching the Watergate scandal on television. "Journalism was about public service for me, a way of making a difference and giving something back to the community, and literally being a watchdog," he said. This zeal was typical for reporters covering the story. "We had some of the best investigative reporters in Los Angeles who were honing their skills on the subway project and who went on to win Pulitzer prizes on other subjects, went to work at the *New York Times,*" Rabin described. "The stakes were high for the [agency] and for the journalists involved. This was the major leagues: the major leagues of subway construction and the major leagues of journalism."[62]

SUBWAY SINKING

The construction process was giving the media plenty to cover. In late August 1993, subway "whistleblowers" sent the *Los Angeles Times* internal agency documents regarding the thickness of the subway walls. The documents indicated that the contractor in charge of pouring the concrete, Tutor-Saliba Corp., left portions of some walls thinner than required. As a result, some experts feared that the tunnels could be vulnerable to a major earthquake. The *Times* ran a Sunday article on the subject on August 29, 1993, producing panic and outrage among residents. The contractor's president, Ronald N. Tutor, told the *Times:* "These are human beings who pour these tunnels." If any walls had in fact been poured with insufficient concrete, "it wasn't deliberate."[63]

Representative John J. Duncan Jr., a Republican from Tennessee, responded by calling for a federal investigation into the subway construction process. Duncan was a member of the House Public Works and Transportation Committee and had positioned himself as a subway opponent and spending watchdog since revelations about shoddy accounting at the LACTC hit the *Los Angeles Times*. Now primed with documents from the same *Times* whistleblowers and the resulting newspaper story, Duncan urged the U.S. Department of Transportation to force the subway agency to launch an independent investigation of tunnel safety. "The House Public Works and Transportation Committee, on which I serve, has and will spend billions of tax dollars on the Los Angeles Metro Rail Project," Duncan wrote Transportation Secretary Federico Peña. "We must be sure that we are funding a project which will be safe for the passengers who will ride the subway."[64]

In response, the Department of Transportation asked local rail leaders to launch an independent review of tunnel safety. In a letter to agency leaders, Gordon Linton, administrator of the Federal Transit Administration (FTA), the successor agency to UMTA that was funding the subway, wrote: "I ask that this review and evaluation be accomplished in an expeditious manner, and with personnel independent of those involved with the [subway] or any other current Los Angeles [rail] project."[65] Linton demanded continued federal oversight of the investigation.

The media firestorm, leaked documents, and questionable agency oversight of construction had landed subway leaders in trouble with the federal government. They would have to redeem themselves to avoid jeopardizing federal funding for the remainder of the subway. At this point, the whistleblowers, frustrated that the federal government had decided not to launch its own investigation, revealed themselves to Secretary Peña as John Walsh and Bob D'Amato of the "Los Angeles Transportation Whistle Blowers."[66] John Walsh was a former substitute teacher in the Los Angeles Unified School District who became a full-time rail gadfly.[67] He began to display increasingly erratic behavior during his Metro Rail protests, including engaging in "street theater" at agency board meetings and getting himself arrested at the opening of the Blue Line for disturbing the peace.[68] Bob D'Amato proclaimed himself director of safety at the American Safety Institute in Northridge, California.[69] In a scathing letter to Secretary Peña, they asked: "Will you receive paybacks [for not launching a federal investigation] once you return to private life?" They closed with a warning: "This is not a local scandal. This is a national scandal. Please do not underestimate the repercussions at your own political risk."[70]

The Whistle Blowers' efforts yielded results. In March 1994, the independent investigation found that the construction management firm, Parsons-Dillingham, had fallen short of "acceptable industry practice" in its inspections of the tunnel walls.[71] Tutor-Saliba Corp., the company responsible for pouring the concrete, would find itself in a multidecade lawsuit with the subway agency over the incident.[72]

HOORAY FOR HOLLYWOOD

Despite the construction mishaps, rail leaders succeeded in getting federal funds to build the subway to Hollywood. This route would take the subway along state senator David Roberti's preferred path from downtown to Hollywood via Vermont, with a terminus at the intersection of Hollywood and Vine. MOS-2 (the second "minimum operable segment" of the subway), as planners called it, also included a "stub line" from downtown along Wilshire Boulevard to the intersection at Western Avenue. Although Waxman's ban prevented the subway from tunneling any farther than Western, RTD planners took the system as far out Wilshire as they could before they hit Waxman's methane zone. They hoped to delay any decision-making on the route to Century City and Westwood in case they could one day arrange a compromise with Waxman.[73]

The Hollywood route had overwhelming support from the Hollywood Chamber of Commerce and institutions along Vermont. Unlike Hancock Park and other residential communities that opposed the subway, Hollywood residents did not voice much organized opposition. "There were a large number of immigrants who were not familiar with the system, senior citizens who had more short-terms concerns about rent control, and the usual dynamic that low-income neighborhoods tend not to be as organized and not be as involved in the process," explained Mike Woo, who represented the area in the Los Angeles City Council.[74] Or as then-congressional negotiator Bevan Dufty put it, "Hollywood was basically a dump at the time."[75]

Despite these dynamics, some individuals in Hollywood remained staunchly opposed, albeit with little organized power. Warren B. Meyers of Tele-Talent, Inc., for example, wrote to Mayor Bradley that the subway "will unleash on this city all the horrors of the New York subway system." He described subways as "havens and spawning places for muggers, vandals, drug pushers, loiterers, and homosexuals seeking random and anonymous sex."[76]

MOS-2 still had strong bipartisan support in Congress,[77] which appropriated $667 million for the segment in the 1987 highway bill. Once again, Ronald Reagan tried to stop the project by vetoing the bill, but Congress overrode the veto. Reagan then directed UMTA to refuse to release the funds. Reagan's vice president, George H. W. Bush, who became president in 1989, continued his stingy rail policies.[78]

Support from the business community[79] and congressional allies such as both California senators (Republican Pete Wilson and Democrat Alan Cranston) and congressional representatives from both parties, including Glenn Anderson, Jerry Lewis, Julian Dixon, and David Dreier,[80] succeeded in overpowering the Bush administration. In March 1990, UMTA finally released the appropriated funds for MOS-2 and signed a full funding agreement the next month. Subway construction would continue to Hollywood and west down part of Wilshire Boulevard.[81]

The journey into downtown Hollywood meant even more scrutiny. "Anything with the name Hollywood in it is going to get enormous attention," Jeff Rabin noted.[82] In May 1994, the *Los Angeles Times* reported that the five existing subway stations all lacked gas sensors to detect hydrogen sulfide, despite reports that hydrogen sulfide was leaking into the tunnels. A panel of experts, including some appointed by Representative Waxman, had recommended that the sensors be installed, but subway engineers had apparently ignored the advice. The article also highlighted how the plastic liner in the tunnels, designed to prevent gas seepage, had numerous punctures.[83] In July, an agency study concluded that there was no hydrogen sulfide hazard to the public or employees in the tunnel, but the agency promised to continue monitoring.[84]

Meanwhile, by the summer of 1994, merchants along Hollywood Boulevard complained that the north side of the street was literally sinking from the tunnel excavation. On August 20, 1994, nine square blocks in the heart of Hollywood Boulevard had to be closed to traffic while an apartment building was evacuated due to water seepage in the subway tunnels and to ground settling along the street.[85] The *Times* reported that a tunneling expert had warned subway engineers of this possibility beforehand, but the agency had refused to employ ground-stabilizing grout during the excavation. According to the paper, local engineers apparently hoped other measures would prevent further sinkage instead.[86]

The agency denied the story. Ed McSpedon wrote to the *Times,* "In fact, the contractor was using contact grouting at the time the settlement occurred and had been doing so for several months." McSpedon bemoaned the article for having "created the misperception that the agency's desire to save money and lack of timeliness" had caused the ground subsidence.[87] Regardless of the cause of the subsidence, however, the result on the street was undeniable evidence that something had gone wrong.

THE SINKHOLE

At 3:40 A.M. on Thursday, June 22, 1995, the subway experienced its most high-profile and symbolic construction disaster. At that time, tunnel workers under Hollywood Boulevard were removing the outer concrete tunnel liner one segment at a time in order to correct a drilling misalignment of more than a foot. But in the process of removing the walls, they failed to use proper supports. Combined with recent heavy rainfall that had driven up the groundwater level and destabilized the soil, the lack of support began causing a problem.[88] The dirt began settling quickly, and the workers rushed to place support beams in the tunnel.[89]

Seeing that something was going wrong, the state inspector, Joe Doyle, ordered the twenty workers on duty out of the tunnel. Fire captain Richard Brunson hurried to the tunnel shaft at that moment. "Suddenly, there was a huge wall of water that just came rushing out of the tunnel," he said. His colleague, fire captain Chris Burton, heard a loud noise and wood cracking and saw the useless wood beams shoot out of the tunnel shaft. The force of the water was enough to bend a metal pipe in half. "It was one of the most destructive forces I've ever seen," he said. "It's incredible we didn't lose anyone."[90]

Aboveground, a half block of Hollywood Boulevard collapsed into a seventy-square-foot, muddy sinkhole. Authorities closed ten stores on the famous street and evacuated sixty psychiatric patients from a nearby hospital. As day broke, television stations around the country aired footage of the scene. Politicians went to inspect, and a sudden ground collapse almost threw Supervisor Zev Yaroslavsky and City Councilwoman Jackie Goldberg into the hole.[91]

The accident led to months of delays and cost the agency upward of $6.7 million in repair costs. Although subway officials first blamed the collapse on a broken water main controlled by the Los Angeles Department of Water and Power, a later study for the agency concluded that two main contractors, Engineering Management Consultants and Shea-Kiewit-Kenny, were at fault. Subway leaders fired both contractors. Denying the charges, Shea-Kiewit-Kenny filed suit against the agency.[92]

More important, the sinkhole put a significant dent in public support for rail leaders and their project. "The sinkhole became a symbol of the ineptitude of the [rail agency] and its efforts to build a subway," the *Times*'s Rabin observed. "Hollywood Boulevard, lined by stars of celebrities, titans of television industries, collapsed. The street collapsed. It makes great video—a wonderful story for television. It's visual, not just dusty documents; a tangible example of something gone wrong."[93]

The negative coverage became so intense that local politicians began pressuring the *Times* to fire their investigative journalists. Rabin's editor "heard from both a mayor of Los Angeles and a county supervisor who wanted my head on a platter. Those are the ones I know about. To [the editor's] credit, I was told to keep doing what I was doing. There was no way they were going to achieve their goal of silencing me, and they didn't."[94]

[handwritten margin note: spread truth, not political opinion]

BRADLEY'S FAREWELL

Despite the ongoing construction difficulties, subway leaders finally readied MOS-1 for its public unveiling. The man who had probably been most responsible for bringing the subway to Los Angeles lived to see it open. In January 1993, Tom Bradley was nearing the end of his twenty-year run as mayor of Los Angeles. With just a few months remaining in his final term, the leader who had made rail a priority during his first mayoral campaign in 1973 presided over the long-awaited opening of the Red Line subway, as it was called. Politics and funding woes had pummeled his grand plans for a subway that would connect all of Los Angeles to an initial 4.4-mile segment, and the construction mishaps and bad press had tarnished the image of rail for the voters. But the event was cause for celebration nonetheless.

The ceremony for the new Los Angeles subway took place in front of officials from all levels of government. California's two senators, now-governor Pete Wilson, the five county supervisors, and city council members were in attendance, with a proud Mayor Bradley presiding.[95] As the mayor called out, "All aboard our new Metro Red Line subway" and blew a whistle, technicians cued up the song "I Love L.A." by Randy Newman.

"I'm very excited, very happy about this day; it's been 20 years coming," Bradley beamed. "The Red Line is going to deliver us to the 21st Century."[96]

SIX

The Wish List

IN 1989, the Southern Pacific and Santa Fe railroads offered a deal that would tantalize Los Angeles rail leaders. The railroads wanted to sell three freight train rights-of-way that crisscrossed valuable urban real estate in Los Angeles: the State Street–Baldwin Park Line, the West Santa Ana Line, and the Exposition Line. But the timing was not great for the Los Angeles County Transportation Commission (LACTC); by the end of the 1980s, money for rail was running out. The light rail lines had cost substantially more than initial estimates, draining Proposition A sales tax funds well before the transit agency could build the envisioned 150-mile system.

LACTC leaders needed a new source of revenue to continue the light rail program and capitalize on these right-of-way opportunities. Despite the construction mishaps, cost overruns, and less-than-expected federal support, the political momentum in Los Angeles still seemed to favor rail. The opening of the Blue Line and the beginning of construction of the Green Line and the Red Line subway emboldened rail leaders to seek voter approval of a new sales tax plan. With more revenue, they could start building new lines from their ambitious rail wish list.

But their efforts to usher in a new era of rail development became ensnared in the politics of homeowner opposition, turf wars among elected leaders, and a system that brought spoils to the most powerful leaders and not to residents of the most populated transit corridors.

PROPOSITION C AND THE RISE OF THE LACTC

Neil Peterson, the LACTC executive director, did not want to miss the opportunity to purchase the freight rights-of way. He arranged for the

LACTC leadership to meet with Southern Pacific Railroad representatives. Commission members like Ray Remy and Jacki Bacharach wanted to purchase the rights-of-way. They advocated that the agency agree to financial terms with the railroad and simultaneously wage a campaign to raise public money to complete the purchase.[1]

The public seemed to be in a prorail mood. In June 1990, California voters approved Propositions 108, the Passenger Rail and Clean Air Bond Act, and 111, the Traffic Congestion Relief and Spending Limitation Act, to raise funds for transit and rail projects through increased gas taxes and bond issuances. LACTC leaders hoped these initiatives would finance the rail line purchases,[2] but they soon realized that this money would not be enough. One month after the June election, Southern Pacific broke off talks with the LACTC when Peterson refused to increase a $335 million offer for the rights-of-way.[3] Southern Pacific, believing the market value to be $440 million, threatened to sell the rights-of-way to real estate developers.[4]

LACTC officials needed more money, and they turned once again to the local sales tax option. The agency's enabling legislation allowed it to seek a full-cent sales tax increase, only half of which was being used by 1980's Proposition A. With the support of the Southern California Rapid Transit District (RTD), the two transit agencies teamed up to campaign for another sales tax measure for the November 1990 election.[5]

Local officials once again debated the wisdom of pursuing a county sales tax increase. Like Supervisor Kenneth Hahn before him in 1980, Neil Peterson was concerned that he did not have enough votes on the LACTC board to put the measure on the ballot. The county supervisors already wanted a sales tax increase to finance jail construction, which meant at least four out of the eleven LACTC board members would probably vote against a tax for public transit. Privately, Mayor Tom Bradley's staff opposed placing the tax on the ballot because they feared that voters would not support a tax increase on the heels of Proposition 111's gas tax increase.[6] Their caution mirrored the mayor's resistance to placing Proposition A on the ballot in 1980.

Railroad lobbyists came to the rescue. Tom Houston was a local attorney who had been Bradley's deputy mayor in the early 1980s, and he now represented railroad interests.[7] He approached the mayor about the possibility of teaming with Southern Pacific Railroad on a sales tax campaign. He promised the mayor that the railroad would finance the campaign for a sales tax hike in exchange for the mayor's aggressive support for the measure. The railroad would then receive assurance that a portion of the sales tax money would go toward the purchase of their rights-of-way. "I believe SP [Southern Pacific] might well be willing to support a 1/2¢ sales tax increase," Houston wrote Bradley, "if at least one of its rights-of-way were to be purchased by LACTC, and positive negotiations on others were back underway."[8]

The deal was sweet: transit advocates would get campaign finance support for a badly needed sales tax hike, while the railroads would help the LACTC raise public money to buy rights-of-way for future rapid transit projects. Houston's entreaty appeared to convince the mayor, and Bradley's initial reticence morphed into strong advocacy for the sales tax measure. He publicly urged the LACTC to place the tax increase on the ballot, expressing concern that important regions, such as Pasadena, the San Fernando Valley, and the South Bay, would not have rail access without it. "There is not enough money," Bradley told Angelenos. "This is the only way we can build" the entire system. The system was short $300 million of its needs for the next ten years, and the additional half-cent sales tax would provide $400 million a year for rail construction.[9] The railroad's backroom deal had unleashed Bradley the campaigner.

But as Neil Peterson feared, the vote at the LACTC to place the measure on the ballot was a nail-biter. In a repeat of Kenny Hahn's battle with the commission over Proposition A ten years earlier, Peterson and other sales tax supporters were unsure that they could survive uniform opposition from the county supervisors—including, ironically, Kenny Hahn. At a joint RTD/LACTC meeting on August 8, 1990, Bradley moved to place the measure on the ballot. Joining him in favor were Jacki Bacharach, Los Angeles city councilman Richard Alatorre, Santa Monica councilwoman Christine Reed, and Bradley appointee Jimmy Tolbert. Opposed were Supervisors Kenneth Hahn, Ed Edelman, Deane Dana, and Mike Antonovich, as well as Long Beach city councilman Ray Grabinsky.

The vote was now tied five to five, the outstanding vote being that of arch-conservative "Pistol Pete" Schabarum, the longtime rail opponent. Schabarum, however, shocked the commission when he voted in favor of the measure. Announcing an unorthodox electoral strategy, Schabarum hoped that the transit tax would fail and drag down other proposed tax hikes on the ballot. "[I'm] trying to present a menu of tax increases so substantial that they are rejected in their entirety," he explained. With his vote, the LACTC approved the tax for the ballot by a single vote, six to five.[10]

The measure became known as Proposition C, although the LACTC board awkwardly dubbed it the "1990 Fast-Track Anti-Gridlock Transit

Improvement Proposition." Claiming to address gridlock and "dirty air," the initiative presented a detailed formula for dividing the funds, similar to how Proposition A allocated funds to different transit purposes.[11] Forty percent of the money would go to either expanded rail or bus transit (giving the LACTC discretion to choose which mode of transport to fund), 25 percent to streets and freeway improvements, 20 percent to local return funds to cities and the county, 5 percent to increased transit security, and 10 percent to commuter rail projects and park-and-ride lots.[12] Unlike Proposition A, Proposition C contained no provision to reduce bus fares.

As the campaign began, LACTC backers made extensive promises about the number of rail lines that Proposition C would fund. Among the forecasted projects was an expansion of the Green Line to Los Angeles International Airport (LAX), a new light rail line to Pasadena, and, of course, the purchase of existing railroad rights-of-way to create commuter rail lines across the county. The measure prohibited using any revenues to fund the subway from Union Station to Hollywood (which was essentially the entire second phase of the subway, dubbed MOS-2), reflecting the subway's unpopularity in the face of cost overruns and construction accidents.[13]

LACTC PURCHASES THE RIGHTS-OF-WAY

A month before the election, the LACTC agreed to purchase 175 miles of rail rights-of-way for $450 million, for what would eventually help form the Metrolink commuter rail service. The purchase included the 21-mile Burbank Branch line in the San Fernando Valley, which would link the Valley to the future Metro Rail subway stop in North Hollywood; the 23-mile Santa Clarita line between Saugus and Burbank; 46 miles between Moorpark and Burbank; a 58-mile line between downtown Los Angeles and San Bernardino; a 12.5-mile branch from Paramount to Stanton; and the 14-mile Exposition Boulevard route from downtown to Santa Monica.[14] Funds for the purchase would come from Propositions 108 and 116 (the Clean Air and Transportation Improvement Act of 1990), but LACTC officials publicly hoped that Proposition C would pass and provide additional money to cover costs.[15]

Southern Pacific claimed that the county was getting a great deal. Robert Starzel, the vice chairman of Southern Pacific, described the rights-of-way as "assets worth more than twice what [the county] is paying.... But we've agreed to the price because we consider ourselves partners in the progress of

Southern California and because we could sell all the lines at this time as a single package."[16] Southern Pacific also laid claim to landholdings around the rights-of-way, which included property that was likely to increase in value once the commuter rail service began.[17]

Shortly after the purchase, Southern Pacific contributed $587,000 to the campaign for Proposition C. The Santa Fe Pacific Corporation, another railroad interest negotiating the sale of additional rights-of-way with the LACTC, donated another $75,000 to the campaign. Together, the two railroad companies accounted for almost two-thirds of the $1 million donated to the campaign.[18] Compared to the $36,000 Proposition A campaign in 1980, Proposition C was well funded.

LACTC members and the railroad companies denied that they had negotiated any sweetheart deal. "Our deal isn't conditioned on passage of Prop. C," Starzel said. "We have been a major contributor because we believe the rail projects . . . [will help] untangle the transportation mess."[19]

On Election Day in 1990, voters once again approved a sales tax increase to fund rail transit in Los Angeles. This time, however, the measure barely passed with a 50.4 percent approval.[20] Proposition C had faced stiff competition from the county sheriff's sales tax measure to fund jail construction.[21] Rail advocates therefore had to compete to raise scarce local funds with other critical local services. The financial support from the railroads proved critical, given the close margin. And because the California Supreme Court had already determined, following the 1980 Proposition A vote, that the LACTC was exempt from Proposition 13's two-thirds majority requirement for raising taxes, Proposition C could go into effect immediately.

As with Proposition A, Proposition C's formula for dividing the funds among various transit needs proved successful in assembling a winning coalition. For example, the rights-of-way purchases for commuter rail were critical to earning the endorsement of the *Los Angeles Times*. The *Times* endorsement also resulted from the recognition that federal funds for the Los Angeles rail system were drying up with the national economic recession.[22] As with Proposition A campaign material, Proposition C boosters exaggerated the number of rail lines that the money could build. Ray Remy, Mayor Bradley's chief-of-staff, recalled that Neil Peterson "went out like Monty Hall on *Let's Make a Deal*. We were going to have rail lines to Diamond Bar, you name it."[23]

For his part, Peterson believed that the opening of the Blue Line just a few months before the Proposition C vote convinced voters that rail could work in Los Angeles. "We had something to show," he commented about the July 1990 Blue Line unveiling. "A lot of people were very skeptical of the reintroduction, after a forty-year absence, of rail in Los Angeles County. So for the Blue Line to open successfully without any incidences, graffiti, on the honor system for fares in Los Angeles, which nobody thought could be done, that was unbelievably important. It stimulated the rest of the regions of the county to want their version of the Blue Line sooner rather than later."[24]

Iraq's invasion of Kuwait in August 1990, which occurred just a few months before the Proposition C vote and caused a spike in gasoline prices, may also have helped secure support. Meanwhile, LACTC rail development director Richard Stanger credited the 1988 movie *Who Framed Roger Rabbit?*, which popularized the theory that car companies had deliberately destroyed the once great Los Angeles streetcar system.[25]

In the end, Supervisor Schabarum came to regret his role as the deciding vote to place the tax on the ballot. After Proposition C's passage, he remarked: "I wouldn't have voted for it knowing what I know now."[26]

THE FOUR RAIL LINES OF THE APOCALYPSE

Following the Proposition C victory, Neil Peterson led the LACTC in drafting the agency's "wish list" of rail projects. He wanted to enshrine the list in a long-term, thirty-year transportation plan for Los Angeles. He viewed the drafting of the plan as fundamentally a political exercise designed to secure regional support across the county for individual rail lines. "If you wanted to create a vision that brought everybody under the tent," he later explained, "you had to do it in a way that everybody could see they'd get their piece of it. They might not get it today, or tomorrow, but it was going to be in there."[27] The thirty-year plan was therefore Peterson's response to the challenge of securing consensus across an enormous county.

As a result of its political nature, the plan quickly became a vehicle to over-promise rail lines based on optimistic financial assumptions. When the LACTC formally adopted it in 1992, the $183 billion, thirty-year transportation plan included $78.2 billion for over four hundred miles of urban rail, commuter rail, and "similar high-capacity transportation improvements."[28] It budgeted for "committed" heavy rail subway lines from downtown to North Hollywood, East Los Angeles, and West Los Angeles, plus a rail extension through the San Fernando Valley and light rail to Pasadena. The plan also identified eight "candidate corridors" for rail. These eight included three Green Line extensions (south, north, and east), a connection to the Burbank Airport, two segments of light rail to Santa Monica, and two corridors in the San Gabriel Valley, including an extension of the planned Pasadena light rail line.[29]

The thirty-year plan guided LACTC rail efforts following the Proposition C victory. LACTC staff soon narrowed the focus to four of the rail routes identified in the plan: the Green Line extension north to LAX, light rail along Exposition Boulevard from downtown Los Angeles to Santa Monica, the San Fernando Valley rail extension from the subway terminus in North Hollywood, and the light rail line from Pasadena to downtown Los Angeles.[30] These lines rose to the top because they satisfied key constituencies in major regions of the county.

While planning for these four rail lines predated the thirty-year plan, the adoption of the plan and the Proposition C victory intensified these processes. But as the implementation efforts began, almost all of these proposed lines faced severe political challenges, primarily from outspoken community opposition groups and disagreements among various leaders. The political process soon bogged down, and the national recession and escalating rail construction costs drained transit funds available for these projects. Delivering on the promise of Proposition C would be more difficult, and the outcome less optimal, than rail supporters anticipated.

THE GREEN LINE MISSES ITS CONNECTION

The first major project that LACTC planners attempted to plan and build in the post–Proposition C era was the extension of the Green Line, then still under construction. The extension would fulfill the promise of the first Green Line segment, which included a station two frustrating miles from LAX terminals at Aviation Boulevard and Imperial Highway. Planners had long wanted to bring rail to the airport, a high-profile travel and jobs center. They hoped that an extension would also serve local neighborhoods and possibly lead to a connection to Santa Monica and a future Exposition Boulevard rail line.

Planning for the Green Line North Coast Extension, as it was known, had begun when LACTC staff completed the environmental review in August 1989 as part of the environmental impact report required by state law for the entire Green Line.[31] In 1990, LACTC staff ranked this route as the highest-priority rail line,[32] and the agency approved a $215 million budget for it.[33] Proposition C money finally provided the opportunity to bring rail to LAX.

The plan for the LAX extension never involved direct train service to the airport terminals. Instead, the extension would deliver passengers to a station close to the terminals, where airport officials had begun studying and planning for a fully automated airport "people mover" rail system that would link the Green Line extension with the terminals. The line would then continue north to serve various population and job centers. Meanwhile, the airport station would serve as a hub for a planned high-speed magnetic levitation ("maglev") rail line from Palmdale, a sprawling desert community in far northern Los Angeles County, which officials at the Southern California Association of Governments (SCAG) hoped to build.[34]

Green Line extension planners wanted to ensure that the light rail, people mover, and maglev trains all converged in one convenient station. The Department of Airports and LACTC planners preferred a station at Parking Lot C, which was airport-owned property next to the terminals. Lot C represented the best option for a transit hub due to its location and available land area. LAX officials envisioned consolidated rental car and shuttle van facilities, bus connections, the three converging rail technologies, and a drop-off and pick-up location outside of the terminals for passengers arriving and departing, thus limiting the need for automobiles to circulate through the airport.[35]

But when the LACTC tried to bring the Green Line directly to Lot C, they encountered turbulence of a different sort. The most promising route took the trains directly in front of the southern runways of LAX,[36] and the Federal Aviation Administration (FAA) was concerned that the overhead catenary lines that powered the trains would create electromagnetic effects that would disrupt navigational aids for incoming planes.[37] The LACTC preferred rail route, wrote FAA officials in May 1991 to Green Line planners, "may now have a significant negative effect on the operation of the airport and FAA navigational equipment."[38] The FAA wanted the route to avoid what became known as the "Runway Protection Zone" or "Clear Zone."[39] FAA leaders transferred legal liability for any negative effects on airplane navigational aids to the city's Department of Airports, which in turn transferred liability to the LACTC.[40]

The FAA concerns forced LACTC planners to evaluate station locations far from Lot C to avoid running trains in the Clear Zone. But airport officials did not like the proposed stations, still wanting a Lot C terminus.[41] The dispute

Figure 3-4
**METRO GREEN LINE ALONG
AVIATION BOULEVARD**

*ICF KAISER
ENGINEERS*
(California) Corporation

Metro Green Line Northern Extension Supplemental Environmental Impact Report

FIGURE 19. Map of the proposed Green Line northern extension stations at Los Angeles International Airport, 1992. The route would travel underground to avoid runway interference and serve a potential transit hub at Parking Lot C, including an airport people mover connection, before terminating in Westchester. (Courtesy of the Los Angeles County Metropolitan Transportation Authority Research Library and Archive. Reprinted with permission.)

prompted protracted negotiations among local elected officials, transit agencies, the FAA, and the airport.[42] By November 1991, LACTC staff were growing alarmed at the increasing costs associated with the revised airport extension plans.[43] With new proposed alignments to accommodate FAA concerns, the estimated costs jumped $100 million above original forecasts. James Okazaki in the city's planning department began to fear the worst for the line. "Not building it because of lack of consensus and loss of opportunity fueled by political grandstanding," he wrote, "... would be a great disservice to the citizens of Los Angeles. We must have a regional rail connection to LAX. It is better to build it sooner than later, and it is certainly less expensive to build it now than later."[44]

Okazaki's words proved prescient. The LACTC was quickly running out of funds to build new rail projects. Sales tax revenues for rail had fallen 15 percent due to the national economic recession by March 1992.[45] LACTC efforts to convince the airport to contribute funds failed.[46] Reluctantly, the LACTC board voted to postpone until 1998 plans to begin service to LAX.[47]

With time and money running out, the parties belatedly narrowed down the options to two alternatives: an all–people mover route from the existing Green Line Aviation Station, on the one hand, and a light rail extension to a Lot C transit hub that avoided the Clear Zone by traveling underneath Aviation and along Century Boulevard, on the other. But both routes required extensive supplemental environmental review that would push the process years into the future.[48]

The postponement of the airport connector meant a potentially unlimited delay as rail funds dwindled, costs for current projects escalated, and the public soured on further rail expansion. As a result, the north coast extension was essentially dead, a victim of bureaucratic infighting and dwindling funds. With its demise went rail service to the airport.

Many local leaders blamed the airport for the impasse, arguing that airport leaders should have been willing to contribute funds for the extension. "If [the airport] had used passenger facility funds to meet the line, we would have gone there and made it happen," said Bacharach. "But we never got help from the airport."[49] According to Ruth Galanter, who represented the area at the Los Angeles City Council, airport officials cited a federal law that prevented airport revenues from funding anything other than airport improvements. "The airlines said, 'No way. The people using the Green Line have nothing to do with the airport, so you can't take this money.' If Bradley had been around for another ten years, he probably could have worked out a compromise."[50]

With the airport connection thwarted, the Green Line that opened along the Century Freeway in 1995 debuted with something of a whimper. The estimated cost in 1984 had been $254.5 million, with a projected daily ridership of 100,000.[51] By the time it was completed, however, the line cost $718 million, with Caltrans spending an additional $242 million to design and construct the stations and parking lots.[52] "A lot of those costs were shifted through negotiations to the LACTC," argued Richard Stanger, "which got a bum deal."[53] Ridership topped out at roughly 34,000 average daily boardings by 2010.[54]

Not only was the opening tainted by disappointment over the lack of service to the airport, but the western terminus of the line now served an industrial ghost town in El Segundo, the result of the recently collapsed defense industry. The end of the Cold War and the resulting defense industry cutbacks had decimated the job centers that planners had once used to justify the construction of light rail to the area.

The eastern terminus was also a disappointment, located in the middle of a freeway far from any urban center. The terminus was supposed to occur in Norwalk, at an Amtrak (and future Metrolink) station that would connect to Orange County and beyond. "We went to the city of Norwalk and said we want to build it to the Amtrak station," explained Bacharach. "But they said, 'Absolutely not. We don't want this thing going through our city.' So we terminated, we found a site, and . . . the design was already going on. Then Norwalk got a brand new city manager who said, 'You've got to take the line through Norwalk.' But we said, 'Sorry, it's too late.'"[55]

Transportation officials like Bacharach sounded defensive at the opening of the line. "In 50 years, let's talk about whether the Green Line was a good idea," she told the *Los Angeles Times*. "Let's not talk about it now."[56] Even the media, which usually celebrated new rail line openings, questioned the Green Line's value. In a *Los Angeles Times* article entitled, "Is New Green Line a Road to Nowhere?" reporter Richard Simon discussed the line's planning failures and inability to reach key destinations. The article featured transit planners who privately blamed airport officials for the Green Line not reaching LAX, suggesting that they resisted public transit to protect airport parking revenues. Airport officials denied the charges.[57]

The Green Line's weak ridership figures and poor supporting land use around station areas, located in the hostile environment of a freeway median, bolstered the case that a busway would have been a superior use of public funds. But the failure of the Green Line to reach the airport, ironically, may not have significantly hurt ridership. The limited scholarship on rail connections to airports indicates that the most successful lines have in-terminal stations or high-frequency connections to the airport from the rail station, a large rail network to access, travel times that generally approximate an automobile trip, one-seat rides, and limited walking distances to the check-in counters.[58] By these measures, an airport connection to LAX would not attract significant ridership. The route would require multiple connections for most passengers and an off-site station requiring a transfer to a bus or people-mover train. For example, a passenger traveling from downtown Los Angeles would have to ride the Blue Line, transfer to the Green Line, and then take either the bus or people mover to the actual terminal. The total travel time would rarely be competitive with that of an automobile or shuttle.[59]

Still, the Green Line's failure to reach the airport and service a significant population or employment center became a psychological black eye for rail in Los Angeles, contributing to a growing public perception that the rail system was a poorly executed waste of resources. Ultimately, the death of the north coast extension became the first casualty of transit leaders' ambitious plans for rail expansion that followed the Proposition C victory.

THE BALLAD OF THE SAN FERNANDO VALLEY HOMEOWNERS

While the Green Line extension was failing, another rail route in the post–Proposition C era would soon meet the same fate—this time in the San Fernando Valley. Elected officials had long sought to deliver rail to the Valley, primarily because of the region's political importance. The relatively affluent and largely suburban area, separated from the urban centers of Los Angeles to the south by the Santa Monica Mountains, lacked the population density necessary to support a heavy rail subway. However, county rail officials needed the Valley's political support for a countywide rail initiative. As a result, the 1980 Proposition A map prominently identified the Valley as a candidate for rail service, while the 1983 LACTC rail transit implementation strategy identified a Valley line as one of only six in the entire county that the agency would consider for light rail.[60] Rail also had support from the Valley's business leaders, who viewed it as a means to boost property values, create and revitalize commercial districts, and provide residents with easy access to job centers in the county.

Rail advocates, however, faced fierce opposition from a small but vocal group of Valley homeowners who lived along the various proposed rail routes. Owing to their relative wealth, they tended to be well organized and determined. They resisted rail because of concerns about noise from loud rail cars passing through previously dormant rights-of-way—some of which were almost in people's backyards. They also feared rail's impacts on the character and safety of their neighborhoods.

These forces were on a collision course as local leaders began narrowing the options on where to locate a rail line in the Valley. The original starter-line corridor in 1975 included a broad route from the east end at Warner Center in Canoga Park to the west end in North Hollywood, with a continuation to downtown Los Angeles. Following the 1980 passage of Proposition A, the LACTC contemplated an east-west route in the Valley to connect to the planned heavy-rail subway terminal in North Hollywood, at the foot of the Valley across the Santa Monica Mountains from downtown Los Angeles. After years of discussion, the agency agreed in 1987 to perform an environmental review of five Valley routes, including one along the Ventura Freeway and one parallel to Burbank and Chandler boulevards.[61]

The Chandler Boulevard route was the favorite of transit planners. Chandler was a wide road running east to west that featured an abandoned rail right-of-way down the middle. The street led to the North Hollywood terminus of the planned subway station, rendering it a natural for a rail connection. Planners also liked the route because it served unmet transit needs in the vast residential area between two parallel freeways that ran to the north and south.[62]

But the route engendered immediate opposition. The trains would pass directly through an Orthodox Jewish community that feared the impact of rail transit on noise levels and pedestrian safety (important for a congregation that walked to religious services on the Sabbath). Rabbi Chaim Schnur of Agudath Israel of California, whose mission was to protect "the civil and religious rights of the observant Jewish community," wrote to Bradley to protest the Chandler route plans. "It is our sincere belief that the construction of this system on Chandler Boulevard will do great harm to the residential community and its outstanding institutions," Schnur wrote. "The synagogues, day schools, and other services . . . would be severely threatened," he added. "Safety risks, noise, traffic disruption would further impede and prevent continued settlement in the area."[63]

The Chandler rail opponents found a political champion in then–City Councilman Zev Yaroslavsky. In a letter to Mayor Bradley, who was advocating the study of the various Valley routes in the environmental impact report, the councilman embraced the role of homeowner advocate. As a representative of a Jewish community in his Fairfax district, Yaroslavsky now extended the solidarity to the Jewish neighborhood in the Valley. He urged Bradley to cease consideration of the Chandler route, citing the "anxiety the entire community has come to feel" at the prospect of light rail down Chandler Boulevard. "I don't want to destabilize this neighborhood; I want to preserve its quality of life," he wrote. He then closed with an argument that essentially refuted the purpose of light rail: "You are trying to send a train through a built-up area whose streets are lined with lovely homes and well-established community institutions. . . . Light rail is viewed not as a service to this community but as a noisy, unwanted intrusion."[64]

As word of the rail proposal spread, Valley residents flooded their local officials' offices with letters expressing concern about noise and the threat to the character of their neighborhoods. In a typical letter received by Mayor Bradley's office, Bruce Varnum of Reseda wrote, "This line would come very close to my house and would create noise, vibration, excessive traffic and undermine the value of my property."[65] The *Los Angeles Daily News* ran a story profiling a Reseda homemaker who made stopping light rail in the Valley her personal cause. Having purchased a home less than 100 feet from Southern Pacific railroad tracks, Julie Fine now enlisted support from homeowner groups along the proposed route to fight the project. In each community, she emphasized different arguments against light rail, from noise and blight to the increased crime and building density that the rail would surely bring.[66]

The public outcry grew, dampening enthusiasm for the project at the LACTC. Jacki Bacharach, a Valley native who now lived on the Palos Verdes Peninsula in the far southern part of the county, headed the committee studying various Valley routes. She held numerous community hearings that resulted in an outpouring of negativity from local residents. "When the Blue Line was being built, I would go to Compton and Watts a lot to go to meetings, without problem," Bacharach said, referring to South Los Angeles communities with a reputation for crime. "But when I went to the Valley to do the public hearings for the development of rail, I asked for an escort to my car, because those people were like crazy people. They were threatening, they felt more entitled, and they were just not really nice people to deal with. And I grew up in the Valley, and I kept thinking these are 'my people.' Nobody could agree with anybody."[67]

Cowed by the opposition, Bacharach persuaded the LACTC board to postpone study of the Valley routes. She suggested instead that the LACTC rely on local Valley officials to develop a different process to achieve consensus.[68] A few months later, she voted to authorize an environmental impact report for a southern extension of the Green Line,[69] taking that line close to her district in Palos Verdes.[70]

In collaboration with local leaders, the LACTC eventually whittled the rail options down to two corridors: an alignment along the median of the Ventura Freeway[71] and the east-west Burbank-Chandler Boulevard corridor.[72] The Ventura Freeway route offered lower costs and less neighborhood opposition, given that the freeway already created significant environmental impacts and had a median ripe for conversion to rail. The Burbank-Chandler route was more optimal for rail ridership and station area development, although neighborhood opposition to surface rail would likely force an expensive underground route.

Valley leaders pushed for and secured LACTC approval in March 1990 for a heavy rail subway route underneath the Burbank-Chandler alignment.[73] This option would serve their political need to underground the line and bring expensive heavy rail service to their constituents. The route would function as an extension of the downtown subway from North Hollywood.[74] Although the Valley subway route was politically palatable, it was an expensive and inappropriate technology for the relatively low-density corridor, especially compared to other, denser corridors in the metropolitan region that did not yet have rail service. "If a subway is required through residential neighborhoods," LACTC executive director Neil Peterson wrote the LACTC board members, "the cost of a project across the San Fernando Valley may approach the current commitment to Metro Rail."[75]

Lacking available funds to build the subway in the Valley, the LACTC sequenced the subway to begin construction after the proposed Pasadena and Green Line extensions, with a projected start date in 1996.[76] The passage of Proposition C that November injected new life into the rail proposal.[77] But enthusiasm for the project waned at the LACTC given the agency's dwindling revenues and competing demands. Perhaps hoping to spur local consensus for a cheaper alternative, the agency announced in May 1991 that the eight-mile subway extension would now be delayed until 2024.[78]

Homeowner groups along Chandler wanted to kill the possibility of a less expensive surface route. They took their case to Sacramento, persuading state senator Alan Robbins of Tarzana to author legislation mandating that any rail line through the residential neighborhoods in North Hollywood and Van Nuys on the Chandler route be built underground to reduce noise and _{OMG} traffic impacts. Robbins's proposal became law in June 1991.[79] As a result, rail in the most optimal corridor in the Valley would now be prohibitively expensive to build. The new law was therefore a major victory for homeowner groups, who had successfully circumvented the local process by enlisting eager state representatives to overrule county transit officials. Sacramento leaders were now deciding the type of rail to be built along Chandler, taking their cues from outspoken opposition groups.

With Robbins's law in effect and no money for a subway, LACTC leaders tried to keep rail in the Valley alive, at one point even considering a monorail above the Ventura Freeway at the behest of Supervisor Mike Antonovich. But the monorail proposal died when new safety standards following the 1994 Northridge earthquake made the technology almost as costly to build as the all-subway alternative.[80] Valley leaders were now left with only the expensive subway option for rail. But they would not have the funds for the foreseeable future.

Ultimately, the combination of political infighting and fierce, well-resourced homeowner resistance had effectively ended the possibility of rail in the Valley. Opposition groups had successfully delayed a decision on rail long enough to ensure that the agency would have no money left to build it. And they had made illegal by state statute the most inexpensive rail option in the most optimal corridor. Homeowner groups and their elected allies in the Valley thwarted rail with more success than anywhere else in the county, most likely due to their relative affluence and sheer numbers in a largely suburban landscape. As a result, the San Fernando Valley would not see rapid transit for more than a decade afterward, and it would not take the form of rail.

EXPO

As the Valley and Green Line extension rail projects withered, local leaders hoped for success with a third rail line in the Proposition C era. Called "Exposition" or "Expo" after the boulevard that it largely followed, this line was arguably the most important of all the rail candidates because it attempted to serve the population-rich Westside of Los Angeles, via a route that paralleled a major freeway. But like the Valley line, it traversed pockets of high-income, suburban neighborhoods that proved equally committed to fighting rail.

The Westside was home to some of the densest jobs and housing centers in Los Angeles County, including cities such as Santa Monica and Culver City and neighborhoods like Venice, Inglewood, and West Los Angeles. The existing network of rail lines failed to serve the area, and planners hoped a light rail line would fill the gap and provide steady ridership. Rail-friendly cities like Santa Monica welcomed the idea. While subway advocates still hoped to bring the heavy rail subway down Wilshire Boulevard to the northern end of the Westside, a light rail line would be the next best thing and could serve residents and workers to the south of Wilshire.

Somewhat conveniently, a rail right-of-way already existed in the area from an old Pacific Electric route, the "Santa Monica Air Line," which once brought downtown residents out to Santa Monica and the beach. The line went out of business in the 1950s and instead began to support freight trains. Southern Pacific operated the line until the early 1980s, delivering supplies to Fisher Lumber in Santa Monica.[81] The route roughly followed heavily traveled Interstate 10 as the only highway to link downtown with the Westside, passing by the University of Southern California before rolling through Crenshaw and residential areas in West Los Angeles. Eventually, it entered industrial sections of south Santa Monica (which became major employment centers starting in the 1990s) and terminated a few blocks from the Pacific Ocean by the famous Third Street Promenade, a street closed to traffic and converted into a successful outdoor pedestrian mall.

LACTC leaders had considered the abandoned railroad line for transit since the initial staff assessment of potential rail corridors following the 1980 Proposition A victory and Supreme Court decision upholding it in 1982. The draft rail implementation strategy from 1983 described light rail on Exposition Boulevard as "relatively low in cost to construct" because of the existing rail right-of-way and noted that it had "good potential as a rail route."[82] The report recommended Exposition as one of the six corridors for the LACTC to continue evaluating for rail. By 1984, agency staff viewed rail on Exposition as superior even to the right-of-way along the more heavily traveled Santa Monica Boulevard to the north, preferring it because it would serve transit dependents and the "different population centers" by downtown near Crenshaw.[83]

Throughout the 1980s, advocates for the line waited their turn while transit officials picked light rail to Long Beach and along the Century Freeway and stalled on subway plans under Wilshire to the Westside. Initially, the Wilshire subway plans had made light rail on Exposition less politically viable. "The point of view of everybody was that each corridor would get one rail line before you built a second line in a corridor, just to be fair," explained Richard Stanger, describing in frank terms how politics in the sprawling region trumped ridership in rail decision-making. "To have two rail lines from the downtown to the west was just not politically possible. Supervisors from the loser part of the county wouldn't have let that happen."[84]

But the prospect of the LACTC purchasing the railroad rights-of-way in 1990, which included Exposition, made the light rail option more appealing. Powerful local leaders and rail advocates supported the purchase for this reason, indicating the widespread support for rail in the corridor. These leaders included Assembly speaker Mike Roos,[85] state senator Diane Watson (who represented the transit-dependent areas of the right-of-way near downtown),[86] Santa Monica city leaders (including former city council member Christine Reed, who chaired the LACTC during part of this time period),[87] and Culver City officials, who viewed the railroad sale as a "once in a lifetime opportunity."[88] Cultural institutions and businesses along the route, such as the University of Southern California, Shrine Auditorium, Coliseum Commission, and other private and public entities, also supported rail on the corridor.[89]

But the suddenly looming prospect of rail on Exposition mobilized homeowner opposition to the purchase along the proposed route. While much of the route traveled through Santa Monica's and Culver City's industrial and retail areas (areas that lacked homeowners as potential opponents), the right-of-way also bisected suburban communities in Rancho Park and Cheviot Hills, two neighborhoods within the city of Los Angeles. Like their San Fernando Valley neighbors to the north, these homeowners organized to fight rail along the line, which was now mostly an abandoned strip of grass. They primarily feared the noise and crime that an eventual light rail line could bring.

Their first stand came at an LACTC community meeting in September 1989 to discuss the purchase. Homeowner groups turned out over four hundred people to oppose the sale. Their city councilmen, Zev Yaroslavsky and Nate Holden, appeared at the meeting to voice their opposition as well. Councilman Yaroslavsky explained at the meeting that he preferred a Westside rail route on corridors farther north, while Holden claimed to want deep-bore subway tunneling.[90] Meanwhile, the West of Westwood

Homeowners held a neighborhood meeting to protest. Their newsletter to nearby residents asked, "Did you know a light-rail train route is being planned to run by your bedroom??? It will create noise, pollution, vibrations, litter, invasion of privacy, and encourage traffic congestion, crime and vandalism!!!" The flyer included a picture of a serious train derailment that occurred in San Bernardino earlier that year, complete with the caption "These tracks [in the photo] are further from homes than the distance between the Exposition right-of-way and adjacent homes!!! Act now, prevent a similar disaster from happening in our neighborhood."[91]

Los Angeles city councilwoman Ruth Galanter experienced the opposition firsthand. "I inherited half of Cheviot Hills through redistricting, and when that happened, I inherited all the people who were hysterical with opposition at having 'those people' come though their backyard," she said in 2008. "They were worried about people coming from the other parts of town and coming into houses and stealing stuff. They said, 'We want a bike path.' But it's much easier to get off a bike, steal something, and get back on than it is to get off a moving train. But I couldn't get through to them." She further noted, "During the time I represented the area, all the homeowner groups were adamant they needed to protect their neighborhood."[92]

But the homeowners lost when the LACTC decided to purchase the route in 1990. The sale "made the corridor more attractive [for rail] because we now owned it," Stanger said.[93] The passage of Proposition C just a few months later elevated the line's prospects tremendously. With sales tax dollars in hand, LACTC leaders approved the commission of an environmental impact report under state law in March 1991. But in a nod to the political resistance farther down the corridor, they commissioned a study for only a short route from downtown to Vermont Avenue.[94] As a consolation, the agency included the entire Exposition corridor in the expanded thirty-year plan for rail deployment. The LACTC decided to study light rail, trolley buses, and a bus/carpool transitway options for the route.[95]

Public hearings on the proposals drew mixed crowds. For every Santa Monica resident who generally considered rail service to be a benefit, angry homeowners in Rancho Park and Cheviot Hills complained about potential crime and noise from the route.[96] Councilman Yaroslavsky appeared determined to be their champion. He called a rail line on Exposition Boulevard a "waste of money" and incorrectly argued that it was "the lowest density corridor in Los Angeles."[97] Instead, he advocated for a rail line through Century City and Beverly Hills. As Galanter observed, "Zev has always been a very articulate and successful supporter of whatever the homeowner groups are pushing for. It's one of the reasons I don't think he's ever had a serious challenge. The homeowner groups love him, and he cultivates them."[98] Unfortunately for Expo rail advocates, however, his opposition as the local city council member made it politically difficult for other elected officials not to defer to him.

Ultimately, the opposition in Rancho Park and Cheviot Hills, combined with the emerging financial problems at the agency, resulted in LACTC inaction on the route. By 1993, the LACTC agreed only to approve the environmental review of the portion terminating at Vermont, far from the angry homeowners of the Westside. Community opposition had therefore reduced the area of study and guaranteed that the line would remain a second-tier priority for the near future.[99] Soon, the LACTC ran out of money and halted new rail construction. Plans for the line gathered dust. Residents walked their dogs on the grass that had overtaken parts of the dormant right-of-way, and commuters obliviously drove over the abandoned tracks that crisscrossed busy Westside streets.

Homeowners had won this round.

PASADENA'S POWERFUL POLITICIANS PREVAIL

Amid the controversies and failures of the Green Line extension, the San Fernando Valley line, and the Expo line, the fourth and final remaining transit corridor in the Proposition C era seemed promising, primarily by default. While the other lines fell like dominoes, the Pasadena light rail line looked increasingly like a safe bet for transit leaders needing to demonstrate success with Proposition C revenues for rail.

The Pasadena line involved 13.7 miles of track from Union Station on the eastern edge of downtown Los Angeles to eastern Pasadena.[100] The ninth-largest city in Los Angeles County, Pasadena was a generally affluent city with a revitalizing historic downtown in the San Gabriel Valley, at the base of the San Gabriel Mountains. The city was famous for the Rose Bowl and the New Year's Day Rose Parade, as well as for institutions like the California Institute of Technology. After leaving Pasadena, the line would travel along a winding right-of-way adjacent to the Arroyo Seco waterway, through residential areas largely consisting of rental housing. Once the line reached downtown, plans called for a connector to take it to the Blue Line terminus at the 7th Street and Flower Red Line station. In fact, the LACTC originally considered the line to be an extension of the Blue Line. Once the agency built the connector, travelers would ride seamlessly from Long Beach to eastern Pasadena on a one-seat light rail ride.[101]

Although rail planners generally supported serving Pasadena with rail, other routes were more likely to have higher ridership based on greater population densities. Following the 1980 victory for Proposition A (which had featured the corridor on the ballot map), LACTC staff recommended the line as one of six corridors for further rail study, noting that it had one of the cheapest cost estimates of any of the lines under consideration.[102] But in the draft Rail Implementation Strategy in 1984, agency planners wrote that the Pasadena line "did not rank highest in the top three criteria relative to the other corridors," though it did appear to have "good patronage potential." Nonetheless, LACTC leaders considered the Pasadena line a "high priority" for future rail projects.[103]

What the Pasadena line lacked in population density, it made up for with powerful political backers. The line had critical support from Congressman David Dreier, a rare Republican rail proponent in the U.S. House of Representatives. Dreier was elected to Congress during the Reagan Revolution, at the age of twenty-eight. Despite Reagan's and the Republican Party's hostility to government spending, Dreier became an outspoken proponent for bringing rail to his congressional district in the San Gabriel Valley. "Dave Dreier was a stalwart all along," Ray Remy, Bradley's chief of staff, recalled. "He was an important voice in supporting the system and wanted the system to come out to his area." Given that the federal government had been so hostile during the Reagan and George H. W. Bush years to spending money for rail in Los Angeles, Dreier's Republican support for transportation appropriations for the region was vital to funding the entire Los Angeles rail network. Remy observed that getting "a prominent member of Congress from the other party who was very helpful in supporting" the line gave the project a significant advantage. Although Dreier represented the San Gabriel Valley and not Pasadena, Remy explained that the Pasadena line "was on the way to his [congressional] district and would get there eventually."[104]

In addition to the federal support of Dreier, the Pasadena line had strong backing within the city of Los Angeles and its business community. Richard Alatorre, the Los Angeles city councilman representing parts of the rail corridor, became a strong proponent of the project and its most outspoken advocate,[105] predicting that the project would be "cost-effective, on time, [and] built to the highest professional standards."[106] The city of Pasadena, including its business community, also strongly supported rail, most likely because the route traversed mostly industrial areas within the city and not residential communities that might have had organized homeowners to oppose the line. Businesses along Colorado Avenue in Old Pasadena meanwhile hoped the rail line would spur a revitalization of the area.[107]

While the route appeared to offer less than competing rail projects, particularly without the downtown connector, local officials still believed the line could be successful. Ray Remy, then a member of the LACTC, explained: "The patronage with Pasadena was pretty good, with people going downtown. It was also a good starting point to get to the San Gabriel Valley," the suburban population center directly to the east of Pasadena.[108] The San Gabriel and San Bernardino valleys were becoming booming bedroom communities, and local officials liked the idea that the Pasadena line could offer a first leg toward serving them with rail.[109] They envisioned turning the line into a commuter rail system for suburban communities.

The Pasadena line seemed to benefit from the travails afflicting competing county rail projects. As the Green Line extension, San Fernando Valley line, and Expo project became enmeshed in community opposition, and while the subway stalled in Hollywood, the Pasadena line slowly moved to the top of the priority list.[110] By 1990, the LACTC listed the route as second-in-line after the Green Line airport extension but ahead of the Valley subway.[111] "There was tremendous support for the Green Line, Expo, and other lines," recalled Neil Peterson. "But when you get to implementation, some of these lines had pockets of resistance," he said, citing Cheviot Hills homeowners opposed to the Exposition line and religious group opposition to rail in the Valley. "With the Pasadena line though, there wasn't a neighborhood or group like that that was comparable."[112]

Then, in the early 1990s, a confluence of events moved the Pasadena route to the top of the rail list. First, in the fall of 1990 the LACTC purchased the railroad rights-of-way, which included the Santa Fe Railroad tracks to Pasadena. As with the Exposition line, transit officials had removed a significant impediment and cost to building the line, because they now owned the land for the tracks. Second, the Proposition C victory provided new revenues for light rail. Finally, and most importantly, the decisions by LACTC officials to postpone the Green Line extension, the Valley line, and the Expo line due to local opposition and infighting meant that the Pasadena line was the last major rail project left that seemed politically viable.[113]

On January 27, 1993, with little fanfare or debate, the LACTC board authorized Proposition C dollars to build light rail to Pasadena from Union Station in downtown Los Angeles.[114] The agency earmarked $841 million for the 13.6-mile line, slated to open in late 1996. LACTC staff estimated that the ride would take about twenty-five minutes, with stops at six stations, including Chinatown and Old Town Pasadena. "This next light rail line is a much-needed corridor for people who use the overcrowded Pasadena Freeway now for travel between Pasadena and downtown L.A.," Stephanie Brady of the LACTC remarked to the media.[115]

Despite its questionable merits relative to other projects, the line appeared to be a sure thing.

RAIL BY DEFAULT

Backers of rail to LAX, the Valley, and along Exposition Boulevard would have to wait their turn—potentially decades. Given the promise of Proposition C and the ambitions of rail planners at the beginning of the 1990s, the outcome of the process must have been disappointing to rail advocates. Dwindling funds and infighting had stymied rail in some high-profile transit corridors, leaving a relatively low-value Pasadena route as the last project standing. Rail advocates in other parts of the region had simply missed their chance, sunk by homeowner opposition and elected officials unwilling to buck them.

The political buzzsaw that these light rail lines faced, however, would soon become dwarfed by a larger political tide that would sweep away the transit bureaucracies in Los Angeles and ultimately threaten to undermine the city's entire rail program.

SEVEN

A Knife in the Seat

THE BEGINNING OF THE END for the two Los Angeles transit agencies, the Southern California Rapid Transit District (RTD) and the Los Angeles County Transportation Commission (LACTC), came on December 18, 1991. That day, the LACTC board made what seemed to be an innocuous decision on a rail car contract, voting seven to three to award a Green Line job to Sumitomo Corporation of America, a company with a history in Japan dating back to 1630.[1] In doing so, the commissioners rejected the bid of Morrison Knudsen, a venerable Idaho-based construction firm that helped to build the Oakland–San Francisco Bay Bridge and the Hoover Dam.[2]

The LACTC planned to automate the rail cars on the Green Line to eliminate the need for drivers. Automation would reduce long-term operating costs from saved salary expenses and allow for more flexible service. Sumitomo and Morrison Knudsen were the only two companies to respond to the agency's competitive bid process.[3] Morrison Knudsen's bid was lower than Sumitomo's by $5 million, at $116.8 million versus $121.7 million.[4] But LACTC staff determined that Sumitomo's proposal was more technically sound and offered greater long-term benefits.[5] Sumitomo had also manufactured more than 40,000 automated rail cars, compared to Morrison Knudsen's 304 in production at the time of the bid.[6]

What the LACTC staff did not anticipate, however, was that the nationality of the companies involved would become a political lightning rod. The ensuing controversy, stoked by the severe economic recession plaguing the country, and Southern California in particular, cost both the RTD and LACTC significant public support. Despite the Proposition C victory, the economic downturn in the early 1990s meant fewer funds for transit and popular backlash against a rail program that seemed to be wasting taxpayer dollars. Harsh media reports and questionable behavior by transit officials only fueled the negativity. While momentum had been building to merge the two agencies for a number of years, given that they each had similar functions and responsibility for governing the same jurisdiction, the political pushback from the rail car vote provided the final impetus.

The bureaucratic rearrangement, however, would fail to address the underlying structural problems that created the adverse financial and management situations in the first place. Local leaders needed more than an economic recovery to improve transit governance in Los Angeles.

THE SUMITOMO TSUNAMI

The Sumitomo controversy was the first sign that the recession and its social impact were going to create political problems for transit leaders. The reaction from the public to the decision was explosive, igniting protests across the United States based on fears of Japanese preeminence and declining American competitiveness. "The week they [the LACTC] announced they were going with Sumitomo was the week [President George H.W.] Bush threw up in the Japanese Prime Minister's lap," recalled Bevan Dufty, then chief of staff at the agency. "I never would have imagined that buying a rail car would be front page national news, but it was."[7]

Local media were overrun by irate Angelenos, shocked that the LACTC would hand money to a Japanese company over an American one with a lower bid. The *Los Angeles Times* ran continuous stories and editorials during the Christmas holidays focusing on the nationality of Sumitomo and the broken promises to support American companies.[8] The *Times* and other media also ran stories about the influence of lobbyists on the decision-making process, including former California governor George Deukmejian.[9]

In defense, LACTC chairman Ray Grabinsky argued to the *Times* that Sumitomo had pledged that 22 percent of its manufacturing on the contract would be done in the United States and that even Morrison Knudsen would have had to partner with a Japanese company to build some of the cars.[10]

But the media fury only increased in the new year, and politicians of all stripes joined the populist outrage. State Assembly speaker Willie Brown wrote duplicate scathing letters to each LACTC member—even those who voted against awarding the contract to Sumitomo—expressing how "very disappointed" he was with the vote and accusing them of voting to "create jobs and tax revenues in Japan."[11] (Brown's letter to Supervisor Edelman, who voted against the contract, prompted the supervisor to write to his staff that Brown "doesn't even know the vote!" while a staff member commented, "This letter is out of line.")[12] The State Assembly then voted 70–0 to ask the LACTC to reconsider the decision.[13] Almost the entire Los Angeles County congressional delegation wrote a letter to Chairman Grabinsky to reconsider this "tragic mistake"—even though the Green Line was not receiving federal funds.[14] Supervisors Deane Dana and Kenneth Hahn came out against automation and Sumitomo, and Councilman Joel Wachs even set up a hotline number for constituents to call to complain.[15] Councilman Zev Yaroslavsky became one of the most outspoken opponents of the decision, challenging an infuriated Mayor Bradley to reverse it.[16]

The LACTC was inundated with constituent complaints.[17] Commissioner Jacki Bacharach told reporters, "We have been bombarded not just with opinion but with a tremendous amount of hatred."[18] Bacharach later recalled how politics had twisted the debate. "It was a nightmare," she said. "I called friends of mine on the Los Angeles City Council and said, 'Let me explain this to you.' They said, 'I know what you're saying, but I can't say it publicly.' That's when politics first hit the commission, when everything started going in a way that wasn't just 'what's the best for here?'"[19]

Privately, the LACTC's general counsel advised Executive Director Neil Peterson that rescinding the contract would likely constitute a breach of contract with Sumitomo, resulting in possibly millions of dollars in damages.[20] But LACTC leaders had few good options given the terrible backlash. On January 17, 1992, the agency relented, issuing a stop work order on the Green Line rail car procurement and train control contracts. Chairman Grabinsky issued a terse statement: "The public comments received since last month's decision deserve to be reviewed and the Commissioners want to discuss this at the next meeting."[21]

The decision came too late to save the LACTC's reputation and the image of rail governance in Los Angeles. Conservative critics of the rail program pounced on the story. The *Wall Street Journal* ran an editorial singling out the Metro Rail subway as one of the "more aching outrages" compared to the Sumitomo affair, criticizing the expense of the project as a "financial bloodletting" and as a waste of national taxpayer dollars.[22] Representative John J. Duncan Jr., the Tennessee Republican who investigated allegations of subway tunnel flaws, lambasted local officials for siding with Sumitomo.

The episode also heightened racial tensions and xenophobia throughout the country. The LACTC had used foreign companies to manufacture cars for both the Red Line and the Blue Line without much of a fuss being raised.[23] But the economic and political climate of the early 1990s changed the context of public perception. Supervisor Hahn's deputy Mas Fukai, who spent World War II in an internment camp, had the awkward assignment of announcing Hahn's decision to reverse support for Sumitomo. "All you see in the newspapers is Japanese-bashing," Fukai told the *Los Angeles Times*.[24]

After the LACTC decision, Koichi Narikawa, general manager of Sumitomo, wrote the LACTC to remind its leadership that the decision to award Sumitomo the contract could be revoked only if there were an "unforeseen material change in circumstances." Yet "here, no change has occurred since execution of the contract," Narikawa wrote. Sumitomo would be reserving "all of its rights and remedies" under the contract with the LACTC.[25]

Nine months later, the LACTC cut a deal with Sumitomo to purchase a reduced order of fifteen cars for the Green Line.[26] Then in December 1992, the agency reopened the entire bidding process, eventually awarding one of its largest contracts ever to Siemens Duewag Corporation, a German company with a California manufacturing facility, along with some U.S. partners. In fulfilling the order for the Green Line rail cars, Siemens pledged to create local jobs in Los Angeles.[27]

Morrison Knudsen, meanwhile, filed for bankruptcy in June 1996.[28]

THE *TIMES* INVESTIGATES THE LACTC

The Sumitomo controversy primed the *Los Angeles Times* for a knockout blow. In February 1992, just a month after the uproar, the newspaper began preparing an investigation into LACTC finances. Following the California Public Records Act, the LACTC had to open its books for the investigation, which was headed by reporter Jane Fritsch. In anticipation, LACTC staff had created a special audit team eight months earlier to address cost efficiency and reduction issues. But the audit team had not eliminated the problems: Fritsch's investigation uncovered questionable expenses that Executive Director Neil Peterson was forced to explain and justify. LACTC leaders moved quickly to devise new policies, such as cutting back on employee meals and instituting carpooling for agency vehicles, but these steps came too late.[29]

In March 1992, with the agency still reeling from the Sumitomo affair, the *Times* published its front-page report, titled "Cash-Rich Transit Agency Spends Freely on Itself." The report documented evidence of "casual spending and lax accounting" at the LACTC, such as $2.9 million spent on meals, travel, and company fleet cars over an eighteen-month period. These expenditures included a "$9,000 Palm Springs retreat for accountants and bookkeepers, catered, staff-only lunch meetings that cost up to $499 per day, and many thousands of dollars worth of free coffee and doughnuts for staff members."[30]

The article also humiliated LACTC executives like Neil Peterson, claiming that he "rarely filed expense accounts" and citing this example as evidence of the weak financial procedures at the agency. "Ten days ago," Fritsch reported, Peterson "reimbursed the commission for $1,267 in personal charges he made on a commission credit card during the 18-month period. One of the bills was from a Scottsdale, Ariz., golf school. Peterson repaid the money after *The Times* requested explanations of his credit card purchases." In addition, Fritsch wrote, LACTC executive Thomas Tanke was able "to charge $1,588 in bicycles on an agency credit card, records show. He repaid the money and $1,136 in additional personal charges six months later, after auditors traced the charges to him, officials said."[31]

The report infuriated the public during a period of economic woes and private budget cutbacks. It also caught the attention of the federal government, just when local officials needed continued funding from Washington for the rail program. Following the *Times* articles and various reports he received from the local "Whistle Blowers," Representative Duncan successfully urged both the Federal Bureau of Investigation and the General Accounting Office to investigate the allegations.[32]

MEET THE NEW BOSS

Both of the city's transit agencies were now in the doghouse. The RTD already suffered politically from frequent bus driver strikes and construction problems plaguing the Red Line subway. Now the LACTC controversies created a critical mass to reform the agencies. Critics clamored to start the process by merging the two agencies into one, finally ending the bureaucratic duplication that had been in effect since Assemblyman Walter Ingalls helped create the LACTC in 1976.

Proposals for a RTD-LACTC merger had met without success in Los Angeles for over a decade. Supervisor Hahn had been exploring the possibility since at least 1983,[33] and two local state legislators, Assemblyman Richard Katz and Senator Alan Robbins from Van Nuys, almost succeeded in 1987.[34] But Governor Deukmejian vetoed their bill,[35] in part because of opposition from local officials like Hahn and Bradley, who were concerned that a merger would jeopardize federal funding and cause administrative confusion and delay.[36]

In the year following Deukmejian's veto, the two agencies became enmeshed in a bitter rivalry that only bolstered the case for a merger. LACTC leaders were convinced that the RTD's poor management of the first phase of subway construction would hurt the region's chances for federal funding for the second phase to Hollywood. LACTC officials tried to take over subway construction from the RTD for this next phase, led by Commissioner Jacki Bacharach. Bacharach and her cohorts felt that the RTD should stick to operating buses and that transit construction should be consolidated with the LACTC, which was already building two light rail lines that at the time lacked the controversy that dogged the RTD.[37] Predictably, RTD leadership refused to cede control of the subway and argued that such a change would not only jeopardize federal funding but also provide enemies with an excuse to kill it.[38] The LACTC, they argued, lacked the staff and expertise to build heavy rail.[39]

The conflict quickly escalated. The LACTC tried to force the RTD to surrender the subway by withholding Proposition A money, which the LACTC collected.[40] The feud became personal between members of the agencies.[41] "It was horrible," recalled Bacharach. "There was a meeting where we brought in seats to show everybody what the Blue Line seats were going to look like. We had put upholstery in our seats, and Nick Patsaouras [board member of the RTD] came to the meeting with a knife to slash the seats. He wanted to show everybody how foolish we were to put fabric on our seats."[42] But Patsaouras's knife did not stop LACTC leadership from continuing with plans to seize control of the subway.[43]

Local leaders attempted to negotiate a compromise. Mayor Bradley, Supervisor Dana, and RTD board member Jan Hall developed in 1988 what came to be known as the "Eight-Point Plan."[44] It allowed the LACTC to become the lead agency for Metro Rail, with the RTD continuing to construct and eventually operate the rail system. The agreement also introduced the concept of a unified rail system under the name "The Metro," with colors for each line.[45] With scant political support, RTD leaders had to accept the agreement. The LACTC emerged as the dominant transit agency in Los Angeles, with the RTD now reporting to it.[46]

But four years later, with accounting scandals and the Sumitomo blowback crippling the LACTC, Assemblyman Katz saw another opportunity to merge the agencies. He introduced AB 152, which he called the "Los Angeles County Metropolitan Transportation Reform Act," and it passed the legislature in Sacramento.[47] This time a new governor, Pete Wilson, signed the bill into law on May 19, 1992.[48] The LACTC and RTD were history.

Katz's legislation merged the RTD and LACTC into a new agency called the Los Angeles County Metropolitan Transportation Authority, referred to as the MTA or Metro, that would become operational on April 1, 1993.[49] It would have a thirteen-member governing board like the LACTC, including the five Los Angeles county supervisors. The mayor of Los Angeles controlled four votes: his own and those of three appointed members—two public members and one from the city council. The Los Angeles County City Selection Committee would choose four representatives from outlying cities. And finally, the governor would appoint one nonvoting member to the board. Significantly, while the RTD had required elected officials to appoint individuals to serve on its board, the MTA board had politicians represent themselves. Katz wanted them to be directly accountable for their decision-making and not hide behind appointees.

Local leaders needed to hire a chief executive officer for the new agency. Mayor Bradley became deeply involved in the selection process, pushing aggressively to have the board hire Franklin White, an attorney and head of New York's Transportation Commission who was close with the mayor.[50] Although White was not Bradley's first choice for the job (he had approached former city councilwoman Pat Russell, but she declined),[51] Bradley's enthusiastic support persuaded the new MTA board to hire him.

Bradley told the media, "Frank White is most impressive. It became clear to me that he had the kind of breadth and knowledge to lead us into a new era of transportation."[52] But questions lingered over how prepared White would be for the difficult job ahead. One transit staffer recalled a disconcerting moment in White's interview for the job: when asked if he was familiar "with the kind of politics out here, with Board members from vast districts with entirely different interests—different from East Coast governments," White responded with apparent dismissiveness, "We have politics in New York, too."[53]

The merger in many ways was cosmetic. Elected leaders and their appointees had not altered their ambitions to build more rail lines than the agency could afford, and many of the tensions between the RTD and the LACTC simply became housed under one roof.[54] "When the MTA was created, the whole creation carried the tension over," Bacharach said. "The first several years of the MTA were a disaster because it was never consolidated. It was political and horrible and done in a way that had nothing to do with best welfare of either agency."[55]

MTA's new leaders wasted no time planning an expansion of the rail system. Despite the budget woes and cost overruns, MTA's first chairman of the board, Los Angeles city councilman Richard Alatorre, pledged to "plan and build the most ambitious rail expansion program in the country."[56] The new MTA board decided to follow the LACTC's thirty-year plan for rail expansion from 1992. But with the northern Green Line extension, Exposition Boulevard route, and San Fernando Valley extension stalled by local opposition, the new board focused on two rail lines: the Pasadena light rail project and the third phase of the subway.

The third and final segment of the subway, called MOS-3 (minimum operable segment), would take the line in three different directions simultaneously: to the entry point of the San Fernando Valley at North Hollywood; to the west from Wilshire, with a jog to the south of Waxman's methane zone; and to the Eastside of Los Angeles. The Eastside extension in particular had powerful congressional supporters from the area. With their backing, President Bill Clinton's transportation secretary, Federico Peña, announced in May 1993 that the Federal Transit Administration (FTA) was awarding $1.23 billion in federal grant funds to cover roughly half of the $2.4 billion price tag of MOS-3. The MTA would begin construction of the North Hollywood extension first to secure the Valley's stake in the system. One month later,[57] the MTA Board selected an Eastside extension route, covering 6.8 miles below ground and serving Little Tokyo, Boyle Heights, and East Los Angeles.[58]

The MTA, however, was running out of money to fund both the subway extension and the Pasadena line. By mid-1993, overall funding for the MTA had dropped below the levels forecast in the thirty-year plan, which the LACTC had adopted just one year earlier. Compounding matters was the significant debt service the agency owed as a legacy of financial risks taken by the RTD and LACTC. To leverage state and federal resources, the RTD and LACTC had borrowed against future sales tax revenues through bond sales. Agency leaders thought it made sense to borrow when $1 million of annual debt service payments could result in a gain of $12 million in bond proceeds, which in turn could serve as a match for state and federal funds. However, the decrease in sales tax revenue meant that the MTA now had to dedicate all of the Proposition A revenue for rail to service the debt incurred to build the Blue Line and to provide the local match for MOS-1 and MOS-2 of the subway.[59] The overall budget for capital projects was now over a half-billion dollars in the red, leaving just $335 million in reserve to complete the Green Line and Pasadena line rail projects.[60]

Accordingly, Franklin White's first budget for fiscal year 1994–95 forecasted that the coming year "will be a difficult year for the MTA financially."[61] The MTA board approved White's budget on August 25, 1993,[62] but hired outside accountants to review the budget and recommend options to navigate out of the fiscal crisis. The ensuing analysis, called the "Solutions Report," recommended further belt-tightening, the transfer of funds for capital projects to cover operations, and continued drawing down of reserve funds. The report also called for an overhaul of the thirty-year plan to better reflect fiscal realities. But even with these measures, the report predicted continued financial gloom and debt for the agency.[63]

Tom Rubin, the MTA controller at the time and former chief financial officer of the RTD, objected to both the budget and the Solutions Report. He believed the true financial picture was far worse than anyone was willing to admit. Foreseeing far more dramatic cost increases and revenue reductions, Rubin called for an immediate disavowal of the thirty-year plan, a cessation of all studies of future rail projects, a delay of MOS-3, and an indefinite postponement of the Pasadena line.[64]

Rubin had stepped into a political beehive. His call to postpone the Pasadena line elicited a strong reaction from the project's powerful supporters, including Chairman Alatorre and backers like Republican congressman David Dreier. These supporters could also count on a strong new ally: Richard Riordan, Tom Bradley's successor as mayor of Los Angeles. Elected in 1993, Riordan was a business-friendly Republican moderate who focused mostly on economic issues, evincing none of the passion for rail transit shown by Bradley. Because Alatorre had provided a critical endorsement of Riordan during the mayoral campaign,[65] Riordan felt compelled to intervene to save the Pasadena line from delay.

The new mayor brokered a compromise. Riordan's plan involved proceeding with the project with some guaranteed funds and some funds contingent on finding cost savings elsewhere. The board approved the plan, and in its resolution adopting the new budget, the members asked MTA staff to spend no more than $97 million on final engineering and planning studies for the line.[66] The MTA would guarantee $40 million of that figure, with $57 million to come from later savings. A relieved Riordan told the *Los Angeles Times,* "Very clearly, Pasadena is something that is going to happen. This is a compromise."[67] Franklin White commented, "The Pasadena line was the single most difficult issue relating to adopting the budget."[68] Rather than placing new rail projects on hold, as Tom Rubin had recommended, the board doggedly committed itself to keeping the Pasadena line alive and on schedule.

To address the continuing budget shortfall, Franklin White developed a scaled-back transportation plan in 1995. Instead of the $183 billion called for in the 1992 LACTC thirty-year plan (which included $78.2 billion for rail),[69] White's plan would cost $72.4 billion.[70] The once ambitious rail system would correspondingly shrink from 296 miles to 95 miles and lose eight rail lines. White told the *Los Angeles Times* that the agency's original plan "incorporated some far-reaching ideas that just aren't attainable," and he blamed the recession and the "overly ambitious nature" of the plan.[71] The MTA board approved White's new plan, but the members voted to reaffirm the agency's long-standing commitment to completing the Pasadena line and to making the San Fernando Valley east-west rail line the next-highest rail priority.[72]

The deteriorating fiscal situation soon caught the attention of the agency's federal overlords. FTA leaders began to express concern over the MTA fiscal situation. Alarmed by reports showing low employee morale and huge budget deficits,[73] the FTA notified the MTA in October 1994 that it would temporarily withhold federal funds for the Red Line pending detailed written plans from the MTA with a revised construction schedule and oversight process.[74]

The combination of the cost overruns and subway construction mishaps led to a national media assault. In December 1995, six months after the subway's Hollywood sinkhole incident, the television news program *60 Minutes* broadcast a report highlighting the corruption, bureaucratic ineptitude, and mismanagement of the subway entitled "Riots, Earthquakes, and Now the Subway." The special highlighted setbacks such as the Hollywood sinkhole and problems with the subway tunnel walls. Subway critic and state senator Tom Hayden, gearing up to run for mayor in 1997, told reporter Leslie Stahl:

"My view is that they ought to stop it in its tracks and declare a victory. . . . They can't finish their fantasy. There are too many problems ahead." A less-than-reassuring Franklin White tried to deflect blame but appeared shifty and uncomfortable in his interview. The public responded with outrage, and local officials worried that the coverage would dampen congressional support for the subway.[75]

Within days of the broadcast, the MTA board fired Franklin White. At his final, acrimonious meeting with the board, White told them: "This is a money train, and if you get between the people who want the money and the people who spend the money, you've got problems." Supervisor Antonovich responded derisively, "For the past two and a half years, the MTA has been led by a General McClellan when what we needed was a General Grant." Riordan, who had tried to oust White for months, described him as "a poor leader."[76] Joseph Drew, the chief administrative officer from neighboring Kern County, would now run the MTA on an interim basis until the board could find a permanent replacement.

But a new calendar year and leader did not bring improvements. By the end of 1996, cost overruns had led Congress to cut the MTA's congressional appropriation of $158 million through the year 2000 in half, and Secretary Peña stated his intention to withhold an additional $31 million in FTA funds. At the same time, the General Accounting Office reported the obvious, that the MTA lacked the fiscal resources necessary to implement its rail plans.[77] In the midst of the crisis, Joseph Drew unexpectedly resigned,[78] his exit hastened by controversy over his decision to reverse a competitive bid analysis and award an Eastside rail contract to a construction team allied with MTA board member Alatorre.[79]

Meanwhile, the local media reported stories of undue special interest influence on MTA board members. "The MTA had an enormous ability to spend money and award contracts. Those contractors were campaign con-tributors to many of the supervisors and certainly to the mayor of Los Angeles, who controls four of thirteen votes," commented Jeff Rabin, who covered the MTA at the time for the *Los Angeles Times*. Noting that political races in Los Angeles require vast sums of money to run expensive television advertisements, Rabin argued that local elected officials felt pressure to raise money from businesses that had MTA contracts. "The stakes were so high for construction companies and engineering firms that they saw it as the cost of doing business to support these candidates," he said. "And the amount of money that flowed in was very large in the early days." Contractors even made unlimited contributions to the Los Angeles County district attorney, who was responsible for enforcing worker safety laws and investigating deaths by job accidents on rail construction sites. "One contractor, Tutor-Saliba Corp, received about $1 billion of the $4.7 billion spent on the subway project," Rabin noted, "and it was an absolute major player in the mayor's race and a significant player in supervisorial races."[80]

To avoid the appearance of impropriety, MTA board members would sometimes have their alternates attend board meetings to vote on whether to award money to their campaign contributors. *Los Angeles Times* reporter David Willman documented how Supervisor Dean Dana's alternate and eventual successor as county supervisor, Don Knabe, voted to award Dana's top campaign contributor, Tutor-Saliba, millions of dollars in change orders, in which the contractor claimed entitlement to additional payment due to unforeseen circumstances.[81]

Although subway critic and legislator Tom Hayden wrote a law in 1993 restricting the amount of campaign money that members of the MTA board could solicit from contractors doing business or seeking business from the MTA,[82] Rabin claimed that "the law's never been enforced and no one has ever been prosecuted." Because so many members of the board had conflicts of interest on specific votes, Rabin noted, the board often had difficulty achieving a quorum. "They have a provision to draw straws to see who of the conflicted must be brought back into the mix as a rule of necessity," he explained. "So even though they received money from the contractor, they will still be allowed to vote. It happens every month at the MTA, and their ethics department is primarily designed to protect the board rather than alert the public about potential campaign money involved."[83]

The agency that reformers had created to improve transit governance in the wake of the rivalry and mismanagement at the RTD and LACTC now seemed to embody the worst of both. Despite numerous attempts by agency staff, the media, and the federal government to control the board's spending, the members were determined to build their pet projects and reward their constituencies and campaign supporters.

REALITY AROUND THE CORNER

The MTA leaders could only persevere for so long before the reality of their fiscal situation and sunken public standing would correct their behavior. The board members' decision to fund the Pasadena line and subway expansion exemplified their ongoing denial about the poor budget situation, the cost overruns, and the negative image that rail was developing. In many ways, rail had become its own beast, fed by the various power centers within the county, and the beast could no longer be tamed. The economic downturn and corresponding revenue shortfalls served only to exacerbate the situation. The ambitious rail plans, however, would soon invite serious blowback from an unexpected source.

EIGHT

Of Race and Rail

AT 12:45 P.M. ON JULY 13, 1994, the Los Angeles County Metropolitan Transportation Authority (MTA) board of directors met for a contentious and politically charged vote that would ultimately haunt rail advocates. The issue involved whether or not to raise bus fares to cover the agency's debts. The down economy had reduced the bus budget, which had begun running an operating deficit of $126 million. MTA leaders hoped a fare increase would generate an additional $15 to $20 million to help stem the losses.

The threat of a fare increase immediately riled bus riders and their advocates. For many of these individuals, particularly low-income residents who could not afford an automobile and who represented the majority of all MTA customers, buses were the only means of transport. As a result, MTA buses were essentially a subsidized social service for the poor. The fare increase was also fraught with racial implications, given that the bus system served primarily minority riders, while new commuter rail lines in the county served a majority white ridership.

The vote that day was the culmination of a heated process overseen by a future mayor of Los Angeles. Antonio Villaraigosa was an upstart local labor leader who served as Los Angeles county supervisor Gloria Molina's alternate on the MTA. When the MTA board initially decided to explore a bus fare increase to cover some of the agency's operating debt, they chose Villaraigosa to chair the Ad Hoc Fare Restructuring Committee, in part because of his reputation as a bus advocate.[1] Villaraigosa had previously criticized the former Los Angeles County Transportation Commission's (LACTC) rail plans for ignoring the transit needs of inner-city residents.[2] His role on the new committee, however, required him to determine the best way to raise revenue from bus fares.

Villaraigosa's committee had held a number of public workshops to discuss the various options, which resulted in heavy turnout by low-income residents opposed to any fare increase.[3] At least one of the hearings was so tense that MTA leaders requested transit police in riot gear. Eventually, the committee proposed raising the base fare from $1.10 to $1.35 per ride. The proposal also included the elimination of the highly popular $42 monthly bus pass, except for students, the elderly, and the disabled.[4]

A hushed room listened as the MTA board voted on the committee's fare increase proposal. The final tally was nine to three in favor, with the proposal becoming effective on September 1.[5] Bus riders and their advocates erupted in anger, convinced that the fare increase was immoral, unnecessary, and done solely for the benefit of more affluent rail riders. As if to stoke their anger, Supervisor Michael Antonovich made a motion to set aside $123 million in construction funds for the Pasadena line light rail—almost exactly equal to the $126 million deficit that the fare increase was supposed to address—despite objections from MTA chief executive officer Franklin White that there were not enough funds available for rail.[6] Antonovich's action cemented the perception among bus advocates that rail expansion for the rich came at the expense of poor, often minority bus riders.[7]

These two modes of transit—bus and rail—were now on a political collision course. The objections of bus riders to the new rail program placed rail advocates on the defensive during a time when the first lines were opening and transit leaders needed federal support to cover local funding shortfalls. The result of the conflict would ultimately damage the political and financial fortunes for rail in Los Angeles and around the country.

RAISING BUS FARES, RAISING CAIN

Eric Mann was an unlikely figure in transit politics, yet he would ride the backlash to the bus fare increase to prominence. Recalling his days as a white, Jewish 1964 graduate of Cornell University, he credited the civil rights and black freedom movements "for saving my life, and giving me a purpose to my life."[8] He moved to Los Angeles committed to fighting for social justice and quickly became involved in a campaign to halt the proposed closure of a General Motors plant that employed many black and Latino workers. Eventually, along with other organizers from that effort, he launched an environmental justice advocacy group called the Labor/Community Strategy

Center (L/CSC). A self-described "anti-capitalist" organization,[9] the L/CSC began organizing low-income minority communities to fight the toxic air and water pollution from industrial plants typically located in or adjacent to these communities.

Mann soon discovered, however, that access to transit was a critical concern for these Los Angeles communities—as much as jobs and pollution. Manuel Criollo, an L/CSC employee who worked under Mann, had a similar revelation. "I got into the environmental justice movement to hold oil refineries, like Texaco in Wilmington [South Los Angeles], accountable," he explained. "Wilmington is primarily Latino and immigrant. One of the interesting things that happened in Wilmington was that, when you start organizing, you get to know a lot about their lives. So while we were primarily, like, 'Can't you see refineries are literally dumping toxics on you?' they would say, 'Look, obviously we're very concerned about that, our kids having asthma and other health problems. But you know, I live in Wilmington, and I work out in Los Angeles or the San Fernando Valley. Do you know my trip takes two to three hours to get there?' That was a very transformative moment for us."[10]

Based on this feedback from community members, Mann and his L/CSC staff became active in local transportation issues, starting in the early 1990s.[11] Mann came to believe that the MTA and its predecessor agencies systematically favored wealthier white riders by building expensive rail systems to serve them while neglecting to invest in the bus system for low-income minority commuters. He viewed the struggle for transit equity as part of a larger socialist revolution. To him, opposing rail in the 1990s was an outgrowth of the civil rights fight against racism.

Although bus advocates like Mann resented the Metro Rail system for its high cost and apparent harm it caused the bus system, they were particularly outraged by the Metrolink commuter rail system. Introduced in the early 1990s, Metrolink operated on the freight railroad rights-of-way purchased with Proposition C money. The system primarily served middle-class riders from outlying suburbs who commuted to Union Station in downtown Los Angeles. Criollo noted that the MTA had "gone into massive debt" to build Metrolink, while creating a "massive disparity" between the new, plush rail lines and the rundown bus system. "The buses would have forty people sitting and forty standing, no air conditioning, completely messed up," Criollo said. "And on Metrolink, people were riding like Disneyland."[12]

When the MTA approved the bus fare hike in 1994, it created a "tipping point" for Mann and the L/CSC. Of particular offense was the provision to eliminate the monthly bus pass for low-income riders. "Every time you get on a bus, given how massive Los Angeles is, you're not just taking one bus," Criollo said. "And the cost can be five, six, seven dollars daily" without the monthly pass. "Eight hundred people showed up begging the MTA not to do it. But they moved ahead."[13]

Mann decided to fight the fare increase any way he could. At the MTA board meeting approving the fare hikes, he and his fellow activists had to be physically removed.[14] Through the L/CSC, Mann had formed an offshoot project in 1992 called the Bus Riders Union (BRU). The BRU successfully attracted media attention, and the *Los Angeles Times* ran one of Mann's op-eds.[15] But whether because of their aggressive lobbying tactics or the indifference of the MTA board to a less powerful constituency, Mann's organization ultimately failed to convince the agency to change its policies.

MAKING THE CASE

With few other options remaining, Mann decided to fight the fare increase in court. In hopes of forming a broad coalition to legitimize their efforts, Mann brought the Korean Immigrant Workers Advocates and the Southern Christian Leadership Conference of Greater Los Angeles County together as co-plaintiffs. Given that members of the Korean and African American communities had fought against each other during the 1992 Rodney King riots, their partnership on the case was politically and symbolically significant.[16]

Mann needed to build a detailed and fact-based case against the MTA for a successful lawsuit, and he received invaluable help from sympathetic figures within the MTA. According to Criollo, Antonio Villaraigosa provided Mann with information.[17] Tom Rubin, the former chief financial officer of the RTD and briefly of the MTA, was now a disgruntled ex-employee who wanted to correct the agency's behavior. He possessed vast knowledge about the financial situation at the agency and wanted to air it. "The agency was totally out of control," Rubin said. "It had no idea what it was doing and was proving that every day. And the people who were trying to inject logic and common sense were not only *not* listened to, they were getting rid of them."[18]

Ironically, Rubin became involved with Mann and the BRU at the behest of MTA leadership after he left his position. "I didn't have a job, so they had this transition facility. So I was still there at the office and I was sending out my recruitment letters and that kind of stuff." When the L/CSC contacted

MTA CEO White for information about the bus fare increase, White referred them to Rubin. "So they called me and said 'Franklin White told us to call you,'" Rubin recalled. "Well, okay, I guess that means I'm supposed to answer your questions. So I started working with them."[19]

Perhaps the most surprising source of assistance was Richard Riordan, the mayor of Los Angeles. Riordan had made no secret of his hatred for the MTA and what he considered to be its free-spending, out-of-control habits. He approached the attorneys in the Los Angeles office of the New York–based National Association for the Advancement of Colored People (NAACP) Legal Defense Fund (LDF), urging them to sue the MTA over the fare increase. "Riordan understood that the MTA was mismanaged and that the transit system was grossly unfair," observed former LDF attorney Robert Garcia, who worked on the case. "He just couldn't do anything about it as the mayor of Los Angeles or chairman of the MTA because of the powers aligned against him."[20]

Riordan's entreaties made an impact on the LDF attorneys' willingness to investigate the case. "If you have a mayor of a major city telling you to look into it," Garcia said, "you tend to look into it."[21] By the time Eric Mann formally approached LDF attorneys Constance Rice and Bill Lann Lee for representation, the attorneys agreed to take the case.

By this time, Rice and Lee had only one week left to file a temporary restraining order (TRO) to prevent the fare increase from becoming effective. Poring over the documents supplied by Mann and Rubin, the attorneys worked day and night researching and drafting the legal brief supporting the TRO motion. "We were literally building the airplane as we flew it," said Garcia.[22]

But at the last minute, internal politics at the NAACP almost prevented the Los Angeles team from filing the case. The New York LDF office, which had final approval of the litigation, was reluctant to wade into such a high-profile matter, especially given the NAACP's ties to the MTA. As Criollo observed, Los Angeles county supervisor and MTA board member Yvonne Burke was on the board of directors of the NAACP. In addition, Supervisor Gloria Molina had won her supervisorial seat only after a lawsuit forced Los Angeles County to redraw the district maps to include more Latinos, with some settlement funds going to the NAACP.[23] "They took a big risk," Criollo observed of the NAACP.[24] As Garcia explained, "LDF in New York didn't know much about the case until we had a draft complaint ready, which was late in the process." The New York office pushed back on filing the complaint, and Garcia remembered "testy exchanges."[25] The New York leaders finally relented, and Rice and Lee went to court on August 31, 1994, to file the complaint, just one day before the fare increase was scheduled to go into effect and six weeks after the MTA approved the increase.

The attorneys filed the complaint as a civil rights class action lawsuit on behalf of all bus riders. They argued that the MTA had violated the 14th Amendment to the U.S. Constitution, as well as provisions of Title VI of the Civil Rights Act of 1964, by intentionally discriminating against racial and ethnic minority groups in the delivery of transportation services. They also charged the MTA with using federal funds to operate a discriminatory transit system in violation of U.S. Department of Transportation (DOT) regulations prohibiting racial discrimination.[26] They wanted the fare hike stopped immediately.

In support of their motion, the plaintiffs submitted the legal brief, thrown together in the mad one-week rush to absorb the facts and the law. The document detailed the funding disparities between bus and rail and generally cast wide-ranging aspersions on the Los Angeles rail program, from its safety record to its inability to serve key destinations. The brief also promoted the value of low bus fares to achieve increased ridership and equity.

The lawyers' primary argument was that the MTA disproportionately funded subway and light rail construction and commuter rail operating costs over inner city bus operations. As a result, rail expenditures had a "disparate impact" on inner city bus riders. MTA had essentially created separate and unequal transit systems in which minority bus riders were denied subsidies, service, and security equal to the services provided to rail riders.[27]

The lawyers cited MTA data showing that 80 percent of bus riders were people of color, whereas in the county as a whole fewer than 60 percent of the population were people of color.[28] By contrast, rail riders on the Metrolink system were 72 percent white in 1993.[29] Yet while MTA buses carried 94 percent of the agency's passengers, bus operations received less than a third of total MTA capital and operating funds. In 1992, for example, MTA leaders devoted only 29.1 percent of the agency's total budget to buses ($752 million out of $2.583 billion), while 70.9 percent of that year's budget went to rail programs that served only 6 percent of MTA ridership.[30]

Although these cost comparisons between transit modes presented stark disparities, they were not entirely fair due to the incomplete nature of the Metro Rail system. The MTA had only recently begun operating just a few lines of the network. With the introduction of new lines reaching additional communities, ridership on the entire system would increase and per passenger cost subsidies would decrease. The agency had also spent significant sums of money during that short time period to build rail lines that would be in operation for decades, so much of the rail expenditures cited in the brief represented an upfront capital investment that would be amortized over time (although rail projects require significant capital expenditures to maintain). Still, the brief accurately pointed out the indisputably higher expense for rail transit over buses, as well as the disparate populations generally served by each transit mode.

For example, the brief compared the capital costs of bus and rail, which the attorneys argued could "vary by orders of magnitude between rail and bus service."[31] Rail capital costs included the rails themselves, overhead catenary lines to power the trains, tunnels, train yards, and other expenses unique to rail. They tended to be significantly greater for trains that operated in partial or exclusive rights-of-way than for buses that shared the street with automobiles. The brief noted as an extreme example that Red Line subway construction costs to date had been in excess of $250 million per mile. In addition, new rail cars typically cost approximately one million dollars each, compared to $250,000 to $300,000 for each bus. Overall, rail lines received 71 percent of MTA's capital and operating resources.[32]

The subsidies for rail riders also appeared unequal. Metrolink riders received a per passenger subsidy of $21.02, Blue Line riders $11.34, and Red Line subway riders $2.92. Bus rider subsidies, however, averaged only $1.17. The subsidies were more equitable when calculated on a per passenger mile basis given the longer distance involved in rail trips, but the disparities still persisted: Blue Line riders received $1.25 per mile, Red Line subway passengers $0.83, and Metrolink riders $0.70. Bus riders netted a mere half of the smallest rail subsidy per mile at $0.31.[33]

The lawyers also cited the comfort of the ride for rail passengers versus bus riders. "MTA and Metrolink trains, and non-MTA municipal operator buses," the attorneys argued, "are uncrowded, comfortable, clean, and safe."[34] By contrast, MTA buses were "crowded," resulting in less expensive per mile service. The brief cited a high average passenger load (determined by dividing the annual passenger-miles by the annual vehicle miles carrying passengers) for MTA buses at 43 percent above the average of its peer transit agencies.[35]

To provide a contrast with the expense of rail, the brief described low bus fares as an effective policy to encourage public transit. When the Proposition A sales tax measure lowered bus fares to 50 cents over three years in the mid-1980s, bus ridership rose 40 percent, from 354 million to 497 million annual riders, while the number of buses in service increased only 1.5 percent.[36] However, systemwide patronage declined 8 percent from 1988 to 1993, "due largely to a fare increase implemented in [fiscal year] 1989 and accompanying service reductions."[37]

While the briefs presented powerful evidence and arguments in favor of bus service, missing from the overall analysis was an acknowledgment that much of the money for the rail system had come from two voter-approved sales tax measures that guaranteed some funding for rail as part of formulas enshrined on the ballot. While buses also benefited from these measures, the tax increases arguably would not have passed without an electoral coalition that included both rail and bus supporters, given their slim victory margins. In addition, money for rail had attracted significant state and federal matching funds that were restricted to rail, such as the federal government's 50 percent matching funds for the subway.

And as a final set of symbolic ironies, the subway that the bus advocates disparaged as racist had been the pet project of Tom Bradley, the city's first African American mayor, and had been almost singlehandedly saved from extinction at the hands of Henry Waxman by Representative Julian Dixon, an African American who represented a predominantly African American district in Crenshaw. Dixon believed that Metro Rail would bring together different neighborhoods and ethnic communities.[38] Meanwhile, the Blue Line light rail was created at the insistence of Supervisor Hahn, a tireless advocate for the African American community of South Los Angeles. Hahn insisted that the Blue Line be built first in order to serve South Los Angeles residents before wealthier communities to the north got access to rail. He justified the decision in part based on the recommendations of the commission that studied the root causes of the 1965 Watts riot in South Los Angeles. The McCone Commission determined that a lack of transit access "had a major influence in creating a sense of isolation" in the communities that rioted and recommended that city leaders improve transit in the area.[39]

MAD HATTER

Nonetheless, Rice and Lee and their LDF team had assembled a persuasive collection of facts to support their position. On the morning of August 31, 1994, just a day before the fare increase was to go into effect, the attorneys journeyed to the court with the brief and motion in hand. After filing the paperwork, the attorneys received some immediate good news from the random judge selection process. The court assigned the case to federal district court judge Terry J. Hatter Jr., a 1979 Carter appointee and the first African American to serve as chief justice of the Central District of California. In addition to having served as a special assistant to Mayor Bradley, Hatter had been the executive director of the Western Center on Law and Policy and a former Chicago public defender.[40] He made headlines in 1992 by ruling that the military's ban on gays and lesbians was unconstitutional, and he later received death threats in 1996 for issuing a temporary restraining order blocking Proposition 209, California's anti–affirmative action initiative.[41] In short, he was probably the perfect judge for a plaintiff filing a discrimination suit. "It was good news from our perspective," Garcia acknowledged.[42]

The hearing for the motion took place at noon that same day, given the urgent nature of the request and the looming fare increase. Rice argued the case. During the hearing, MTA attorneys informed the judge that all the bus tickets had already been printed and labeled to reflect the increase. Hatter turned to Rice. "Why is it you waited until the eve of the fare hike and the cessation of bus passes?" he demanded.[43] The judge wanted to know how the MTA could even comply with an injunction at this late date. The last thing Hatter wanted to see was a logistical nightmare that could undermine bus service the next day. "Fortunately for us," Garcia said, "Tom Rubin told us beforehand, and Connie Rice responded, 'Your Honor, MTA has a roomful of tickets with no pricing for exactly this situation when pricing is unclear and they need to get tickets out.'"[44]

Rice successfully addressed Hatter's concerns and made a strong showing on the merits. On September 1, 1994, the judge issued a temporary restraining order to stop the fare increase that same day.[45] The temporary order would last a few weeks until a more formal hearing could be held on whether or not to issue a preliminary injunction, which would prevent the fare increase from going into effect until the conclusion of litigation, possibly years in the future. Although temporary, Hatter's decision was a monumental setback for the MTA and a significant victory for the Bus Riders Union and their attorneys.

ON THE MAP

Hatter's decision sparked an outpouring of support and offers of assistance for the LDF. "The minute we filed the case and it hit the *L.A. Times* and all the papers," recalled Garcia, "we started getting phone calls from Marty Wachs, Brian Taylor, Jim Moore [transit experts at UCLA and USC who were generally critical of rail investments]. They all came the same day or shortly after. Essentially, the message was, 'We read about the case in the papers and would like to offer you our services on a pro bono basis. We write articles, we write books, we get tenure, and nothing happens. Here's an opportunity for us to get our ideas implemented by working on this case.'"[46] The case had also succeeded in uniting the far left and the far right, as prominent conservative scholars at the University of Southern California, including Peter Gordon (the longtime rail gadfly), Harry W. Richardson, and James Moore offered expertise and resources.[47] Despite the far left-wing nature of the plaintiffs, conservatives were drawn to their antirail stance. "We're odd bedfellows," Moore told the *L.A. Weekly*.[48]

The victory also brought criticism on Judge Hatter. Supervisor Antonovich called it a "reckless ruling" that illustrated Hatter's "unfitness to serve" as a jurist.[49] Garcia conceded that Hatter's background and experience as a civil rights advocate "were pluses" for the plaintiffs. "The fact of his professional and personal background may have contributed to his better understanding of what the issues were from a civil rights law perspective," Garcia observed, "and also from the human perspective of the people being asked to pay even more of their meager salaries to get on a bus. He also lived in Diamond Bar and used to take the train in and out of L.A., so he saw the differences between commuter rail and bus service in L.A."[50] But the LDF attorneys believed that no matter who the trial court judge was, the case was likely to be appealed to the Ninth Circuit and then to the U.S. Supreme Court.

Hatter appeared to find the plaintiffs more credible, despite, as Garcia described it, giving the MTA plenty of "daylight" to offer countering evidence. "Early on," Garcia related, "we submitted proposed findings of fact and conclusions of law as part of the papers. We knew we were looking good when the judge's law clerk called to ask when we would have the documents in an electronic file to make it easier for them so they wouldn't have to retype everything. That was a good sign. We got it over there, and sure enough, the findings of fact and conclusions of law that Judge Hatter issued were only five pages out of some twenty we submitted, but virtually all of it was in the language we proposed."[51]

Three weeks later, with the temporary order set to expire, Judge Hatter struck another blow against the MTA, issuing a preliminary injunction to stop the fare increase. In explaining his decision, Judge Hatter found that

MTA policies systematically disadvantaged lower-income bus riders and that the plaintiffs had met the burden of showing undue hardship if the fare increase were to go into effect before a full trial. Then in November, as part of a compromise with the MTA, Hatter partially lifted the injunction to allow the daily pass increase to go into effect. But he kept the monthly passes at the pre-increase level.[52]

The preliminary injunction hurt the MTA both financially and in terms of its public image. In the context of the agency's cost overruns and construction mishaps, the public could now stereotype the MTA not only as incompetent and insolvent but also as pushing a rail program that came at the expense of society's most vulnerable members.

THE LOAD FACTOR

Over one year later, as the BRU lawsuit progressed toward a full trial, MTA attorneys moved to have the case dismissed based on the evidence gathered to date. The MTA's summary judgment motion was its last-ditch effort to have the case thrown out before the cost and spectacle of a full-blown trial. Judge Hatter denied the motion on December 22, 1995.[53]

A trial would be bad for the MTA. It would force board members (including local elected officials) to testify publicly and face hostile cross-examination, result in negative publicity as MTA lawyers went up against advocates for the poor and discriminated, and possibly lead to an adverse judgment. If the MTA lost the case, the remedy ordered by the court could be a dismantling of the entire rail program.

Behind the scenes, the LDF attorneys lobbied their friends in high places to pressure the MTA to settle. "The NAACP legal defense and educational fund had very, very good connections with many members of Congress," observed Rubin, by now an expert witness in the case. "MTA needed money to complete the Red Line, and a couple of key Congress people told them, 'What you need to do is settle this lawsuit, and then we'll be happy to talk to you about getting your funding for the Red Line.' And that's never been widely acknowledged, but frankly, that was the key factor in getting the settlement agreed to by MTA."[54]

Perhaps buckling under this congressional pressure, MTA leaders entered into settlement negotiations. The court appointed Richard Bliss, a local attorney who had served in the U.S. Department of Transportation under

William Coleman during the Ford administration, as the special master to mediate. Negotiations carried on throughout 1996 until finally in September the two sides appeared close to an agreement.

MTA staff had drafted a proposed agreement that both sides appeared willing to sign and that appeared to contain reasonable concessions. The proposal included an agreement on the fare structure and increases, as well as provisions to expand the bus fleet, reduce crowding, and improve security. The agreement required the MTA to adopt, "as its highest priority, improvement of the quality of bus service in Los Angeles."[55] The MTA could keep the daily fare at the increased amount of $1.35, but the agency would have to introduce discounted weekly and semimonthly passes and abandon plans to raise the monthly pass rate.[56] Most significantly for rail, the MTA would have to give priority to bus service for transit dependents when allocating bus-eligible revenue. In other words, if the MTA had discretion to use open funds for either rail or buses, the agency had to spend the money on buses as its first priority.[57]

But the agreement contained an inadvertent poison pill for rail. The MTA negotiators agreed to decrease the ridership threshold at which the agency would have to add new bus lines to a given route. The "load factor," which represented the total number of passengers divided by the total number of seats on a bus, would decrease from 1.45 to 1.2.[58] If too many standees on a bus pushed the load factor ratio above 1.2, the MTA would have to add more buses to the line.[59]

At the time, MTA negotiators did not believe that the agency would have difficulty complying with the load factor requirement. As a 2001 internal memo from MTA staff revealed, "The internal debate among MTA management and staff was focused on not committing to specific bus purchases or increased bus service demanded by plaintiffs." In their haste to avoid committing to specific numbers, the negotiators had agreed to a formula of "performance-based measures that linked bus investments to overcrowding." The staff assumed that new rail lines would reduce heavily used bus lines. Therefore, the agency would not have to purchase new buses because it would actually have fewer bus riders. "If MTA buses were not overcrowded," the staff concluded, "then no new buses would have to be bought or added into service."[60]

MTA negotiators took their conclusions on the load factor provision to the agency's board, which had ultimate responsibility for signing the settlement. "During a closed session briefing," the 2001 memo continued, "MTA staff claimed that the MTA could comply with new overcrowding standards *without* diverting *any* additional funds away from rail or other projects" (emphasis in the original).[61]

When Rubin first heard about the MTA's willingness to reduce the load factor, he was ecstatic. The LDF attorneys had checked with him after the MTA negotiators offered the provision, he recalled. "So I started running the numbers on the load factor, started running and running. I finally went back and said [to the LDF attorneys], 'Take the deal. I mean, bitch and moan and yell and scream like crazy, but they're idiots. This is the best.' I could not begin to tell you how good a deal this was." The MTA appeared to have badly miscalculated. "They thought that they would be adding a hundred buses, and it wound up adding hundreds of buses," Rubin said. "We knew it was going to happen. We were going to lower the fares and we were going to relieve overcrowding, which was going to serve as a magnet to bring in more people, which would increase load factors, so they'd have to add more buses. And so the service frequency goes up, and we had that multiplier effect."[62]

But when the LDF attorneys brought the agreement to Eric Mann, he rejected the deal. As Garcia recounted, "Eric Mann and the L/CSC wanted to go to trial and convict the MTA of racist civil rights crime. Eric's concerns were to have a public trial to air all the evidence." LDF attorneys, though, were convinced that the settlement was better than anything the plaintiffs could get at trial, even with a victory there. Garcia described one such benefit of the settlement: "The consent decree kept the monthly pass available not only for low-income bus riders but for the elderly and students, something a judge could not have ordered as part of a judgment because the elderly and students were not protected under civil rights law."[63] Coupled with the prospect of a lengthy and expensive trial and, even with victory, an appeals process that could take years and possibly end up going to the Supreme Court, the LDF attorneys felt bound to accept the proposal in the best interests of the plaintiff class.

Unwilling to back down, Mann and the BRU, along with all the plaintiffs except the Southern Christian Leadership Conference, fired the LDF attorneys. They hired a new attorney who was willing to reject the settlement and proceed to trial. Now representing just one of the original plaintiffs on behalf of all MTA bus riders, the LDF attorneys went to court to ask the judge to accept the proposed settlement. The BRU's new attorney argued against them, but Judge Hatter agreed with the LDF that the settlement was in the best interests of the class of plaintiffs.

On Monday, October 28, 1996, more than two years after the LDF attorneys filed the original complaint, Judge Hatter formally approved the agreement and retained jurisdiction over it for a length of time agreed to by the parties. The settlement now became known as a judicially enforceable consent decree.[64] Eric Mann and the rest of the plaintiffs promptly rehired the LDF attorneys to oversee the implementation of the consent decree. "It was kind of like a married couple decides to get a divorce and the husband moves out," Garcia said, "and then they decide to get back together again for the sake of the children."[65]

"IT WAS NOW RACIST TO BUILD SUBWAYS"

The MTA experienced significant fallout from the signing of the consent decree. Its leaders appeared to concede that rail disadvantaged low-income riders of color, which dampened enthusiasm for rail among its liberal supporters in Los Angeles. "It became accepted wisdom that rail was being built on the backs of people of color whose civil rights were being abused so white people could ride the train," commented Roger Christensen, vice chairman of the MTA Citizens Advisory Council at the time. "Rail lost a major liberal base because it was now racist to build subways."[66]

The consent decree also forced the agency to spend money on buses that did not substantially increase ridership. As Tom Rubin predicted, the load factor reduction ultimately required the MTA to purchase a lot of new buses, but the better service did not attract the riders that Rubin envisioned. By the time of the MTA memo in 2001, it was clear that the negotiators' predictions about the load factor reduction were wildly inaccurate. "The end result," wrote the memo's MTA author, "was that bus ridership has *not* increased due to the addition of new buses. Instead, the same riders now have less crowded riding conditions" (emphasis in the original).[67] By 2005, the special master had ordered a one-third increase in the size of the bus fleet, though bus ridership remained largely flat.[68] MTA officials later blamed Special Master Bliss for enforcing the decree in ways they did not anticipate. But as Rubin concluded, "The person they had who was the main expert support for the negotiation process was an idiot. He literally didn't know what he was doing."[69]

Mayor Riordan had ultimate responsibility for approving the agreement with the load factor provision, and he bore most of the blame. The mayor felt pressured to sign the consent decree owing to the agency's poor public image, as well as political considerations: as MTA staff later noted, the MTA board approved the consent decree "just months before Mayor Richard Riordan's re-election bid."[70] Riordan also detested the agency and its spending habits and was not likely to vigorously defend its interests in settlement negotiations, particularly on a case that he helped encourage in the first place.

The MTA's poor public image contributed to the decision to approve the agreement. As Christensen observed, "The mayor and the MTA were so freaked out about the subway scandals. They wanted to change their image." Riordan and the MTA leadership also feared the moral authority of a plaintiff class that included poor and minority residents. Christensen recalled the consent decree's signing ceremony: "There was this scene with all these BRU people wearing yellow shirts with messages about fighting transit racism. Riordan hugged them all and said this was the beginning of a new day and we're going to make buses a priority."[71]

Almost a decade later, Riordan acknowledged the mistake. In interviews with the *Los Angeles Weekly* and other local media, Riordan expressed regret but refused to accept complete responsibility. "Quite honestly, I was misled by the [MTA] staff. I should have known better because I didn't think they were very bright," he told the *Weekly*. "I kick myself, but I'll take some of the blame. I thought the load-factor requirements could be met by the ongoing MTA budget." MTA board member Nick Patsaouras summed up his view of Riordan's record more succinctly: "Riordan is an ignoramus. Riordan fucked it up with the consent decree."[72]

The signing of the consent decree, however, was not the end of the war, as both parties soon learned. Instead, they became locked in a ten-year fight over the terms of its implementation. Disagreements arose over the load factor requirements, as MTA leaders began to realize the magnitude of their miscalculation. The agency fought implementation of the load factor provision at every turn, recognizing the dramatic cost of compliance.[73] After repeated complaints and public campaigns by the BRU against the MTA's intransigence, the matter went to Special Master Bliss. Bliss sided with the plaintiffs and in March 1999 ordered the MTA to purchase 532 new buses.[74]

The MTA board contested Bliss's ruling, which had the force of a federal court order. They appealed first to Judge Hatter, who quickly ruled against them and affirmed Bliss's authority. Subsequent appeals to the Ninth Circuit and the U.S. Supreme Court similarly failed. The agency had no choice but to comply with a decision that it estimated would cost $463 million to implement.[75] The agency experienced further judicial setbacks over the years as it fought implementation, such as in April 2005 when Bliss ordered the MTA to expand its rapid bus fleet to 134 buses.[76] By September 2005, the MTA had approved the purchase of 200 buses at a cost of $100 million, still short of the BRU's original demand for 450 new buses.[77]

The consent decree forced the MTA to enter a new era where the focus of transit planning would be on buses and not on rail. Implementation took a financial toll on the agency's rail plans, as the BRU had hoped. For their part, agency leaders took a dim view of the impact of the consent decree on Los Angeles transit riders. Roger Snoble, MTA's CEO in 2005, blamed the consent decree for actually making traffic worse. After nine years under the agreement, he noted, "the actual number of people we carry on the bus has remained flat. . . . We're not taking cars off the street. In fact, we're adding buses to the streets, which is causing more traffic jams."[78]

By contrast, bus rider advocates celebrated the positive impact that the consent decree had on bus service in the county, noting the increased service, which meant less crowded buses and more seats for riders, and steady fare values. However, the advocates were unable to demonstrate that the consent decree had resulted in a significant increase in bus ridership. For example, James Moore of USC and Tom Rubin could only conclude in a *Los Angeles Times* op-ed piece that, as a result of the consent decree, "users of public transit gradually started to increase again."[79] The BRU cited just a 1 percent increase per year in bus ridership.[80] "It's not bad in contrast to other MTA projects being built," argued Criollo. "But it's also the comfortability of the ride. Buses can't be seen as a burden on the agency. [The bus] has to be central."[81] Ultimately, this improved service and recognition for bus riders cost the MTA over $1 billion in consent decree compliance.[82]

THE END OF AN ERROR

The original consent decree gave the federal court jurisdiction over the parties for ten years. The court would allow the agreement to expire if the MTA could show "to the Court's satisfaction that it has substantially complied with the Consent Decree and that it has in place a service plan that will enable continued adherence to the principles and objectives of the Consent Decree during the five years subsequent to the termination of this Consent Decree."[83] Desperate to escape the self-inflicted burdens, the MTA petitioned the court in 2006 not to extend the decree.

On October 25, 2006, almost ten years to the day after he approved the settlement, Judge Hatter ruled that the consent decree could expire. In his order, he wrote that it had "served its purpose and will not be extended." He credited it with improving the quality of life for "Los Angeles' public transit–dependent poor population." But even Judge Hatter recognized that the load factor requirements constituted a severe burden for the agency. Noting that the agreement was a "less than perfect document," the judge wrote that "it is impossible [for the MTA] to achieve absolute compliance" with its terms.[84]

The BRU vowed to keep fighting. "I've been here ten years," Criollo said a few years later, "and with each new rail project that opens, it has an impact on our people. The Green Line opens, and fares go up 25 percent. The MTA has to take those impacts into account. An operational deficit comes from building things you don't have money to run." Believing that rail supporters lack awareness of rail's impact on low-income bus riders, Criollo added: "The answer to rail enthusiasts from our perspective is, look at the choices being made and the costs associated with them."[85]

Seven months after the consent decree expired, the MTA board voted to raise bus fares.[86] Arguing that the consent decree terms had created huge and lasting operating deficits to cover the costs of the increase in bus service, the agency believed that it had no alternative. MTA CEO Roger Snoble noted that the current fares for buses in Los Angeles were among the lowest in the nation.[87]

The BRU immediately sued.[88] But in the years since the first lawsuit, the Supreme Court had deprived advocates like the BRU of a critical legal weapon that had afforded them victory in 1996. As noted, the plaintiffs in the original lawsuit based their legal claim on Title VI of the Civil Rights Act of 1964. Under this law, the plaintiffs alleged that MTA decisions to fund rail over bus had created a "disparate impact" on poor bus riders of color versus wealthier, whiter rail riders. But in 2001, the Supreme Court, in a decision written by Justice Antonin Scalia, ruled that private individuals, as represented by the BRU and NAACP, could not sue under Title VI anymore for disparate impact claims. Under the ruling, *Alexander v. Sandoval,* these plaintiffs now had to show that a government agency had an actual intention to discriminate. Showing disparate impacts as evidence of discriminatory intent was no longer sufficient. As a result, plaintiffs had to produce evidence of a discriminatory mindset among decision-makers, an attitude that was challenging to document in written agency documents or public comments.[89]

As a result of the *Sandoval* decision, bus advocates had to base their case on a less helpful California law requiring environmental review for certain government actions. The BRU argued that the bus fare increase would harm the environment by causing more driving, and as a result, the agency was required to engage in a potentially lengthy and costly process of analysis and justification. The BRU hired the Natural Resources Defense Council (NRDC), an environmental organization well versed in the law, instead of the NAACP. The initial rounds in California Superior Court were unsuccessful, and the BRU lost an attempt to get a temporary restraining order to prevent the fare increase.[90] NRDC and the BRU then lost the case entirely in California Superior Court in August 2008.[91]

THE CASE HEARD 'ROUND THE WORLD

Although the litigation efforts had come to an end for the foreseeable future, the Bus Riders Union and their allies had secured significant and long-term victories. They forced the MTA to make tangible improvements to the bus system, including more frequent service, newer and more comfortable buses, and innovative lines like "Rapid Buses" that skipped less-frequented stops to shorten end-to-end travel times.

The plaintiffs also brought the plight of low-income, minority bus riders to the consciousness of rail advocates. To be sure, many rail advocates continued to dismiss the Bus Riders Union's arguments and their tactics, and the organization developed a reputation as being strident and unwilling to compromise. BRU activists also made enemies by being quick to label rail plans and rail advocates as racist. But following the lawsuit, rail supporters were more likely to acknowledge and consider bus riders and the impacts that transit decisions had on them. In many ways, the BRU's greatest success was forcing policy makers to be more conscious of how their decisions affected bus riders.

The BRU litigation also inspired similar suits around the country by environmental justice activists, becoming a model for a successful challenge of the status quo when it comes to transit and the urban poor. But nowhere else did bus advocates manage to change the debate about rail and halt the progress of an existing system like they did in Los Angeles.

NINE

Switching Tracks

LOS ANGELES COUNTY SUPERVISOR ZEV YAROSLAVSKY wanted to stop spending money on the subway. He believed, with reason, that the subway would drain funds for cheaper, aboveground transit lines, such as a potential light rail route in his San Fernando Valley district.

Despite the Bus Riders Union (BRU) lawsuit and settlement and the dire fiscal conditions plaguing the Los Angeles County Metropolitan Transportation Authority (MTA), however, powerful leaders both on the MTA board and in Congress were loath to give up the opportunity to bring subway and light rail service to their communities. By 1998, subway expansion plans included an extension to the Eastside of Los Angeles, North Hollywood in the San Fernando Valley, and the Mid-City area, still dodging Waxman's methane zone. Agency leaders were also committed to building the Pasadena light rail line.

But if Yaroslavsky could halt the subway, the MTA would have funds to build a number of light rail lines to serve more parts of the county, all for potentially the same price as one subway line. These light rail lines included the Pasadena line, one along Exposition Boulevard to Culver City, and another to the Eastside in place of the subway. It would also free the agency to experiment with innovative rapid bus service.

Yaroslavsky's machinations would ultimately divide rail transit supporters and place the region on a new, more modest trajectory for bringing rapid transit to the people.

By the late 1990s, annual payments on the MTA's debts were crippling the nation's second-largest transit agency. The MTA and its predecessor agency, the Los Angeles County Transportation Commission (LACTC), had never funded its rail construction on a pay-as-you-go basis. Instead, the LACTC, and then the MTA, tried to leverage more dollars each year by going into debt. As a result, debt service alone devoured more than 30 percent of the MTA's nearly $1.2 billion operating budget, with the annual payments on the outstanding debt amounting to almost $360 million a year. These payments represented the agency's single largest operating expense, more than the salaries of all employees.[1] Worse, according to former *Los Angeles Times* reporter Jeff Rabin, the MTA board members were receiving campaign contributions from Wall Street financiers and investment bankers who were advising them to issue bonds backed by sales tax receipts thirty years into the future. "They told the board members, 'You can spend money now,'" Rabin recalled. "And they did."[2]

The dire budget situation did not seem to dampen enthusiasm for specific rail lines, notably the Eastside subway extension and the Pasadena light rail line. But leaders at the Federal Transit Administration (FTA), a significant funding partner for the local rail program, believed that the agency needed to scale back these rail plans in light of fiscal realities and the agency's mismanagement problems. FTA leaders demanded in 1997 that the MTA develop a "recovery plan" to restore confidence in the management of the subway project.[3] They also asked Congress for less money for the subway, essentially delaying the Eastside subway extension for at least two years and the Mid-City subway extension for seven. FTA Administrator Gordon Linton even had to warn MTA Board Members to behave with more professionalism. "If the board slides back into some of the lack of decisions and bickering that have occurred in the past," he admonished, "then our efforts to receive the support of Congress will diminish."[4]

But the MTA Board kept fighting, particularly over the next subway extension. Powerful congressional representatives from the Eastside, including Lucille Roybal-Allard, Xavier Becerra, and Esteban Torres, threatened to withhold federal funds for future Metro Rail funding requests if their demands to extend the Eastside subway route were not met. Tempers flared as the board debated a motion in February 1997 to seek $44 million from the federal government to fund part of the Eastside line. Representing the San

Fernando Valley, Supervisor Yaroslavsky fumed, "I know exactly how this game is played: that money will put the Eastside ahead of the Valley, and we will watch them leapfrog right over us." City councilman Alatorre responded, "The reason that the east-west line in the Valley isn't further along is because they couldn't get their act together."[5] MTA board member and city councilman Hal Bernson told the board, "I see it as an attempt to screw the Valley." On a regional vote, the board approved the motion seven to three.[6]

In response, the FTA took a hard line, rejecting multiple recovery plans submitted by the MTA.[7] In July 1997, the FTA separated the financing of "MOS-3" (the third phase of the subway construction) into three separate segments: the North Hollywood, Eastside, and Westside/Mid-City extensions. The agency also executed a revised funding agreement that covered just the North Hollywood extension. This action placed the Eastside and Mid-City extensions on hold indefinitely, but allowed subway construction to continue to the Valley.[8]

Undaunted, the MTA's third long-range plan for the federal government in 1997 retained plans to finish the Eastside and Mid-City segments, as well as the Pasadena light rail line. Although the FTA found the new budget to be more in line with reality, FTA leaders complained about MTA's underestimation of the cost of future rail service expansion and faulted the agency for its poor decision-making processes. The FTA refused to release funds to the agency until it addressed these problems.[9]

Los Angeles mayor Richard Riordan had seen enough of the MTA infighting and the continued effort to build rail lines despite the lack of funds. Riordan pushed through the hiring of Julian Burke, a corporate reorganization specialist, to run the MTA. Burke went to work like the Harvey Keitel character in the movie *Pulp Fiction,* who performs a disciplined and rapid cleanup of a messy situation. Burke's review of the agency's budget splashed cold water on the rail plans, finding it impossible to build the two subway extensions to the Eastside and Mid-City and the Pasadena light rail. He informed the board that it should cancel these projects.[10]

Burke's sober review and credibility with the board finally seemed to make an impact. The MTA board followed his recommendations and suspended all new rail projects in January 1998, pledging to complete only the already-funded subway extensions to Hollywood and North Hollywood. However, Councilman Richard Alatorre and Supervisor Gloria Molina introduced a successful motion to reaffirm the board's commitment to an Eastside subway extension, upon completion of further studies and efforts to secure funding.[11]

The board also approved a new restructuring plan that projected deficits through 2004.[12]

The suspension satisfied FTA leaders, and they approved the MTA recovery plan.[13] Congress eventually released approximately $62 million in rail transit funds to the MTA (along with $31 million for bus purchases),[14] but only after a political arrangement brokered by Representatives Julian Dixon and Esteban Torres. The two politicians represented areas that would receive the Eastside and Mid-City extensions of the Red Line (Dixon's district having benefited from the Waxman ban and the subsequent Waxman-Dixon compromise). They agreed that Congress could resume funding the Red Line subway, provided that the MTA consider alternatives to the Eastside and Mid-City extensions. In other words, the two congressmen received assurances that if a subway extension was unlikely, the MTA would still address the transit needs of their constituents.[15]

A STAKE THROUGH THE SUBWAY

Supervisor Yaroslavsky knew that the suspension would only temporarily halt his fellow board members' desire to expand the subway. Fearing that his San Fernando Valley constituents would lose transit funds if all the remaining money went to the Eastside subway, he decided to starve the subway beast. In 1998, he introduced a ballot measure to restrict future spending of county sales tax revenues on the subway, while leaving funding for surface rail (like light rail) and buses intact.[16] Dubbed the "MTA Reform and Accountability Act," Yaroslavsky described the measure as a "two by four that will finally knock some sense into this out-of-control agency and take it back from the special interests."[17] His plan prohibited the use of any local tax revenues for further subway construction beyond completion of the Red Line to North Hollywood. Ironically, the measure appeared as Proposition A on the ballot—the same designation as Supervisor Kenneth Hahn's successful 1980 ballot initiative that provided the local sales tax funds to begin the subway.

"The reason I proposed it," Yaroslavsky later explained, "is because everybody wanted a subway. The Eastside wanted a subway, the Valley wanted a subway, Pasadena Gold Line wanted a subway under Pasadena. Because if you build one subway in the Eastside, or one subway in Pasadena, or one subway across the San Fernando Valley, you've basically for a generation shot your wad. And at the time this was going on, the MTA board of directors was getting ready to fund multiple subway projects."[18]

Yaroslavsky was effectively declaring war on the subway and the elected officials of the MTA who wanted an extension in their districts. "There was not a lot of support among the elected officials" for his ballot measure, the supervisor noted.[19] Jeff Rabin described Proposition A as an "ugly clash between Democratic politicians in Los Angeles" because it pitted Eastside Latinos like Supervisor Molina and Councilman Alatorre against the Westside, as represented by Yaroslavsky, over future subway funding. "It was hardball politics between those sides of the city," he observed.[20]

The supervisor's decision to introduce the measure was made easier by his longtime antipathy toward the MTA and its poor track record at the time. "The MTA was under perpetual investigation by the FBI and other investigative bodies because of contract fraud," he recalled. "We were watching the construction of the subway with big sinkholes and buildings sinking and buildings cracking. It was becoming nothing but a pain in the behind of the communities in which it was going. And we could not get the attention of the MTA to try to reform the contracting process and hold the contractors accountable."[21]

Yaroslavsky's opponents questioned his motives. They noted that he had helped stall the Exposition line to Santa Monica by championing homeowner groups' objections. Indeed, Yaroslavsky had never been shy about channeling homeowner opposition to rail in Los Angeles. Many political observers also expected him to make a run for mayor, and a victory at the ballot box would raise his standing in the city. As one exasperated transit official and subway supporter commented, "The initiative against the subway funding gets his name out there. But if you're against the subway, just vote against it. Why go to all the trouble of funding an initiative?"[22]

But even critics could not deny that the supervisor's initiative tapped into a deep well of public frustration with the MTA. A *Los Angeles Times* poll from February 1997 had shown declining public support for the subway, with a narrow majority opposed to the project altogether. Latinos supported the subway the most of any group, while African Americans and whites were mostly opposed. Westside residents were narrowly split, and respondents in the San Fernando Valley were generally opposed to the subway.[23]

Eastside Latino politicians and transit advocates joined together to oppose the measure. Local Eastside activist groups and environmentalists argued it was unfair to punish the Eastside for past subway mismanagement. They also argued that it was unfair to deprive one of the most densely populated and transit-dependent parts of the region from getting a subway.[24]

Despite these objections, in November 1998 Yaroslavsky's ballot initiative passed overwhelmingly with 68.1 percent support. Even in the Eastside, residents voted decisively in favor of the measure (although some observers argued that the heavily transit-dependent residents there opposed the subway out of fear that rail investments would lead to bus service cutbacks).[25] The measure ultimately meant that the Eastside would not receive its promised subway extension. "The initiative drove a stake through the Eastside subway," Rabin said, "and Zev won. The Westside stopped the Eastside from getting it."[26]

Many observers considered the measure to be a referendum on the MTA. The MTA, for its part, declined to mount an opposition. Officials knew that their agency and the subway project were deeply unpopular. They privately expressed hope that they could overturn the measure after a few years, when the negative news stories about mismanagement and construction accidents faded from people's memories and as the convenience of the subway became apparent to more voters.[27]

Thanks in part to Yaroslavsky's measure, the MTA's era of funding subway expansion was now ended, and the tab for years of fiscal mismanagement was finally coming due. Yaroslavsky believed Proposition A saved the MTA. Given the MTA's crippling debt service payments, Yaroslavsky argued that Proposition A averted fiscal ruin at the agency and allowed it to build more light rail lines and bus rapid transit projects than it otherwise could have afforded.

"One subway would have stopped everything else," he said.[28]

A HOLLYWOOD ENTRANCE AND EXIT

With no further funds for new lines, the existing subway construction reached its end. The Red Line subway extension to Wilshire Boulevard and Western Avenue had already opened in July 1996. The 2.1-mile extension was just a spur line, stopped in its tracks by indecision and lack of funds in the face of Waxman's ban on federal funding.[29] Next, the Hollywood extension opened on June 12, 1999, closing the books on "MOS-2" (the second phase of subway construction) and giving the subway a more visible and important connection to an urban center. The $1.75 billion project came in $288 million over budget and about six months behind schedule. But subway advocates were pleased when the Red Line experienced 110,000 boardings during the daylong festivities. Mayor Riordan, along with local officials and Administrator Gordon Linton of the FTA, rode the line with characters from the Wizard of Oz, in true Hollywood style.[30] "Clearly there have been some bumps and hurdles along the way," Linton commented. "But . . . without pressure there are no diamonds. We today have a diamond." It was now possible to travel 11.1 miles by subway from Union Station to the intersection of Hollywood Boulevard and Vine Street.[31]

Then, in June 2000, after over a decade of work, subway construction ceased with the opening of the final remnant of MOS-3 at North Hollywood in the San Fernando Valley. At the opening ceremony, reporters asked Mayor Riordan if the $4.7 billion for the 18.6-mile subway was worth it. He responded, "No, no it's not worth it. We could have spent the money more efficiently."[32]

Mayor Riordan was now in his final days as chair of the MTA. Media summaries of Riordan's accomplishments with the MTA pointed primarily to his hiring of Julian Burke to stabilize the agency and stop the bleeding. "If I did nothing else for the MTA," Riordan told the *Los Angeles Times,* "I should be deified for bringing Julian Burke." The mayor had never been a believer in the value of rail for Los Angeles. "I wish we had never started the whole thing," he commented. "Fixed rail is not the answer to the transportation needs of our city." He was now happy to leave the chairmanship: "A day away from the MTA is like a month in the country."[33]

Riordan's negative feelings about the subway stood in stark contrast to those of his predecessor, Tom Bradley. But Bradley was not in attendance. Just nine months earlier, he had passed away at the age of eighty-one following a debilitating stroke.[34] The man who had done more than anyone to bring a subway to Los Angeles would not live to see its inglorious, though temporary, conclusion.

SAVING PASADENA

With the subway completed for the foreseeable future, the action shifted to light rail lines. Chief among them was the Pasadena light rail line, with its powerful backers in Congress, the state legislature, and among local government officials. The MTA had postponed the line, as declining funds meant that the agency would no longer be able to authorize new transit lines. In response, the Pasadena line's backers attempted an end-run around the MTA. State senator Adam Schiff, who represented the Pasadena area in the state legislature and later in the U.S. House of Representatives, authored legislation in 1998 to create the Pasadena Metro Blue Line Construction Authority (with the clunky acronym PMBLCA), a separate agency that would replace the MTA in overseeing construction of the line. (The new agency had "Blue Line" in its title because planners at the time considered the line to be an extension of the Blue Line, once the MTA completed a downtown light rail connector.)

Schiff's goal was to remove the MTA from responsibility for constructing the line because the agency lacked the financial resources to complete the job. In addition, the agency's burden of compliance with the terms of the settlement with the Bus Riders Union meant even less likelihood that the Pasadena line would pass muster. The Bus Riders Union reacted with outrage to the plan, describing it as a backhanded way to avoid MTA compliance with the settlement consent decree. They staged protests and disrupted meetings of the PMBLCA. Although the PMBLCA would construct the line, the plan was to transfer it to the MTA to operate it.[35]

With a strong coalition to support the effort, including state senator Richard Polanco of the Latino Legislative Caucus and Assembly speaker Antonio Villaraigosa, Schiff's bill became law in September 1998. The PMBLCA had a five-person governing board, but the MTA had only one voting member on it. The legislation transferred funds programmed for the Pasadena line in the MTA's restructuring plan to the PMBLCA. Schiff's plan set a new precedent for what essentially amounted to a state circumvention of a local transit agency.

The PMBLCA eventually completed the Gold Line, as it became known, in 2003, finishing a route from Union Station to Pasadena (Supervisor Mike Antonovich wanted the color to be rose for the Rose Bowl, but leaders in other parts of the city did not want the train to become so closely identified with Pasadena). The light rail line cost $900 million to build, surprisingly close to the 1993 estimate of $841 million, and it featured thirteen stations. Neighbors along the route objected to the noise from the trains, which due to the curving right-of-way required sharp turns that made the wheels squeal. The curving right-of-way also meant that the line was generally slower than automobile traffic, which contributed to poor ridership. By April 2009, ridership on the Gold Line had topped out at approximately 24,000 weekday boardings, the weakest of all rail lines.[36] A few high-profile, multistory real

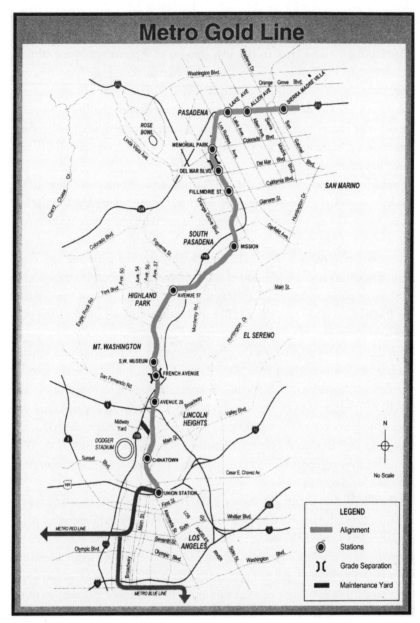

FIGURE 20. The 2013 Los Angeles Metro Rail Gold Line from downtown Los Angeles to Pasadena. (Courtesy of the Los Angeles County Metropolitan Transportation Authority Research Library and Archive. Reprinted with permission.)

estate projects sprouted around some of the station areas,[37] however, leading to positive media coverage in the local papers and the *New York Times*.[38]

The Pasadena line came into existence not necessarily because transit and planning experts decided it was the best use of public funds but because it had strong bipartisan political support, while other rail corridors suffered from community opposition and political infighting. The line's political supporters had first persuaded the MTA to prioritize their preferred rail line, despite lingering questions over its effectiveness relative to other potential corridors and a limited budget for rail. Then, when MTA funds dried up, state backers managed to save the line from a potentially indefinite postponement by creating the PMBLCA. Gold Line supporters now hoped to extend the line deeper into the San Gabriel Valley.

EASTSIDE STORY

Yaroslavsky's Proposition A ensured that any rail service to the Eastside would not take the form of heavy rail subway. A few years after the Proposition A vote, the MTA had a new CEO who wanted to make a light rail project to the Eastside a priority. In June 2001, Roger Snoble left his position as the head of Dallas Area Rapid Transit, where he received a national award as transit official of the year, to come to Los Angeles and run the MTA.[39] He replaced Julian Burke, who was happy to step aside after four years of establishing financial stability for the MTA.

Snoble brought experience successfully building new light rail lines in Dallas. "We had the opportunity and the money to do things right," he said of his Dallas experience. "It made it fun, and we opened up line after line, facility after facility, light rail and commuter rail." Now, with the subway stopped and a new emphasis on building light rail, Snoble had an opportunity to open new lines in Los Angeles. "There's been a structural deficit since I got here," Snoble commented in 2008 about his time at the MTA, "and we've been struggling to taking care of it. But there was still lots of money, one billion ready to go."[40]

The MTA's fiscal situation had improved since the Proposition A period. Thanks to increased revenues from a growing economy, scaled-back rail expenditures, and Burke's leadership, Snoble was able to deliver the MTA's first under-budget fiscal year, which decreased spending by 5 percent without raising fares. "We had a big bus system, with one person overseeing seven to eight thousand people," Snoble explained about some of the reforms he insti-tuted. "One person can't pay attention to everything, so we divided it up into five service sectors, with the general manager of each sector having two to three divisions so they could pay attention to that area."[41] His budget included cuts to workers compensation payments to MTA employees and streamlined bus operations that encouraged cost savings through decentralization.

Snoble's ability to deliver on the finances gave him political support to start new rail lines. "I'm getting more and more encouraged by what I'm seeing," Hal Bernson commented after seeing Snoble in action. "There's a lot of innovation."[42] As a result, the board began planning again for an increase in rail and bus rapid transit. Its 2001 Long Range Plan included rail to the Eastside, Santa Monica via the Exposition corridor, the San Fernando Valley in the north-south corridor, and Los Angeles International Airport (LAX) via the Green Line. It also tried to revive the Red Line extension west along Wilshire, the Green Line extension south to Redondo Beach, and the Pasadena line out to Claremont.[43] The MTA leadership's ambition for rail expansion was reemerging.

Snoble prioritized the light rail expansion to the Eastside of Los Angeles. Having been denied the subway promised to them by fiscal woes and Supervisor Yaroslavsky's ballot measure, the Eastside's political representa-tives secured financial support for Snoble to proceed with rail. First, Eastside congressional representatives salvaged the funds that Congress had already dedicated to the aborted subway line. The original legislation authorizing funds for the project had set aside money for a "heavy rail subway" on the corridor. Now that a subway would be virtually impossible to build, the con-gressional delegation changed the language to "any fixed guideway project," thus giving transit advocates greater flexibility to bring rail to the region. Although MTA board members selected a busway in March 1999 to replace the subway, they voted to approve rail instead after completing environmen-tal review on the route at the end of 2001.[44]

Now Snoble had to get federal funding for the rail line. "The Eastside extension was fairly well planned," he said, "but it didn't have the full fund-ing grant agreement [with the FTA] and it wasn't ready to go yet." Snoble, however, had help from a powerful Eastside congresswoman. "It helped a lot that we have Lucille Roybal-Allard on the [congressional] appropriations committee, and the line is in her district," he said. "She was fabulous. She did exactly what she needed to do, and she did it big time. So she's quite a hero of everyone who will benefit from this line."[45]

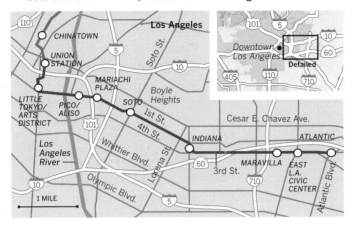

FIGURE 21. The Eastside Gold Line from Union Station near downtown Los Angeles to East Los Angeles. (Map by the *Los Angeles Times,* published November 16, 2009, on page 8A. © 2009, 2013. Reprinted with permission.)

With Roybal-Allard's help, the federal funding arrived and Snoble went to work getting the line built. "I wanted from the very beginning to be able to build that project and really take everything I've learned and really apply it, particularly the community relations piece of it," Snoble said. He credited community support with easing the planning and building of the line.[46]

The MTA considered the Eastside rail extension to be part of the Pasadena line, as both lines connected at Union Station. The Eastside line therefore became the Gold Line extension. As a result, the Gold Line looked like a sideways horseshoe with Union Station at the apex. It would be a six-mile route from Union Station through Little Tokyo, Boyle Heights, and ending in unincorporated East Los Angeles at Atlantic Boulevard.[47] Construction began in 2004, and all funding came from a combination of state and federal money—no local sales tax revenue went to the project.[48]

In November 2009, Eastside residents rode light rail in their neighborhood for the first time since the Pacific Electric streetcars closed half a century earlier on First Street.[49] The route's six miles included a two-station underground section. Major flaws included a slow travel time of twenty-five minutes for the route (owing to dramatic turns over the freeway leaving Union Station and because the train shared the road with cars and pedestrians along First Street) and a route that did not serve downtown Los Angeles directly. Although the First Street tracks took the train on a direct bearing for downtown Los Angeles, the tracks curved almost backwards to serve Union Station on the outskirts of downtown. To fix the lack of access to downtown, MTA planners set their sights on a downtown "regional connector" to link the Eastside line to the Blue Line. Overall, the Eastside extension of the Gold Line boosted ridership from about 24,000 weekday boardings in April 2009 to approximately 32,000 boardings by April 2010.[50]

The revival of rail construction, starting with the Eastside Gold Line, marked a dramatic turnaround for an agency plagued by bad publicity and debt. It reflected the improved finances of the agency, which resulted from a stronger local economy and better fiscal leadership by MTA staff and the board. It also reflected the continuing desire of local leaders to bring rail to their communities. Although the Eastside had originally been promised a heavy rail subway, light rail was the compromise choice as a nod to fiscal and political realities. And without strong political support at all levels and a receptive community clamoring for better transit, the line would never have been built.

EXPOSING EXPOSITION

With the opening of Eastside light rail, the Westside was one of the only major regions of the county that still lacked access to rail transit. Although the MTA owned the dedicated right-of-way along the Exposition corridor from downtown Los Angeles to Santa Monica, that corridor (or Expo, as it came to be known) represented a painful reminder of the MTA's inability to build rail in the most populated areas. Despite owning the route for over a decade, a high-profile location serving the Westside from downtown, and a ridership that was likely to be higher than any other light rail line under consideration at the time, the LACTC and the MTA had failed to deliver. Homeowner opposition and lack of funds had successfully thwarted the line since the early 1990s.

In the late 1990s and early 2000s, however, a building boom of offices on the Westside changed the political calculus. The new development created traffic gridlock, and the imbalance between jobs (too many) and housing (too little) in the coastal communities meant that more people were driving from downtown to the Westside, a reverse of the historical pattern. As a result, by the afternoon most residents feared to take their cars out as traffic congestion became the worst in the region. Popular support for rapid transit on the route was overtaking the dominant homeowner interests in Cheviot Hills and Rancho Park. Zev Yaroslavsky no longer represented their interests on the city council, and now that he was a county supervisor he had begun to change his attitude about rail along the route. More important, the improved MTA fiscal situation in the early 2000s allowed the agency once again to contemplate building light rail lines.

Longtime Santa Monica resident Darrell Clarke decided to seize the opportunity. When he was an engineer for IBM at the company's downtown Los Angeles office a decade earlier, he read about the proposed Expo rail line along the former Pacific Electric and freight train right-of-way in the *Santa Monica Outlook*. Clarke was a rail aficionado and a native Angeleno, and he came from a family with a deep appreciation for the Pacific Electric trains and an equal sense of loss at their demise. His father shared with him photos he took of the Red Cars' last day of operation in 1961. As a UC Berkeley student in the early 1970s, Clarke watched construction of the Bay Area Rapid Transit (BART) system and was on the first BART train from Oakland to San Francisco in the summer of 1974. For Clarke, rail was "a classy way to get around."[51]

In the late 1980s, when Expo was just being proposed, Clarke joined a community group organized by the city of Santa Monica to counter the Cheviot Hills and Rancho Park opposition. Combing through academic literature and U.S. census data, Clarke put together a slide show on the economic benefits of rail and went door to door in Cheviot Hills to lobby residents. "Half of the residents' eyes turned red, and the other half said, 'We need it,'" Clarke recalled. Although his group helped convince the LACTC to purchase the Exposition Boulevard right-of-way for rail transit, the homeowner opposition and budget woes kept the right-of-way dormant. "All the money was going into the subway," Clarke said, "and the agency realized they couldn't build all the rail projects in their thirty-year plan."[52] Meanwhile, Clarke watched as traffic congestion on the Westside worsened.

The year 1998 provided renewed opportunity. Yaroslavsky's Proposition A created an opening for light rail along Expo. "It killed two and a half bad projects," Clarke observed of the initiative's effect on the proposed subway extensions. "With the demise of the Pico–San Vicente subway extension, with federal money for both that and the Eastside extension, the MTA did a hurry-up reengineering study to qualify new routes for the federal money already allocated," Clarke recalled. "I went to an MTA community meeting in the latter part of 1998, and what stood out, along with bus rapid transit on

Wilshire with dedicated lanes, was bus rapid transit on Expo. As it happened, there were one or two other people at the initial meeting who were old Expo supporters, along with some newcomers. We decided it was time to reestablish the focus on Exposition."[53]

Along with these activists, Clarke cofounded the all-volunteer group "Friends4Expo." Composed of self-described "transit nerds" from communities along the Expo right-of-way, Friends4Expo set about organizing and running community meetings, knocking on neighborhood doors for supporters, and researching transit and population data—the flip side of homeowner activists who spent their time lobbying against rail. And like those opposition groups, Friends4Expo began getting attention from local officials and the media.[54]

The group's efforts came at an important time. The MTA was considering the route for a busway only, but the initial environmental review presented an opening to consider rail as an alternative. "In 2000 there was a pivotal board meeting," Clarke recalled. "The recommendation from the environmental study was to study both bus rapid transit and light rail on the Expo corridor, as well as bus rapid transit on Wilshire. In the course of the meeting, there was a motion from Jaime de la Vega, fresh out of UCLA planning school and an appointee of Mayor Riordan, only to do bus rapid transit on Expo, and only on a detour route. It was sort of like, 'Oh my god, we've lost it all.' But John Fasana, a councilman from Duarte who was pushing hard for light rail in Pasadena and an extension farther east, said, 'How about we add light rail?' It passed with a slim majority."[55]

Friends4Expo then mobilized to vanquish bus rapid transit as an option. At a spring 2001 MTA meeting on the project at the Veterans Hospital in West Los Angeles, the group mobilized a major turnout of rail supporters. "We organized and built a big email list, sort of early internet organizing," Clarke explained. "So many people turned out in support, and there were only a handful of opponents from Culver City and Cheviot Hills. With one exception, they left the room without speaking, they were so outnumbered."[56]

The timing was perfect. By July 2001, Los Angeles had a newly elected mayor, James Hahn, and Pam O'Connor, an ardent Expo supporter from the Santa Monica City Council, was serving on the MTA board. The new board voted to approve light rail along the route from downtown to Culver City.[57] Representative Diane Watson cited Friends4Expo's persistent meetings with local officials and ability to gather signatures in support of the project as one of the reasons for the decision. "If it wasn't for their willingness to show there was a community that wanted rail, the Expo line would not have gotten this far," she remarked.[58] As Clarke related, "A former state senator that we met with told us, 'You guys start the parade, and I'll march out in front of it.'"[59]

With the decision to go with light rail, the MTA still needed to find funding for the project. Expo supporters would also have to wait their turn and let the Pasadena line finish and the Eastside light rail line begin construction.[60] Meanwhile, some residents along the right-of-way expressed opposition to the project based on the potential for accidents with pedestrians, and the MTA board voted to perform additional safety studies. But the MTA leadership, thanks to a motion by O'Connor, expressed their "vision and intent to complete the LRT [light rail transit] line to Santa Monica."[61]

Soon, though, state politics and an economic downturn combined to stall efforts to secure funds for the Expo line. In response to a 2003 state budget crisis that resulted in the diversion of gas tax money to nontransit uses, as well as a decrease in federal support, the MTA once again had to scale back rail plans.[62] The state cutbacks had a negative multiplier effect because the MTA lost money that it was using as a match for federal dollars. The agency decided to borrow up to $1.1 billion over the next ten years, through a bond issue backed by future Proposition C revenues, to secure the federal match. The upside for the Exposition line was that the plan would provide $240.9 million for the project on a faster construction timetable.[63]

Fearing that the MTA's fiscal situation might doom the Expo line, the state government took over construction of Expo in 2004. State senator Sheila Kuehl, an Expo supporter representing Santa Monica in the legislature, authored legislation, modeled on the Pasadena line authority, to create a separate authority to build Expo.[64] The new authority was called the Exposition Metro Line Construction Authority and would build the project, while the MTA would prepare the environmental documents and eventually operate the line.[65]

As the search for funding and political consensus on the first phase of the line continued, light rail on Expo received a critical endorsement from the *Los Angeles Times* in December 2004. The paper argued that the line would reduce traffic and was wide enough to be safe for pedestrians.[66] Just a few months earlier, however, the paper ran a story somewhat critical of the route for being too far to the south of population centers in a less densely populated industrial and residential corridor.[67]

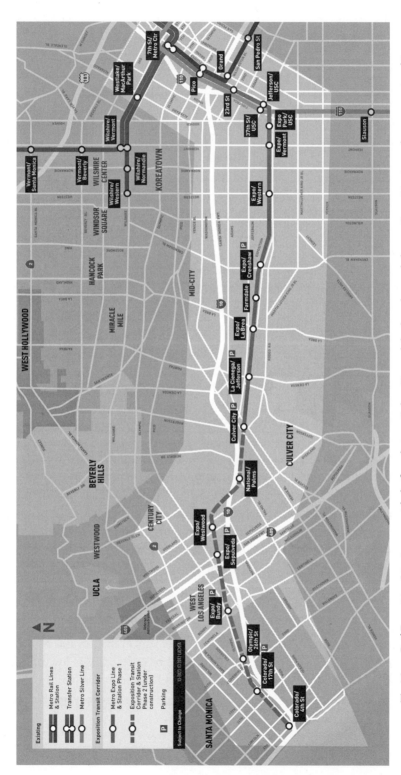

FIGURE 22. The Metro Rail Exposition Line in 2012, with the first phase to Culver City and the dotted second phase to Santa Monica under construction. (Courtesy of the Los Angeles County Metropolitan Transportation Authority Research Library and Archive. Reprinted with permission.)

Environmental review on the line finished in 2005. Officials at the MTA identified $590 million in federal and state funding for the project, which was just $50 million shy of the total required to build the proposed line. The route would cover 9.6 miles, beginning at the existing 7th Street Metro Rail station where the Blue Line and Red Line subway converge. It would then follow the former freight right-of-way through southwestern Los Angeles, past the University of Southern California, before ending in downtown Culver City. The line contained ten stations.[68]

In 2006, final funds for the project came together, and the MTA held a groundbreaking ceremony on the route on September 29. The local Dorsey High School jazz band played while local elected officials gathered to have their pictures taken holding shovels over a ceremonial dirt pile. The projected date of completion to Culver City was 2010. At the ceremony, local officials mingled with community members. The volunteers from Friends4Expo prided themselves that the day had finally come, and Supervisor Burke publicly thanked the group for their efforts.[69]

One of the group's leaders, Ken Alpern, described the battle for light rail given the tight transit budget. "It's hard to fight over pieces of the pie when the problem is the pie is so small," he said. "It's better if we all get together and try to make the pie bigger. The Gold Line people want the extension out there, the subway-down-Wilshire people want that, then there's the Green Line extension. But we've waited our turn, and now we can say to them, you've had your first shot, now it's our turn."[70] His comments reflected the challenges of advocating for a transit line in a large and diverse county.

Even with a victory under their belts, however, Friends4Expo was still in fighting mode. A minor controversy had emerged over what color to give the Expo Line (now the official name). As the volunteers stood up to be acknowledged publicly for their efforts, they were conspicuously dressed in aqua, their color of choice for a rail line destined to go to the ocean.[71]

THE EXPO REALITY

The construction process for the Expo line became plagued by some of the same challenges that afflicted other rail lines in the county. Construction management issues and local opposition bogged down the effort and increased costs. The original opening date of 2010 to Culver City for the first phase became delayed until 2012, with the Santa Monica phase not scheduled to open until 2015 or 2016, pushed back from the initial projection of 2014. Meanwhile, the project ended up $260 million over budget by the end of 2010.[72]

Community members along the first phase of the route objected to its proximity to the Foshay Learning Center and Dorsey High School (ironically, the same school whose jazz band played at the groundbreaking), given that the trains traveled at grade. They worried that rogue students would get hit by the trains trying to cross the tracks. They wanted the trains to run below ground or on an elevated platform. "You're going to need something that is reminiscent of the Berlin Wall," commented rail critic Tom Rubin of the safety precautions needed, "because kids do not like to be detoured and they do not like to go vertical. If there is a way, they will find it."[73] As an eventual compromise, the MTA agreed to site a new station to slow the trains by the schools and introduce various safety precautions, at a significant cost in time and money to the project.[74]

As with the Blue Line construction, betterments to the project along the route and agency coordination challenges drove up costs. For example, because of delays related to work done by the Los Angeles Department of Water and Power on power lines over the La Brea crossing, the authority was one year late building a bridge over that intersection. The California Department of Transportation (Caltrans) also had to approve a new bridge over the Harbor Freeway, while the California Public Utilities Commission was responsible for approving grade crossings. "Half of the budget is for improvements," noted Darrell Clarke. "They also brought extra money to build an aerial station at Culver City on Phase 1 instead of Phase 2, and they added a complete station at USC rather than a shell."[75]

Adding to the challenges was a controversial construction management process implemented by Rick Thorpe, head of the Expo authority, who had successfully shepherded the Pasadena Gold Line and its Eastside extension to completion. In an attempt to save costs, Thorpe introduced a modified bidding process. On Thorpe's other rail projects, to make the design as cost effective and practical as possible, he had builders package the design bids with their building bids. Thorpe believed that this process resulted in occasional windfall profits for builders who completed their tasks substantially under budget. With Expo, he attempted to remedy this problem by including a second step in the process. First, the authority agreed to design-build parameters with a contractor. Second, once the design was finalized, the authority would negotiate with the builder on the actual construction price. In a scathing article, the *L.A. Weekly* claimed that this process flew in the face of advice from experts and resulted in huge cost overruns (critics believed the procedure left the construction authority with little leverage in practice to hold down construction costs).[76] Thorpe maintained that the cost overruns were due to higher material costs and betterments added late to the project. "It didn't go as well as hoped," Clarke summarized.[77]

Doubts also began to surface about the travel time of the trip from Santa Monica to downtown Los Angeles. With the at-grade crossings and multiple stations, some less than half a mile apart, the optimistic total trip time would be forty-five minutes. Express trains on the route that could skip some stations would be impossible without building passing lane tracks. Given that travelers could drive the route along the parallel freeway in as little as fifteen minutes (without traffic), coupled with travel times getting to and from the stations, the route could suffer from the same low ridership affecting the Pasadena Gold Line. Clarke acknowledged the time challenges but cited other benefits: "You have the freedom of getting around without a car, to go downtown, and you don't have to worry about where to park or how much it's going to cost."[78]

But Expo supporters bristled at the idea that the route should be built as bus rapid transit to save costs. "You don't have the ride quality with buses, the smoothness of steel wheel on rail, the electric drive, with the fast acceleration," Clarke said. "With buses, you have a big engine in the rear, with noise, vibration, and unevenness of the pavement. It's better than taking a bus down Wilshire Boulevard where buses are creating all these potholes. I mean it's just bang-bang-bang in a bus down Wilshire. It's horrible." Converting a busway later to light rail would also entail delay and demolition and new construction costs. "If at all possible, build what you need to end up with up front," said Clarke.[79]

Ultimately, the success of the light rail investment on Expo will be determined by the ridership and the development of the station areas to maximize the utility of the train service. Future light rail lines will also enhance the value of the Expo Line, by providing connections to other parts of the city and county. But the history of the Expo Line illustrates two primary dynamics in rail politics. First, building light rail through existing communities is challenging both politically and practically. Opposition from homeowners successfully delayed the project for over a decade, while the at-grade nature of the route through a dense urban environment resulted in additional construction costs and slower travel speeds that hurt ridership. Second, the

FIGURE 23. Ribbon-cutting celebration for the opening of the first phase of the Expo light rail line on April 27, 2012. From left to right: Los Angeles Metro board member Richard Katz *(back left)*, Los Angeles mayor and Metro board president Antonio Villaraigosa *(front left)*, Los Angeles county supervisor and Metro board member Zev Yaroslavsky *(front center)*, Los Angeles city councilman and Metro board member Mark Ridley-Thomas *(back second from right)*, California state assemblyman Mike Feuer *(back right)*, and Metro board member Pam O'Connor *(front right)*. (Courtesy of the Los Angeles County Metropolitan Transportation Authority Research Library and Archive. Reprinted with permission.)

democratic process and decentralized nature of governance in Los Angeles presented opportunities for residents to be engaged in pushing policy forward, rather than merely opposing projects. For possibly the first time in Los Angeles history, a community group like Friends4Expo, composed of residents from the diverse communities along the route, was instrumental not in stopping or delaying a rail line, but in making it possible to build.

WHERE RAIL MEETS RUBBER

San Fernando Valley leaders had hoped to bring rail transit to their constituents. But when Valley residents resisted at-grade or aboveground rail transit, elected officials looked to the city of Curitiba, Brazil, as a model. Curitiba had considered building an expensive subway, but the price was too high. Instead, city leaders there conceptualized a "surface subway" of buses on exclusive lanes that radiated out from the city's center. The cost was dramatically less.[80]

Curitiba's low-cost transit solution attracted Los Angeles leaders after the 1998 voter backlash against subways. In 1999, at the request of Los Angeles architect Martha Welborne, a contingent made up of Mayor Riordan, Supervisor Yaroslavsky, Supervisor Yvonne Braithwaite Burke, and other leaders traveled to Curitiba to see the bus rapid transit system in action.[81] The buses there functioned like light rail cars on rubber tires, traveling in dedicated rights-of-way at faster speeds than a bus in traffic. They provided many of the benefits of rail, such as fast travel times and reliability, without the expense and construction difficulties of rail.

The effect was immediate. Supervisor Yaroslavsky said that, after one look at Curitiba's system, "it took me about thirty seconds to say that this will work on the Southern Pacific railroad tracks" along Chandler Boulevard in the San Fernando Valley. The supervisor said he drew what became the Valley's bus rapid transit (BRT) line "on the plane ride back, on the back of a Varig Airlines napkin."[82]

Bus rapid transit represented a significant cost savings over rail. Estimates for the San Fernando Valley BRT ran from $12.4 million to $14.9 million per mile (in 1998 dollars), while light rail lines would cost between $51.7 million and $81.6 million a mile. By contrast, heavy rail subway costs ranged from $237.3 million to $271.2 million a mile. Without the need for wiring and track, BRT was also faster to build than light rail lines, which were in turn faster to build than heavy rail subway lines.[83]

As a result, the MTA completed the fourteen-mile Valley BRT line, dubbed the Orange Line, in just two years at a cost of $330 million.[84] The route, which was finished in 2005, followed the exclusive rail right-of-way from the North Hollywood Red Line station to the Warner Center in Woodland Hills, across the San Fernando Valley. It included thirteen stations at major centers, including five with park-and-ride lots. To mollify residents along the route, the MTA installed five miles of sound walls with anti-graffiti coating, used rubberized asphalt to quiet the bus noise, and planted 5,000 trees and 800,000 plants along the route.[85] In 2012, the MTA opened a four-mile extension to the Chatsworth Metrolink station.

The Orange Line was arguably a more appropriate mode of transit than rail for the San Fernando Valley. The Valley did not possess the same population or job density, and hence the same ridership potential, as other transit routes like the Exposition or the Eastside lines. And given the homeowner opposition that forced any rail to travel below ground by state statute, BRT was a reasonable compromise. The MTA also retained the option

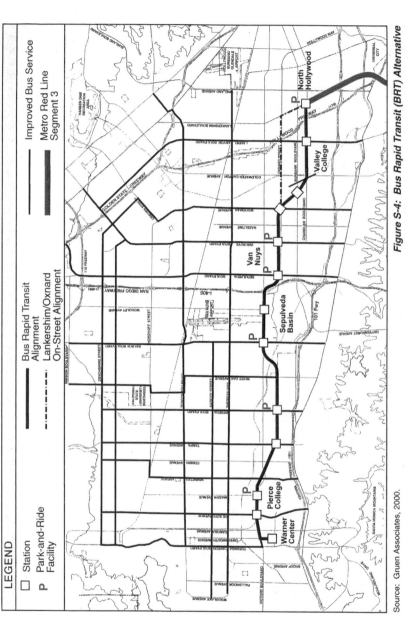

Figure S-4: Bus Rapid Transit (BRT) Alternative
(Full BRT and Lankershim / Oxnard Variations)

page S-13

San Fernando Valley
East-West Transit Corridor
EIS/EIR

FIGURE 24. The Metro Orange Line Bus Rapid Transit route and stations, as planned in 2000. (Courtesy of the Los Angeles County Metropolitan Transportation Authority Research Library and Archive. Reprinted with permission.)

FIGURE 25. The Metro Orange Line Bus Rapid Transit vehicles travel on a landscaped, dedicated right-of-way through the San Fernando Valley with a parallel bike path, June 30, 2012. (Photo by Gary Leonard for the Los Angeles Metro. Courtesy of the Los Angeles County Metropolitan Transportation Authority Research Library and Archive. Reprinted with permission.)

of converting the busway into light rail to satisfy increased demand, albeit at additional cost and with significant disruption to existing service. Ultimately, the Orange Line served as an efficient feeder to the Red Line subway at North Hollywood and as a model for less expensive rapid transit in the region.

LIGHT RAIL DREAMS

The completion of the light rail lines to Pasadena, the Eastside, and Culver City, as well as bus rapid transit in the San Fernando Valley, meant that the Metro Rail system could reach whole new sections of the vast area of urban Los Angeles, much as Supervisor Yaroslavsky had intended with his ballot initiative. Because light rail costs significantly less than heavy rail subway, MTA board members and staffers became eager to plan new lines and extensions of existing routes. These lines included an extension of the Gold Line farther east into Congressman David Dreier's district in the San Gabriel Valley, a Green Line extension along the Crenshaw corridor, and a downtown regional connector to link the Pasadena Gold Line with the Blue Line. "Because we didn't piss away the money on subways in places that didn't warrant it," argued Yaroslavsky about his Proposition A, "we ended up having money to spend on light rail and busways where it was warranted."[86]

To be sure, the desire to continue funding heavy rail was not dead. The only factor preventing expansion of the subway and the additional light rail lines was a lack of money. But that situation was about to change.

TEN

Subway to the Sea

FIVE YEARS AFTER CONSTRUCTION ENDED, subway advocates were eager to get their train going again. They found a new champion in 2005 mayoral candidate Antonio Villaraigosa. Ironically, Villaraigosa did not start his career as a subway proponent. As an appointee of Supervisor Gloria Molina to the Los Angeles County Metropolitan Transportation Authority (MTA) board in the 1990s, he had been a strong advocate for bus riders and low-income residents who did not feel they would gain from increased rail expansion. He had also been a supporter of the Bus Riders Union (BRU) lawsuit against the MTA. In fact, Manuel Criollo of the BRU credited Villaraigosa with helping the organization launch the lawsuit, saying that Villaraigosa "would literally come to our office and tell us that we should call bus riders and advocates about the proposed fare increases."[1]

But Villaraigosa's views on rail evolved. By 2004, as a Los Angeles city councilman, he had helped secure federal funding for the Eastside light rail line.[2] And when he ran for mayor in a 2005 rematch against James Hahn, son of late supervisor Kenneth Hahn and successor to Richard Riordan, Villaraigosa coined the phrase that would become iconic in his campaign and future rail efforts: he wanted the region to build a "Subway to the Sea."

Villaraigosa's run for mayor sparked renewed political momentum for the subway and launched an effort to bring new funding for the long-sought Westside subway extension along the Wilshire Boulevard corridor.

Villaraigosa's embrace of a subway down Wilshire to Santa Monica was if nothing else a smart political move. Transportation was a big issue for voters during the 2005 campaign. A *Los Angeles Times* poll showed that 24 percent of registered voters listed transportation-related issues as their top concern, more than any other issue except education, also at 24 percent.[3] New Los Angeles mayor James Hahn had not appeared to seize the political momentum to address transportation. He spent the first term of his mayoralty focusing on small-scale solutions to traffic, like fixing problem intersections. He also declined to assume the chairmanship of the MTA board because of his battles with San Fernando Valley secessionists, and he developed a reputation for missing MTA board meetings and losing control over his appointees.[4]

Villaraigosa took advantage of Hahn's perceived failure to lead. Alone among the mayoral challengers, he vigorously supported the repeal of the Waxman ban and extending the subway down Wilshire Boulevard.[5] His bold transit agenda injected life into his campaign. Like Bradley before him, Villaraigosa extolled the virtues of the subway, and he began using the "subway to the sea" phrase as part of his standard campaign speech. He recognized that traffic on the Westside had reached crisis proportions and that enough Angelenos either lived or worked there to create broad electoral appeal. The bad memories of subway construction seemed to have faded.

Villaraigosa defeated Hahn in May 2005 and became the first Latino mayor of Los Angeles in 130 years. While Bradley had predicted a subway groundbreaking within eighteen months of his assuming office, the new mayor had learned the lessons of transit planning. His goal was to begin groundbreaking on a Wilshire subway extension before he left office in eight years.[6] Despite seemingly insurmountable obstacles, including the Waxman ban on tunneling in methane areas and a lack of funding, he brought an enthusiasm to rail transit that had been missing since the days of Supervisor Hahn and Mayor Bradley.

Upon taking office, Villaraigosa assumed the chairmanship of the MTA board and began vigorously selling the idea of the subway to the sea. "It would be the most utilized subway in the nation, maybe the world," he said. "It would also be the most cost-effective public-transportation project in America."[7]

Villaraigosa's victory and the public's frustration with traffic brought renewed scrutiny on Henry Waxman's two-decade-old ban on federal funding for a western subway extension, a ban the congressman had obstinately continued to defend.[8] But Villaraigosa's election sent a strong signal that it was time for him to reconsider. Los Angeles city councilman and former MTA board member Tom LaBonge had been advocating for a Wilshire extension, and he now stepped up his effort with Villaraigosa's backing. LaBonge journeyed to Washington, D.C., to lobby Waxman. As MTA CEO Roger Snoble recalled, "Tom LaBonge got up on our board and said, 'By God, that's got to get done' and started beating the drum." Snoble offered to provide Waxman technical input on the impacts of rescinding the ban. "I said, we got a great tool from APTA [American Public Transportation Association] peer review, let's ask Waxman to name people to the board and see if it's possible or not possible and how much it would cost. Let's just find out."[9] Waxman agreed to the plan. Shortly after this lobbying effort, he reported that he had spoken to "LaBonge, Antonio Villaraigosa, and Roger Snoble about this, and I indicated I would remove the federal prohibition if we could arrange a study to show that we could tunnel through the methane safely."[10] The door was now open for another study to document the safety of tunneling down Wilshire.

The city of Los Angeles quickly provided the money for the study from funds allocated in 2004 under Hahn's leadership,[11] and the MTA approved it by an 11–2 vote. LaBonge then rallied the support of leaders from Santa Monica, Beverly Hills, West Hollywood, and Culver City. Even Waxman's most ardently antisubway constituents had softened. Diana Plotkin, who rose to local fame opposing the subway in the 1980s as president of the Beverly Wilshire Homes Association, now complained about the traffic on the Westside. "Things have gotten progressively worse over the past 20 years," she told the *Los Angeles Times,* "and today we need rapid transit more than we ever did. . . . We do need a solution to this horrible traffic problem."[12] It was a change of heart from a community activist who had originally opposed the subway by predicting that "the problems that we would suffer would be tremendous"[13] if Metro Rail came to her neighborhood.

Former subway foes like Supervisor Zev Yaroslavsky also supported the effort. "If there's ever going to be another subway in L.A., it's going to be going down Wilshire, no doubt about it," he said. "It's got the density, and that's where it was originally supposed to go. Eventually, it's going to happen because it's the only way to move people east/west. You're not going to do it with an elevated and you're not going to do it at grade, so you're going to have to go underground."[14] The supervisor's 1998 Proposition A, the antisubway ballot measure, also contained a loophole that could help the subway: because the measure banned local funds only for tunneling, funds were still available for all nontunneling costs.[15]

Waxman wanted to control which experts the MTA selected for the study. "We've got to get him a panel he's comfortable with," Villaraigosa said.[16] By October 2005, Waxman had chosen two people for a five-member panel of experts to study the safety of tunneling through Wilshire: Fred Kissell, a retired methane expert from Pennsylvania mining country, and John T. Christian, a veteran engineer from Boston's "big dig" freeway tunnel. The American Public Transportation Association appointed the other three members.[17]

Surprising almost nobody, the panel unanimously found that tunneling underneath Wilshire Boulevard was safe. "By following proper procedures and using appropriate technologies, the risk would be no greater than [with] any other subway system in the U.S.," the experts concluded. Perhaps to provide political cover to Waxman, the experts acknowledged that technology for tunneling and gas detection had improved in recent decades.[18] "A couple of them thought that in the mid-1980s it might not have been done safely because there were genuinely new techniques, but they didn't have those new techniques back then," Waxman explained. But when asked what the new developments in engineering were, the man who had diverted and almost stopped a then-$3 billion subway line based on methane fears responded, "You know, I have no idea."[19]

Nevertheless, the panel's conclusions gave Waxman the information he needed to reverse the ban. "Waxman had appointed some pretty good choices, very good technical people," Snoble observed, "and he was really glowing about it when they came back and said it was not particularly a big problem and that we ought to be able to do it. Now he had more community support and not opposition, and he was satisfied we could do it safely. Safety really was a concern for him."[20]

In December 2005, after reading the engineers' report, Waxman announced, "I am very pleased with the panel's unanimous finding, and I will make lifting the prohibition a priority."[21] Waxman had finally come around to supporting the system, albeit reluctantly. "I think since the mid-

1980s the MTA has filled in other aspects of the whole system; they're not relying solely on this one subway system. And in my mind, I have other things to work on and very little expertise to try to figure out an alternative route or any other alternative plans, since this is the one they're all committed to. And my role as a congressman is to try to get the funds and keep it moving." When asked if he had any lingering concerns about safety, Waxman replied, "I accept the fact that they're able to tunnel. I don't know how airplanes stay up in the air particularly, but I have faith in the experts."[22]

After legislative delays in the Senate, the House of Representatives voted to repeal the ban in February 2007 by a voice vote on Waxman's one-page bill. California senators Barbara Boxer and Dianne Feinstein introduced similar legislation in the Senate,[23] which passed the bill. On December 26, 2007, President George W. Bush signed the bill into law as Public Law 110–161.[24] Waxman's ban was now history.

While many subway proponents were jubilant about the end of the methane ban, at least one elected official believed that the ban had served a positive purpose. "In reality, the Ross Dress-for-Less [impact on rail plans] may be the best thing that ever happened," argued Supervisor Zev Yaroslavsky. "The explosion forced us to reroute the line through Hollywood, which it wasn't going to be in in the first place. And so it goes all the way down Hollywood and has been and will continue to be a constructive catalyst for Hollywood. It got us to the San Fernando Valley, which is very important for both transportation and political reasons, leaving us the [Wilshire] corridor, which was unaddressed, until now."[25]

With the ban lifted, the only thing standing in the way of the subway was finding the estimated $4.8 billion needed to build it.[26]

A NEW OLD MEASURE

Denny Zane wanted to get the money for the subway. The former mayor of Santa Monica and environmental activist saw a golden opportunity with the coming presidential election of 2008. Voter turnout would be at an all-time high with the Barack Obama–John McCain matchup, and locally, frustration with traffic congestion was creating a strong political tide to expand public transit, specifically rail transit. He credited Villaraigosa's "subway to the sea" mayoral campaign as creating an iconic image to galvanize the public to fund new rail lines. He also saw a political and practical storm coming:

Los Angeles would have to accommodate an additional two million people in the next few decades, with zero dollars to expand new public transit capacity. In the fall of 2007, Zane moved quickly to line up support among environmentalists, business, labor, and social justice advocates for expanded funding for rail transit.

At first Zane looked to fund just the subway to the sea. But the deteriorating fiscal situation for the MTA meant that money had run out even for the projects MTA leaders originally thought they could fund. The causes were myriad. For starters, prices for raw materials and labor had risen faster than the MTA anticipated. For example, in late 2007, the Expo line construction authority had to ask for an additional $145 million to build the first phase, which represented a 23 percent increase.[27] The state government, facing structural budget deficits under Governor Arnold Schwarzenegger, routinely diverted rail funding to other uses. Even the fare hike that the MTA implemented after the consent decree expired had failed to shore up the budget. The agency was looking at a $1.8 billion deficit over the next ten years, which would jeopardize the entire rail program.[28] And in the meantime, it was delivering budgets that spent down its reserves.[29]

Zane approached Terry O'Day of Environment Now, a Santa Monica–based environmental nonprofit, to organize a conference of business, labor, and environmental leaders to address funding for the subway and for transit in Los Angeles in general. The goal was to get a region-wide consensus on the best approach to raise funds. They quickly realized that a sales tax measure, in the mold of Proposition A and Proposition C, was the only hope. "We looked at a long list of potential revenue sources," O'Day recalled, "such as property tax assessment districts, vehicle license fee surcharges, public-private partnership agreements to fund rail. But the sales tax emerged as the big item that could get done. Denny had arranged to look at past polling before the conference, and it was polling already very close to two-thirds support."[30]

A sales tax measure, however, would require quick action, given that the election was just a year away. "We were thinking, holy cow, if we get something on the ballot in November, we need the state legislature to say okay, and the legislature convenes in January," Zane said. "We need to get a bill in the hopper and get it out by the summer to meet the deadlines for the November ballot." Zane and O'Day set a date for the conference of January 10, 2008 and formed an organization called Move L.A. to host it. "We put it together in less than a month," Zane said. "We were thinking it can't be a show-and-tell, it needs to be coalition-building." The tight legislative timeline and importance of the issue helped attract attention, and Zane's long-standing ties to various stakeholders helped. "I called thirty-five different organizations, divided among business, environmentalists, social justice groups, academics, and labor," he said. "Thirty-four showed up. We were amazed. We were expecting twenty-two or twenty-three people, but we had CEOs of national corporations sitting on tabletops. It was a bigger response than we expected."[31]

At the conference, all the participants agreed on the sales tax measure strategy. Zane's polling data helped convince them, and immediately following the event, State Assemblyman Mike Feuer from Los Angeles submitted a bill to the legislature with the sales tax proposal. Meanwhile, Pam O'Connor, the current mayor of Santa Monica and chair of the MTA (and longtime friend of Zane's), made the motion at the MTA board to place the measure on the Los Angeles County ballot that fall.

O'Day's organization, Environment Now, found a useful sales tax model for Los Angeles. "Denver provided an interesting case study," O'Day explained. "They increased their sales tax one-half percent and raised $150 million for the region. But they got the electorate to go for it with a specific plan. They said, 'We'll build this and this' and pointed to direct projects, mostly light rail, which is how they funded light rail to their airport. Now they have a vibrant downtown with transit links."[32] This strategy contrasted well with Mayor Bradley's 1974 failed sales tax effort, which died in part due to the vagueness of the proposed rail corridors. O'Day's reliance on the Denver model also mirrored Supervisor Kenneth Hahn's use of the Atlanta sales tax model in crafting his Proposition A in 1980.

Fortunately for sales tax measure supporters, the MTA already had a working list of projects that the tax money could fund. MTA staff had developed its long-range transportation plan (LRTP) for the county (a new version of the 1992 thirty-year plan), which contained an updated wish list of the highway, rail, bus, and other transportation projects they wanted funded. Supporters could therefore go to the electorate with specific projects from the plan that would get built with the money, rather than simply presenting voters with a map of various corridors that might get money. The list generated widespread enthusiasm among supporters of the various projects across the county.

The MTA draft long-range plan listed four rail projects that agency leaders hoped to fund: the in-progress Eastside Gold Line extension, the first phase of the Expo line to Culver City, phase two of the Expo line to Santa Monica, and a light rail line down Crenshaw Boulevard.[33] The plan also contained an unfunded wish list of projects. Ranked from highest priority to lowest, they included the downtown regional connector, which offered a light rail link from the Blue Line to the Gold Line for a transfer-free ride from Long Beach to Pasadena; a Red Line subway extension down Wilshire to La Cienega; a link from Union Station to the Green Line's Aviation Station near Los Angeles International Airport (LAX); a further Wilshire subway extension to Santa Monica; light rail from Union Station to Burbank; an extension of the Gold Line Eastside line; a Pasadena Gold Line extension to Azusa; a Green Line extension to the South Bay; another Gold Line extension to Montclair; a Green Line extension from Norwalk; an LAX Green Line connection; and a maglev train from Union Station to Santa Ana.[34] If an Angeleno voted for the sales tax increase, supporters argued, he or she would now know exactly what projects would be built and in what order.

I WANT *MY* PROJECT

While the wish list may have been enticing to voters, it raised the hackles of many elected officials whose local projects were not ranked high enough. Politicians in the western part of the county demanded that the Green Line extension to LAX be moved up, while the mayor backed the subway to the sea as his first priority, along with the downtown regional connector.[35] In one visit to Washington, D.C., Mayor Villaraigosa tried to lobby the Los Angeles congressional delegation for federal funds for public transit. The representatives instead ended up lobbying the mayor: Representative Jane Harman advocated for the Green Line extension to LAX; Representative Waxman called for making the Expo line the top priority; and Representative David Dreier pitched the San Gabriel extension of the Gold Line.[36]

Of all the elected officials, none seemed as willing to jeopardize the sales tax measure to get their projects funded as the representatives from the San Gabriel Valley. State and local officials from the area wanted to extend the Gold Line from Pasadena to Azusa, in the heart of the San Gabriel Valley, and, thanks to Congressman David Dreier, they thought they had an inside track to federal funding to pay for it. Dreier had been a critical advocate for bringing the Gold Line to Pasadena, which stopped just short of his district. Now he wanted to bring that project home. In the intervening years, Dreier had risen through the ranks of the Republican House leadership to become chairman of the powerful House Rules Committee.

Almost single-handedly, Dreier had kept the extension alive since the completion of the first Gold Line phase to Pasadena in 2003. With congressional earmarks, he secured $4 million in 2003 to continue studying the extension.[37] When the MTA board voted in December of that year to shift $21 million for the San Gabriel extension to the Eastside light rail extension, which was low on funds, Dreier personally lobbied the MTA to reverse the decision. The next month, after intense lobbying by San Gabriel Valley officials, including Dreier, the MTA partially relented. The board gave $11 million back to the region through its freight rail project in the Alameda corridor.[38]

But the MTA staff was not convinced that the Gold Line Foothill extension, as it came to be known, deserved a fight. Although the agency wanted to build the project at some point, it prioritized other rail lines well ahead of it. So Dreier and his congressional allies from the region tried to force the MTA's hand. Employing an unconventional strategy, the Foothill advocates went directly to Congress. They had powerful allies: Dreier locked down the Republicans, who were in the majority at the time, while the Democratic delegation included all three representatives whose districts touched on the route. This group comprised Adam Schiff, the former state senator who rescued the original Gold Line in the late 1990s by creating a separate state-sanctioned agency to build it, and Representatives Hilda Solis and Grace Napolitano. Together, they got the Congress to deem the extension a "high-priority project" and to earmark $21 million it. The legislation also changed the designation of the project as being in the "final design" stage, which made it eligible for more federal funding in coming years.[39]

The congressional action sent a message to local transit officials that the line had clout and could get money directly from Congress. Given that finding funds for rail projects was the critical hurdle, the Gold Line Foothill extension brought with it a convenient ATM: the U.S. Congress in the form of Dreier. While the Red Line subway advocates had to beg Congress for an appropriation, the Foothill line delivered cash in a bipartisan gift-wrap.

The MTA understood the message. Richard Katz, Villaraigosa's appointee to the board, commented: "Clearly, the fact that you have federal funds available—it's one of the considerations going forward." A deputy to another MTA director noted Dreier's clout as chair of the Rules Committee: "It would be stupid for anyone in Los Angeles County to think you can call on

Congressman Dreier for [funding] projects like the Eastside and Exposition ... and snub him on a project so important to him."[40]

The Foothill extension now had new life after being on the low-priority list for the MTA.[41] But the MTA still could not guarantee that it could build it. By 2008, the MTA listed the extension to Azusa as the seventh priority in the long-range plan's "unfunded" list.

The problem for Dreier and his Gold Line backers was that the route did not merit an extension to the San Gabriel Valley ahead of other lines that would serve more densely populated corridors. The right-of-way mostly traveled through low-density industrial sections of the valley (although planners along the route vowed to steer future growth around the station areas to create transit-oriented districts).[42] And the ridership for the existing Gold Line was disappointing. Just eight months after it opened, it was only attracting 15,000 boardings a day, or 7,500 round-trips. That total represented half the original projected ridership.[43] Part of the problem for the line was its curvy and slow route to Pasadena. An extension through the Valley to Montclair might boost ridership, but not enough to make the route competitive with other planned light rail routes, such as through Crenshaw or out to Santa Monica.

The first signs of discontent from the San Gabriel Valley representatives came during the MTA vote to authorize the sales tax measure for the ballot. The MTA had dubbed the plan Measure R (as in "Relief"), which agency officials predicted could raise $30 to $40 billion over thirty years. The MTA would use roughly two-thirds of the revenue to expand the bus and rail systems, while one-third would go primarily to road improvements. Villaraigosa had helped draft a compromise that promised some of the revenue to pay for a delay in bus fare increases for a few years. On July 24, 2008, the board voted nine to two to place the measure on the ballot,[44] no repeat of the narrow 1980 and 1990 LACTC votes to approve Propositions A and C for the ballot. San Gabriel officials complained that Measure R did not prioritize the Gold Line Foothill extension enough. The two votes against the measure accordingly came from San Gabriel officials, including John Fasana, a city councilman from Duarte, and Supervisor Mike Antonovich, whose district covered much of the valley. Supervisor Gloria Molina abstained from the vote, but she appeared to oppose the measure, complaining that her Eastside district only got a light rail line while the Westside got a subway. She also represented Azusa, where the first phase of the Foothill extension would terminate.

Fasana, Antonovich, and Molina wanted assurance that the MTA would fund the extension immediately. Specifically, they wanted the MTA to dedicate $80 million to the line, believing this money would serve as a local match for a federal commitment of $320 million.[45] They were threatening not to support the sales tax measure in November.[46]

MTA chief executive officer Roger Snoble bristled at the argument. "There's this myth in the San Gabriel Valley that they're going to get all this funding," he said. "But it's an administrative process, not an earmark process, and it's not easy getting these things. You need congressional support for it, but that doesn't get you the project. They felt that if they had the $80 million from us, they could leverage $320 million. But I talked to the FTA [Federal Transit Administration] administrator, and he said there was no commitment on anybody's part to do anything, other than if Metro put the line in its long-range plan and had the local match to operate it for twenty years, they could advance into engineering. But somehow it got convoluted into $80 million now could get $320 million to start right away." The regional discord reminded Snoble of why Los Angeles took so long to secure federal funds to start and expand the rail system in the first place. "We used to laugh all the time at L.A. when I was in Dallas, that L.A. couldn't get its act together, so we'd come in and grab the money and laugh."[47]

The FTA was the final arbiter of which rail projects the federal government would fund, and the agency was supposed to look at objective criteria in ranking projects to fund—not the political support of various lines. MTA officials worried that it would be futile to submit a poorly justified line for the FTA to consider among hundreds of potential new rail lines around the country. The FTA had already rated the San Gabriel Valley line as "medium low" on the financial rating. Instead, Snoble argued that it would be better to begin the line with local revenue. Once the region built the first phase by itself, it could approach the federal government for continued funding. This strategy would allow the line to avoid the competitive "new starts" FTA process.[48] The agency was also likely concerned that a federal commitment to the Foothill extension would discourage the FTA from funding more meritorious lines in the region, such as Crenshaw and Expo to Santa Monica.

Supervisor Antonovich, however, refused to follow Snoble's strategy. He wrote to Snoble that the only reason the FTA did not rank the project higher was that the MTA itself did not prioritize the project. He accused Snoble of preventing the local congressional delegation from seeking federal funds for it.[49] From MTA staff's perspective, however, the project ranked low on the list because of the same data about its relative merits that the FTA evaluated.

Having failed to stop the sales tax measure at the MTA, San Gabriel Valley officials now tried to stop it at the county level. Following the MTA vote to approve Measure R for the ballot, the Los Angeles County Board of Supervisors now had to vote to place it on the general county ballot. The vote should have been a formality to consolidate all county elections in one ballot. But Supervisors Molina, Antonovich, and Don Knabe joined to vote down the measure three to two. Molina again complained about the Westside getting more than the Eastside. She commented that the measure seems to "get more for one side of town versus the other side" and that "it's a very funny way this little choo-choo is getting on the ballot." Knabe, meanwhile, declared himself a fiscal conservative who generally opposed more taxes.[50]

The supervisors' vote meant that the MTA would either have to pay between two and four million dollars to print a second ballot or sue the supervisors to get it on the same ballot.[51] Either way, the measure would go before the voters. Realizing that the attempt to deny Angelenos a chance to vote on the measure was pointless and costly, the supervisors embarrassingly had to reverse course when Knabe changed his vote.[52] "We saw that as a game of chicken to get them more money for their projects," O'Day said. "The Los Angeles Times and public opinion kind of lashed them the next day, so they reversed course."[53] The sales tax increase was heading to the ballot in November.

But the battle was still not over. Assemblyman Feuer needed to shepherd his bill through the California legislature to authorize the MTA to raise the sales tax money. State politicians began threatening the measure's passage unless their pet project got higher priority or more funding. State senator Gil Cedillo threatened to kill the bill in the appropriations committee, in which he was a member, unless the MTA gave more money for a tunnel for Interstate 710 in his district. State senator Jenny Oropeza held the bill hostage in the same committee for a Green Line extension to LAX. "There is no doubt this should be one of the highest priorities in L.A. County," she told the media. "This project would impact travelers and their families throughout the region."[54]

The actions of these leaders provoked outrage among residents following the debate. An angry article in the Los Angeles Times suggested that the politicians' behavior stemmed more from personal grudges than sound judgment, noting that Cedillo and Villaraigosa had been rivals since high school and that Molina and Yaroslavsky had experienced tension since Yaroslavsky's subway ban kept the subway out of her district.[55] "In part, it reflected two communities that thought they hadn't gotten their fair share of transit money over the years," Denny Zane reflected. "It was basically the cities along the 710 corridor down to Long Beach. Those cities had in mind that they had been screwed before, and they were therefore trying to get guarantees in the bill because they didn't trust the MTA to do it. They tried to hang their projects on the bill."[56]

Feuer refused to relent, and he got the bill to pass out of the committee unanimously, assuaging Oropeza and Cedillo by assuring them that their projects had some safeguards.[57] The bill then passed both houses, got held up during a state budget stalemate, and, like a paper ship on a stream, bobbed its way home. "Mike Feuer put up a solid no," Zane recalled. "And in the end, none of the legislators who were playing chicken with the bill wanted to be the final vote to deny Los Angeles County its opportunity. There was a growing sense of a big turnout, a once-in-a-generation opportunity, and the pressure on recalcitrant legislators not to hold up the bill became strong. In effect, they all caved, and the bill went forward without their projects."[58]

THE CAMPAIGN FOR MEASURE R

With the backroom hurdles overcome, the campaign now turned to the voters. MTA polling indicated strong support among the county population for a transit sales tax, particularly with ridership nearing all-time highs amid a spike in gas prices.[59] However, this support depended on the initiative offering a balanced dispersal of revenues among rail, buses, and roads. The MTA had learned the lessons of the successful 1980 and 1990 ballot measures not to dedicate all the money to one form of transit.

Rail transit leaders pursued support for the measure from the original stakeholders who attended the Move L.A. conference that January. The Valley Industry and Commerce Association and the Automobile Club of Southern California both endorsed the measure.[60] Villaraigosa lobbied business leaders, including the Los Angeles Business Council, to support the tax.[61]

Zane had pulled together an unusual coalition of environmental, labor, and business leaders. Environmentalists liked the transit measure because they wanted to reduce air pollution and promote transit over driving. The business community wanted a more livable city for their employees and less congestion to conduct commerce. And labor saw an interest in both constructing the system and providing their members with better public transit.

"It's not rocket science to figure out that the labor movement is a vital constituency, not only because it represents a large number of people who would vote and because it can raise money, but they've got a compelling reason to be interested," Zane said. "It doesn't require reading somebody's dissertation to figure that out."[62]

Despite the benefits for labor, unions had never before been so involved in transit planning in Los Angeles. "They would get involved politically project by project," Zane said, "but we were trying to get them involved in discussions about development. We had one meeting with business, labor, and enviros in the board room of the Los Angeles County Federation of Labor, and the joke was that this was the first time that any business leaders had been at the Federation of Labor building. It probably was."[63]

The San Gabriel region was still the major source of concern, though. Without those voters, it would be hard for Measure R to secure the two-thirds majority needed to pass. In one editorial, the *Pasadena Star News* argued against Measure R because it would only benefit the Westside, particularly a subway down Wilshire "that has not been deemed feasible," although the paper neglected to explain who had deemed it infeasible. It also argued that outlying areas of the county "account for more of the region's population" while failing to mention the significant population and job density of the Westside compared to the San Gabriel Valley.[64]

Zane and other Measure R supporters were incredulous at the San Gabriel Valley position. "So San Gabriel Valley folks didn't get their local money? Instead they got a measure that would give them twice as much money," Zane argued. "So you lose that vote for local funds, and you're miffed? And then somebody offers you a way to win twice as much money, and you're still miffed?"[65]

Ultimately, these opposition forces, which included the Bus Riders Union, failed to coalesce for a funded campaign to fight Measure R. "We thought there might be a [Howard] Jarvis antitax group that would get in the fight," O'Day recalled, citing the advocacy organization that launched itself with California's Proposition 13 tax revolt initiative in 1978. "And if any real opposition had emerged and funded itself, this would have died. Two-thirds is a very big hurdle to cross."[66] Added Zane, "In the end, their opposition was simply ineffectual. They didn't raise any money, which they needed to do to be effective."[67]

On election day, November 4, 2008, Los Angeles County voters went to the polls to vote on a host of sales tax measures. Nearly three dozen cities, .

FIGURE 26. Los Angeles County Metropolitan Transportation Authority chief executive officer Roger Snoble *(left)* and Los Angeles mayor and Metro board chair Antonio Villaraigosa *(right)* hold a framed Measure R poster, March 26, 2009. (Photo by Gary Leonard for the Los Angeles Metro. Courtesy of the Los Angeles County Metropolitan Transportation Authority Research Library and Archive. Reprinted with permission.)

school boards, and community college districts had their own tax measures on the ballot, while Los Angeles, Long Beach, and El Monte each had three tax measures. Smaller cities, such as Pico Rivera and El Monte, also had sales tax hikes on the ballot.[68] Perhaps as a strategic effort to win more votes, Measure R promotional material downplayed rail funding amid discussion of fixing potholes, improving highways, and synchronizing traffic lights. For example, the MTA placed the pledge to fund the controversial subway second to last on its brochure list, above the promise to distribute revenues to local governments "for traffic relief."[69]

The next morning, the vote was too close to call. "I've said from the beginning that this was going to be a tough fight," Villaraigosa told the media that day. "Were it not for the recession, I believe there would be overwhelming support for this measure."[70] The next day, with 100 percent of precincts reporting and still some provisional and absentee ballots to be counted, Measure R passed the two-thirds threshold. Proponents declared victory.[71] A few weeks later, the final victory margin stood at 67.9 percent of the vote, a substantial increase from the bare majorities won by Proposition A in 1980 and Proposition C in 1990.[72]

Supporters exhaled in disbelief. "Right up until the end I wasn't even out promoting my involvement to even my closest friends," O'Day said a month later. "I didn't really believe it would pass and that voters would tax themselves in a recession. I was shocked, and I'm still pinching myself."[73]

A NEW RAIL ERA

The Measure R victory represented a significant triumph for rail advocates and a political and cultural shift in the attitudes of voting Angelenos. In the time between the previous sales tax vote in 1990 and 2008, local leaders had launched a rail program, suffered construction and financial setbacks, and emerged with a more sound and chastened organization. The MTA deserved credit for improving since the subway disaster years. "People have more confidence in the system," argued Yaroslavsky. "We see that in the public opinion surveys and we hear about it anecdotally. If the MTA was a joke, you couldn't have gotten sixty-seven and a half percent to support a half-cent sales tax."[74]

The voting public had also shifted on the question of rail. Whereas in 1990 urban rail was an unknown in Los Angeles County, inciting fears of methane explosions, collapsed tunnels due to earthquakes, and drained streams in the hills, the advent of the rail system and the years of relatively uneventful service had allayed many of the concerns. The worsening traffic, caused in part by population increases and the imbalance between job and housing locations, also led to greater frustration with the status quo. Finally, demographic changes probably contributed to the shift, as retiring baby boomers and a new generation of urban-oriented professionals expressed greater preference for living in transit-oriented communities.[75]

Elected officials promised to act on the voter mandate. "People are sick and tired of traffic," Yaroslavsky said at the victory news conference. "They were willing to pay for it. Our job is to deliver on the promises."[76]

Rail leaders now had some of the money they needed to realize their vision, and an era of rail expansion in Los Angeles was beginning again.

Conclusion

THE FUTURE OF LOS ANGELES RAIL
AND THE AMERICAN CITY

WHEN SUPERVISOR KENNETH HAHN PRESIDED over the opening of
the first modern rail line in Los Angeles, he told the crowd: "The Blue Line
is here, now use it."[1] Angelenos responded. Although overall system ridership
is less than hoped for (and promised), Metro Rail has achieved some notable
successes. The Blue Line light rail is the busiest in the country, connecting the
two largest cities in Los Angeles County and helping to bring new development and urban amenities to neighborhoods along the route, such as downtown Long Beach.[2] The subway lines have helped spur the revitalization of
neighborhoods like Hollywood and Koreatown and coincided with the rapid
transformation of downtown Los Angeles into a vibrant residential hub with
significant new commercial and entertainment activity. Nationally acclaimed
transit-oriented development projects have sprouted on the Gold Line, near
subway stations, and along the new Expo line.[3]

But Metro Rail supporters still have work to do. When compared to rail
systems in other cities, Metro Rail ridership and cost-effectiveness rank in the
middle-to-lower end of the spectrum. It had approximately 350,000 weekday
boardings as of 2013 on 87.7 miles of heavy and light rail. To put these numbers in some context, the San Francisco Bay Area's Bay Area Rapid Transit
(BART) system averaged almost 400,000 weekday boardings in May 2013
(not including ridership on the region's extensive light rail network) with 104
miles of heavy rail service and a smaller population than Los Angeles, while
the Washington, D.C., Metro had 745,000 riders on 106 miles of heavy rail
in 2012 (also with a smaller population). Metro Rail farebox recovery ratio,
meaning the percentage of operating costs covered by fare revenues, generally
exceeded 40 percent by 2012, according to the Southern California
Association of Governments, compared to over 60 percent for BART and

66 percent for Washington, D.C., Metro. Meanwhile, a 2012 analysis of fifty-four light- and heavy-rail investments between 1970 and 2006 in twenty U.S. cities found that Metro Rail lines generally measured in the middle or bottom third on a per-passenger mile cost-effectiveness basis.[4]

Given this mixed history to date, what does the future hold for Metro Rail? What steps should the region take to address its shortcomings? And what can other cities learn from the Los Angeles rail experience?

THE NEED TO WEAR SHADES

In the 1970s, Mayor Tom Bradley envisioned a comprehensive network of heavy rail subways linking most major corridors and urban centers in the region. But the actual system that rail leaders managed to build contained only a relatively small heavy rail line and a larger network of less-costly light rail lines. To make matters worse, the heavy rail line never fully served the one corridor it should have from the beginning: Wilshire Boulevard. The light rail network had more success but still failed to reach Santa Monica and West Hollywood, connect through downtown Los Angeles, or serve the Crenshaw corridor. As the history of the system shows, fiscal and political challenges prevented rail leaders from building some of these critical lines, resulting in the current scaled-back, hybrid rail transit system.

In the coming decades, however, Los Angeles transit officials stand poised to correct some of these deficiencies. The passage of Measure R by an overwhelming two-thirds majority in 2008 provided the seed money and political support needed to build crucial missing links. Most prominently, with Waxman's tunneling ban rescinded, plans are under way to extend the subway west along Wilshire to Fairfax and Century City, with an eventual destination of Westwood, near the UCLA campus. A potential privately financed toll road tunnel to the San Fernando Valley may create an opportunity to fund and site rail transit alongside paying private vehicles, providing an innovative way to deliver rail service to the jobs and housing center on the other side of the Santa Monica Mountains.

Measure R also benefited the light rail system, with new lines either completed or in planning or construction. The Expo Line opened in 2012 from downtown to Culver City, with a second phase under construction to Santa Monica made possible by Measure R. In addition, the MTA approved a

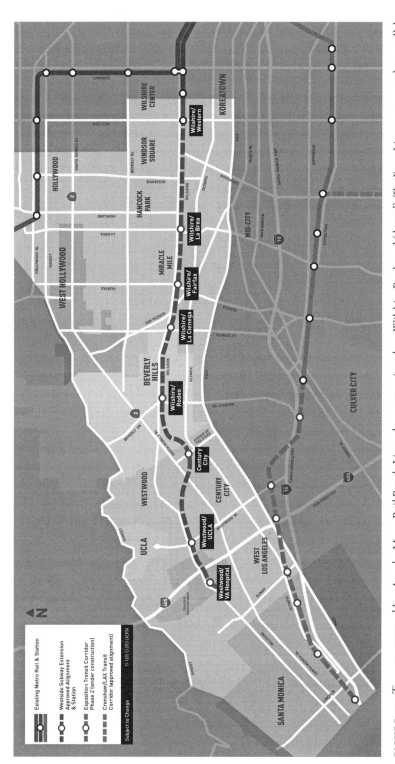

FIGURE 27. The 2013 proposed Los Angeles Metro Rail Purple Line subway extension along Wilshire Boulevard (dotted). The Expo Line runs somewhat parallel to the south. (Courtesy of the Los Angeles County Metropolitan Transportation Authority Research Library and Archive. Reprinted with permission.)

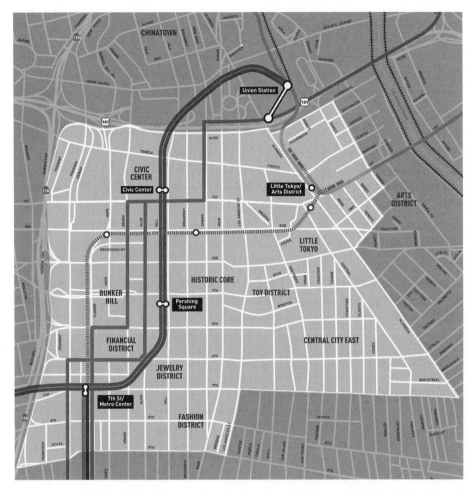

FIGURE 28. The 2012 proposed light rail regional connector through downtown Los Angeles (dotted). The line will connect the Blue and Gold lines from the Seventh Street/Metro Center to the Little Tokyo/Arts District stations for a "one-seat" connection. It will also provide additional rail service for downtown, presently served by the heavy rail subway (detailed here in bold lines). (Courtesy of the Los Angeles County Metropolitan Transportation Authority Research Library and Archive. Reprinted with permission.)

route for the $1.367 billion, 1.9-mile underground downtown regional connector. The line will provide a seamless light rail connection to the Expo, Gold, and Blue lines that converge downtown, boosting ridership on all lines and providing more transit stops in the dense downtown area.[5] The agency hopes to begin construction in 2014, with an opening in 2019. Downtown property owners also voted in 2012 to fund a surface-level streetcar system to provide rail access around the commercial core. And while not rail, a four-mile extension of the San Fernando Valley's successful bus rapid transit Orange Line to Chatsworth opened in 2012, as discussed previously.

Perhaps the most significant light rail line to be built with Measure R funds, however, is the 8.5-mile Crenshaw line, a $1.7 billion project that will connect the Expo Line to the Green Line near Los Angeles International Airport (LAX).[6] The advantages of the line are apparent from looking at a map of the current rail network (see fig. 1): it will make the existing system into a true grid by providing a missing north-south axis to parallel the Blue Line farther east. In terms of ridership, Crenshaw Boulevard represents the second-most traveled corridor in Southern California, after Wilshire Boulevard.[7] The Crenshaw buses are already some of the busiest in the county, with 35,000 riders per day. Officials therefore project that the rail line will garner at least 43,000 boarding per day, boost ridership on other light rail lines that connect to it, and provide opportunities for new development along the route. The Crenshaw line will also travel close to LAX near the Green Line terminus, offering rail planners another opportunity to connect light rail to the airport.[8] The MTA hopes the line will open in late 2018.

Overall, these new lines will provide a significant boost to ridership and finally complete the system that Mayor Tom Bradley and others originally envisioned. But finding the money to operate and construct these lines will be challenging. Local rail advocates have responded by taking on a national leadership role in spearheading creative funding efforts. For example, in 2010 Denny Zane, one of the architects of Measure R, helped develop a concept to speed up the rail-building process through low- or no-interest federal loans on future Measure R revenues. Originally called the 30/10 plan (to build thirty years' worth of Measure R projects in ten years), the model gained national traction among leaders of other cities with local transit revenue. It became known as "America Fast Forward," and Congress passed legislation in 2012 to expand funding and eligibility for a transportation loan program. Zane also continues to advocate nationally for a new class of tax credit bonds to finance more rail construction.

Despite the push for federal assistance, more transit funding will have to come from local sources in the coming years, particularly if the federal government continues to reduce its support for urban rail. Recognizing these trends, Zane and other advocates have begun exploring the possibility of a state ballot initiative to lower the voter-approval threshold for local transit-related tax measures from the current two-thirds to 55 percent. The need for this lower threshold became clear in 2012 when Los Angeles County voters failed to

FIGURE 29. The 2012 proposed Crenshaw light rail line in the Los Angeles Metro Rail system from the Aviation/LAX to Expo/Crenshaw stations. The Expo Line and the Green Line run roughly perpendicular to the north and south of the line. (Courtesy of the Los Angeles County Metropolitan Transportation Authority Research Library and Archive. Reprinted with permission.)

pass Measure J, an initiative to extend the Measure R sales tax an additional thirty years beyond its current sunset date. Even though Measure J achieved a remarkable 66 percent approval, it fell about 15,000 votes short of the two-thirds threshold.[9] New legislation pending in the state legislature, which as of 2013 had a two-thirds majority of Democrats likely supporting it, would place this proposal before the voters.

Rail advocates will also look to other local funding sources, such as increased real estate transfer taxes, tax-increment financing (where local governments borrow against future increases in property tax stimulated by rail investments), and benefit assessment districts (where property owners vote to fund transit improvements in their vicinity via assessments on their property tax bills). These local measures could present innovative means to capitalize on the private benefits bestowed upon property owners from rail transit. Ultimately, too, they may help regions like Los Angeles become less dependent on the whims of the federal government when it comes to funding transit projects.

THE STORM CLOUDS

Despite the positive developments, history indicates that rail proponents will continue to face significant challenges. As happened to the grand rail plans of the early Metro Rail days, new rail lines are likely to take years to plan and build and to incur far higher costs than projected. The Wilshire subway extension, for example, is now not scheduled to reach Westwood until 2036, and possibly later given the inaccuracy of past predictions. The Expo line connection to Santa Monica will now open in 2015 or 2016, years after the original 2012 estimate at the time of groundbreaking. The delays and higher costs will probably force the postponement or cancellation of other important rail lines in unserved corridors. For example, the West Hollywood area, despite its heavily urbanized and generally walkable layout, has been largely left out of rail transit plans and may not receive service for decades to come.

Voter backlash, at some point, is inevitable. While the public tends not to pay attention to the planning process, the construction phase usually leads to relentlessly bad headlines. Construction almost always results in accidents and mishaps, such as the Hollywood sinkhole and Hollywood Freeway tunnel fires. The disruption to businesses will also engender resentment and negative stories. In addition, the delays and higher price tags will embolden critics, particularly during economic downturns. As occurred during the 1990s in Los Angeles, these recessions often lead to heightened scrutiny on public officials and their management of public funds. An ensuing voter revolt could slow rail construction beyond even the current distant projections.

As in the past, rail corridors that should not receive priority funding will likely manage to secure rail service. An extension of the Pasadena Gold Line to the suburban bedroom communities of the San Gabriel Valley fits this description. Groundbreaking took place on the $735 million, 11.5-mile Foothill Gold Line extension east from Pasadena to Azusa in 2010.[10] Like the original Pasadena extension, this line has tremendous political support but lacks merit compared to other corridors. Service to these suburban communities largely via a freeway median should not come before rail to places like West Hollywood that have far more people and opportunities for station-area development. But local leaders seem to approve these politically motivated lines as simply the price the region has to pay to secure consensus for more effective rail transit elsewhere.

SOLUTIONS

What can Angelenos do to avoid these negative outcomes? They can start by ensuring better rail route selection. Residents should insist that no public money be spent on rail or fixed-guideway transit unless the proposed corridor either already has a minimum level of population or job density (or other factors to generate sufficient ridership) or has the land use, infrastructure, and financial plans in place to enable the needed density and ridership. As Friends4Expo demonstrated, voters can organize in favor of effective rail lines to counter opponents of good ones and proponents of bad ones. At the least, they can educate themselves about and hold accountable the elected leaders who champion ineffective rail lines or hold regional rail hostage to their preferred projects.

Improving rail planning and construction processes will require more fundamental changes to laws and regulations. If rail proponents seek federal dollars for a rail line, the United States requires a host of analysis and justification, often taking years to produce. National and state environment laws, as well as California Public Utilities Commission jurisdiction over intersections, also require extensive analysis of the likely impacts of a rail system and implementation of feasible mitigation measures. Efforts to expedite the planning process will have to involve reform of these laws and regulations. But proponents should tread carefully: In many instances, these requirements have improved planning by involving community members and forcing decision-makers to consider sometimes more effective and less costly alternatives. But in other cases, these laws have enabled small opposition groups to wield litigation threats to exact unfortunate concessions. Rail advocates should therefore undertake a careful review of which planning processes tend to improve ridership and cost-effectiveness, among other outcomes, and which are likely to lead to wasted time and resources. Based on those assessments, they can offer recommendations for reform to federal and state policy makers.

Rail leaders can improve the construction process through regulatory changes and better oversight. As Richard Stanger, rail development director for the Los Angeles County Transportation Commission, commented, "The biggest obstacle throughout my career to efficient rail is the traffic engineer."[11] According to Stanger, traffic engineers and the desire to accommodate private vehicles over rail have unnecessarily slowed trains and increased construction costs. For example, light rail trains without traffic signal priority over vehicles have to stop at red lights, while cities exact costly concessions from rail budgets for street widening and traffic mitigation. The Expo line is a prime example. Its many stops at red lights near the downtown portion of the route add tremendous delays to an already long trip from or to Santa Monica. Finally, elected leaders should exercise better oversight of the construction firms building the rail lines. They should hire public officials who are familiar with construction and can therefore demand reasonable and timely completion of tasks. This oversight may only be possible with improved and enforced campaign finance laws that limit construction firms' contributions to local politicians' campaigns.

Perhaps most important, rail supporters need to ensure better development patterns around existing and proposed rail stations and corridors. The Los Angeles County Metropolitan Transportation Authority (MTA) should insist that cities with rail stations lift restrictions on development within walking distance of stations.[12] The MTA should withhold regional transit funds for local governments that refuse to engage in this process. For communities with station areas in undesirable industrial or blighted areas, the MTA and other rail supporters should work with local leaders to direct public investment to infrastructure and "anchor" projects that catalyze private

FIGURE 30. An example of the transit-oriented development projects that have been built around some subway and rail stations in Los Angeles, 2010. This apartment and retail complex is located at the Wilshire and Vermont subway station. (Photo by author.)

investment and utilize nonmonetary tools, such as assistance with parcel assembly and environmental remediation. Without this investment, Metro Rail supporters will continue to miss opportunities to generate higher ridership and improve station neighborhoods.

THE CHANGING FACE OF LOS ANGELES AND THE AMERICAN CITY

In 1987, author Scott Bottles predicted in his book *Los Angeles and the Automobile:* "It will take astronomical gasoline prices, horrendous traffic congestion, or government fiat to force most people out of their automobiles."[13] But since Mayor Bradley first proposed Metro Rail in Los Angeles in 1973, the American city, including Los Angeles, has evolved both physically and culturally. While the region can expect to see more suburban, car-oriented development at the fringes, an increasing segment of homebuyers is demanding more transit-oriented housing and neighborhoods in the urban core. Nationally, as market surveys and government studies attest, development in America's downtowns has been increasing steadily. The trend has been particularly noticeable in Los Angeles, where demand for urban-style apartments and housing has grown significantly in recent years.[14] This demand, and the resulting effort to meet it, have already begun changing the character of Los Angeles, adding vibrant new walkable neighborhoods to the cityscape, from Long Beach to Pasadena to Koreatown.

Rail transit is central to this urban-oriented lifestyle. If the trends continue, which seems likely given the emergence of younger generations embracing urban connectedness and the wave of retired baby boomers moving back to the city, Metro Rail may yet be ahead of the curve. Rail planners and motivated residents therefore have extra incentive to improve the existing system and ensure that new rail lines are built effectively.

Metro Rail is now a permanent part of the Los Angeles landscape and is poised to grow. In the not too distant future, the rail system will likely reach a tipping point where it becomes indispensable to a dominant segment of Angelenos. When that moment occurs, as has happened in regions like greater Washington, D.C., and the San Francisco Bay Area, rail leaders will have an easier time securing public involvement and support. Perhaps in the coming decades, the city that once showed the world the joys of the auto-oriented life will be equally known as a twenty-first-century railtown.

NOTES

First epigraph, page xxi: Juan Bandini, "A Statistical Description of Alta California," in Rose Marie Beebe and Robert M. Senkewicz, eds., *Lands of Promise and Despair: Chronicles of Early California, 1535–1846* (Berkeley, Calif.: Heyday Books, 2001), 378.

INTRODUCTION

1. Interview with Bevan Dufty by the author, December 17, 2012, San Francisco.

2. Interview with Henry Waxman by the author, April 13, 2009, by telephone.

3. Eric Berkowitz, "The Subway Mayor: How a Bus-Only Politician—and a Car-Obsessed City—Are Learning to Love the Uunderground," *Los Angeles Weekly,* August 18, 2005; available at www.laweekly.com/news/features/the-subway-mayor/349/?page=1 (accessed June 19, 2013).

4. Rich Connell, "Metro Rail Supporters Try to Heal Rift," *Los Angeles Times,* August 28, 1985, B-1.

5. Rich Connell, "House Compromise Clears Way for Metro Rail Funds," *Los Angeles Times,* September 12, 1985, 1.

6. See Brian D. Taylor, Eugene J. Kim, and John E. Gahbauer, "The Thin Red Line: A Case Study of Political Influence on Transportation Planning Practice," *Journal of Planning Education and Research* 29, no. 2 (2009): 185–186.

7. John R. Meyer, John F. Kain, and Martin Wohl, *The Urban Transportation Problem* (Cambridge, Mass.: Harvard University Press, 1965).

8. Perhaps the most extreme of these critics was Jonathan Richmond, who wrote a book seeking to explain the "bizarre decision . . . to construct a comprehensive rail passenger system in an environment where it appears incapable of providing real benefits." He labeled support for rail as "mythical" or "fantasy" thinking and analyzed the psychological reasons why leaders supported so obviously (to him) a bad transit policy. Among his theories were people's need for the "simplicity" and "symbols" of trains, male elected leaders' pasts as adolescent boys obsessed with toy trains (which had some grounding in truth in the case of Los Angeles County supervisor

Baxter Ward), and the similarity of trains to sex objects. See Richmond, *Transport of Delight: The Mythical Conception of Rail Transit in Los Angeles* (Akron, Ohio: University of Akron Press, 2005), 218 and 310.

9. See Peter Gordon and Harry W. Richardson, "Transportation and Land Use," chap. 3 in *Smarter Growth: Market-Based Strategies for Land Use Planning in the 21st Century,* ed. R. Holcombe and S. Staley (Westport, Conn.: Greenwood Press, 2001), 6: "Today's interventionists promise that the specifics of smart growth plans will be conjured up and wisely implemented by the powers that be. They will specify minimum and maximum allowable densities for various locations plus a raft of other specifications, asserting repeatedly that any departures from these standards would be (by definition) 'wasteful.'"

10. See Ryan Snyder and Brian D. Taylor, "MTA on Wrong Road with Rail-Line Focus: Transfer Transit Funding to Buses to Provide Better, Cheaper Service," *Los Angeles Daily News,* January 14, 1998. They argued that Los Angeles was too low density for rail and that bus-only lanes and other low-cost transit options would be better for everyone.

11. Boris Pushkarev and Jeffrey Zupan, in *Urban Rail in America: An Exploration of Criteria for Fixed-Guideway Transit* (Washington, D.C.: Urban Mass Transportation Administration, U.S. Department of Transportation, 1980), proposed specific ratios for the density needed to support rail adequately. Brian Taylor, Eugene Kim, and John Gahbauer, in "The Thin Red Line," 185, summarized the criteria broadly as consisting of traffic congestion, high parking costs, high-density development, and concentrated jobs and housing. They also advocated that rail proponents should focus on heavily traveled transit corridors. Robert Cervero used a qualitative approach, noting that successful "transit metropolises" like Singapore and Copenhagen have a "tight 'hand in glove' fit between their transit services and settlement patterns"; see Cervero, *The Transit Metropolis: A Global Inquiry* (Washington, D.C.: Island Press, 1998), xi.

12. For example, residents living near transit stations are roughly five times more likely to commute by transit than the average resident in the same city, according to Hollie M. Lund, Robert Cervero, and Richard W. Wilson, "Travel Characteristics of Transit-Oriented Development in California," CalTrans Transportation Grant, January 2004, iii (available at *www.bart.gov/docs/planning/travel_of_tod.pdf* [*accessed June 19, 2013*]).

13. Erick Guerra and Robert Cervero, "Transit and the 'D' Word," *ACCESS: The Magazine of UCTC [University of California Transportation Center],* no. 40 (Spring 2012): 4–5; available at www.uctc.net/access/40/access40.pdf (accessed June 19, 2013).

14. The average urban American resident in 2005 had a smaller carbon footprint (2.24 metric tons per year) than the average American (2.60 metric tons), primarily as a result of less car travel and energy use. See Marilyn A. Brown, Frank Southworth, and Andrea Sarzynski, "Shrinking the Carbon Footprint of Metropolitan America," Brookings Institution, May 29, 2008, 3.

15. See Taylor, Kim, and Gahbauer, "Thin Red Line," 177.

16. Melvin M. Webber, "The BART Experience: What Have We Learned?" Institute of Urban and Regional Development and Institute of Transportation Studies, University of California, Berkeley, Monograph No. 26, October 1976, 35; available at www.nationalaffairs.com/public_interest/detail/the-bart-experience-what-have-we-learned (accessed June 19, 2013). By the mid-1970s, transit experts were well aware of the shortcoming of the San Francisco Bay Area Rapid Transit (BART) system—the first modern subway since the 1920s. A few years after opening, BART attracted only half of the projected ridership and incurred building and operating costs that were 150 and 475 percent higher, respectively, than anticipated.

17. Martin Wachs, "Autos, Transit, and the Sprawl of Los Angeles: The 1920s," *Journal of the American Planning Association* 50 (1984): 297–310; available at www.tandfonline.com/doi/abs/10.1080/01944368408976597#.Ubu8opzDvuc (accessed June 14, 2013).

18. Ibid., 300.

19. See Scott Bottles, *Los Angeles and the Automobile: The Making of the Modern City* (Berkeley: University of California Press, 1987), 13.

20. William Fulton, *The Reluctant Metropolis: The Politics of Urban Growth in Los Angeles* (Baltimore: Johns Hopkins University Press, 2001), 8.

21. Alan Altshuler and David Luberoff, *Mega-Projects: The Changing Politics of Urban Public Investment* (Washington, D.C.: Brookings Institution Press, 2003), 178.

22. Between 1919 and 1929, automobile registration in Los Angeles County surged from 141,000 to 777,000 (a 550 percent increase), and the ratio of people to cars dropped from nine-to-one to three-to-one during that time. See Wachs, "Autos, Transit, and the Sprawl of Los Angeles," 308. According to Bottles (*Los Angeles and the Automobile,* 211), with the decentralization allowed by the automobile, city planners believed that "no longer would urban dwellers have to suffer from the crowded and unhealthful conditions of the walking city."

23. Residents also had become exasperated by the high cost and poor service. "People in Los Angeles during the first three decades of the century constantly complained about the quality of rail transit. From their point of view the railways sought to benefit at the public's expense" (Bottles, Los Angeles and the Automobile, 4). Angelenos ultimately voted down a rapid transit proposal in 1926 that included elevated rail lines. See Wachs, "Autos, Transit, and the Sprawl of Los Angeles," 23.

24. Altshuler and Luberoff, *Mega-Projects,* 178.

25. "In their defense," wrote Robert M. Fogelson of the municipal leaders, "official inaction, however misguided, corresponded with popular opinion" (*The Fragmented Metropolis: Los Angeles, 1850–1930* [Berkeley: University of California Press, 1993], 185).

26. Martin Wachs, "Learning from Los Angeles: Transport, Urban Form, and Air Quality," Seventh Smeed Memorial Lecture at University College, London; published as Working Paper No. 166, University of California Transportation Center, May 1993, 8; available at www.uctc.net/papers/166.pdf (*accessed June 14, 2013*).

27. Mark Garrett, "The Struggle for Transit Justice: Race, Space, and Social Equity in Los Angeles," Ph.D. diss., University of California, Los Angeles, 2006, 385–90.

28. William Fulton (*Reluctant Metropolis,* 2) recalled driving 130 miles from the western to the eastern end of the greater Los Angeles metropolitan region in the 1990s: "I traveled through suburb after suburb, past shopping center after shopping center and tract after tract," he wrote about his half-day drive from Ventura to Moreno Valley. "The suburban monotony was so continuous that it was numbing."

29. By 2011, a Texas Transportation Institute study of U.S. traffic documented that Los Angeles metropolitan drivers spent 61 hours per year stuck in traffic, with a total loss of approximately 501 million hours and more than 219 million gallons of fuel, at a cost to the region of almost $11 billion per year. See David Schrank, Bill Eisele, and Tim Lomax, "Urban Mobility Report 2012," Texas A&M Transportation Institute, December 2012, 28; available at http://mobility.tamu.edu/ums /report (accessed May 8, 2013).

30. Bottles, *Los Angeles and the Automobile,* 18.

31. Garrett, "Struggle for Transit Justice," 385.

32. In the Bay Area, first San Mateo and then Marin County dropped out, leaving San Francisco, Alameda, and Contra Costa Counties. See Stephen Zwerling, *Mass Transit and the Politics of Technology: A Study of BART and the San Francisco Bay Area* (New York: Praeger, 1974), 38. In Atlanta, Cobb County dropped out, while Clayton and Gwinnett County voters ultimately rejected the Atlanta rail proposal, leaving Fulton and DeKalb Counties. See Clarence N. Stone, *Regime Politics: Governing Atlanta 1946–1988* (Lawrence: University Press of Kansas, 1989), 100; and Doug Monroe, "Where It All Went Wrong," *Atlanta Magazine,* August 1, 2012 (available at www.atlantamagazine.com/features/story.aspx?ID=1742459 [accessed June 19, 2013]).

33. Jack Schneider, "Escape From Los Angeles: White Flight from Los Angeles and Its Schools, 1960–1980," *Journal of Urban History* 34 (2008): 997; available at http://juh.sagepub.com/cgi/content/abstract/34/6/995 (accessed June 19, 2013).

34. In a 2011 National Association of Realtors survey, 47 percent preferred to live in a city (19%) or in a suburban neighborhood with a mix of houses, shops, and businesses (28%). Only 12 percent preferred a house-only suburban neighborhood, while 58 percent overall preferred neighborhoods with a mix of houses, stores, and businesses within walking distance. See "2011 Community Preference Survey," National Association of Realtors, March 2011; available at www.realtor.org /reports/2011-community-preference-survey (accessed December 21, 2012).

CHAPTER ONE

1. Interview with Ray Remy by author, February 3, 2006, South Pasadena, California.

2. Carl Greenberg, "Bradley Has Word for Opponent: 'Dirty,'" *Los Angeles Times,* May 24, 1973, D1.

3. Thomas Bradley, "The Impossible Dream: Oral History Transcript," Oral History Collection, Dept. of Special Collections, University Library, University of California, Los Angeles, 1984, 198–199 (interviewed by Bernard Galm, 1978 and 1979); available at http://archive.org/details/impossibledreamooobrad (accessed June 19, 2013).

4. Remy interview.

5. Interview with Ed Edelman, former Los Angeles county supervisor (1973–1993), by author, December 9, 2004, Los Angeles.

6. U.S. Congress, Office of Technology Assessment, *Assessment of Community Planning for Mass Transit,* vol. 6: *Los Angeles Case Study, Critical History of Transit Planning* (Washington, D.C.: OTA, February 1976), 17; available at www.fas.org/ota/reports/7607.pdf (accessed June 19, 2013).

7. Nora Zamichow, "Once-Scorned Red Line Poised to Open New Era Subway," *Los Angeles Times,* January 24, 1993, A1.

8. Bill Boyarsky, "Bradley Proposes Rapid Rail System, Bus Fleet Expansion," *Los Angeles Times,* February 8, 1973, sec. 2, 1.

9. Quoted in Zamichow, "Once-Scorned Red Line Poised to Open New Era Subway," A1.

10. Edelman interview.

11. Quoted in Zamichow, "Once-Scorned Red Line Poised to Open New Era Subway," A1.

12. Presentation by Norman H. Emerson, "Planning a Rapid Transit System for Los Angeles; Merging Political and Technical Issues: A View from the Mayor's Office," 25th Annual Meeting, Transportation Research Forum, October 11, 1974, 2, in Tom Bradley Papers, Dept. of Special Collections, University Library, University of California, Los Angeles (hereafter cited as TBP), Box 828, Folder 8.

13. Doug Shuit, "Bradley Campaigns in Sacramento for LA Transit System," *Los Angeles Times,* June 15, 1973, sec. 1, 3.

14. Starting with the 1964 federal Mass Transit Act and culminating in 1970 legislation that quintupled federal funding levels for transit, transit spending grew faster than almost any other federal budget item in the 1970s. See Alan Altshuler and David Luberoff, *Mega-Projects: The Changing Politics of Urban Public Investment* (Washington, D.C.: Brookings Institution Press, 2003), 182–87.

15. Shuit, "Bradley Campaigns in Sacramento," 3.

16. Matt Barrett, Introduction to the Los Angeles County Metropolitan Transportation Authority, MTA Archives, 2.

17. Ibid., 3.

18. Ray Hebert, "Bradley Opens Drive for Rapid Transit Plan," *Los Angeles Times,* August 6, 1974, sec. 2, 1.

19. Bradley, "Impossible Dream," 199.

20. Hebert, "Bradley Opens Drive for Rapid Transit Plan," 1.

21. Ray Hebert, "Tax Hike for Improving Transit," *Los Angeles Times,* November 3, 1974, H1.

22. Advertising Executive Memorandum, author unknown, April 1976, 3, in TBP, Box 3894, Folder 2.

23. Memorandum to Maury Weiner from Norm Emerson (Marcuse's report included), "Re: Peter Marcuse's draft," May 9, 1974, in TBP, Box 1744, Folder 8.

24. Ibid.

25. Proposition "A" Community Days Speech, October 29–November 2, 14–17, in TBP, Box 828, Folder 8.

26. Ibid., 8.

27. Southern California Rapid Transit District (SCRTD), "Summary Report on Rapid Transit Starter Line Corridor as of July 15, 1975," 1, in TBP, Box 1986, Folder 6.

28. Tom Bradley, "Where Do We Go Now on Rapid Transit?" *Los Angeles Times,* December 20, 1974, sec. 2, 7.

29. Bradley, "Impossible Dream," 204.

30. Remarks by Mayor Tom Bradley before the Assembly Transportation Committee, 3, in TBP, Box 4732, Folder 1.

31. Bradley, "Impossible Dream," 205.

32. Ibid., 202–3.

33. Mitchell Landsberg, "Why Supervisors Let Deadly Problems Slide," *Los Angeles Times,* December 9, 2004, A1.

34. Remy interview.

35. Stacey Klein, "Baxter Ward, L.A. County Supervisor, 1974–80: Newsman, Ex-Supervisor Succumbs to Battle against Lung Cancer," *The Signal,* February 5, 2002; available at www.scvhistory.com/scvhistory/sg020502.htm (accessed June 19, 2013).

36. The 1974–75 SCRTD Annual Report (TBP, Box 2889, Folder 1) mentions this purchase after describing the available rights-of-way from the old Pacific Electric tracks. It states, "The County has purchased eight passenger rail cars [and] is refurbishing them for service" (14). Eventually, the train cars ran on existing tracks to San Diego for a period of time.

37. Edelman interview.

38. Ibid.

39. SCRTD, "Summary Report", 18.

40. Southern California Association of Governments (SCAG) Staff Report, 1–1, in TBP, Box 1986, Folder 8.

41. On the action of the city council, see Letter from Los Angeles City Clerk to Bradley, Hamilton, Ferraro, Braude, June 16, 1975; on the board of supervisors, see Letter from James S. Mize, Executive Officer, Executive Office of the Board of Supervisors, County of Los Angeles, to Tom Bradley, Los Angeles Mayor, June 20, 1975; both in TBP, Box 1986, Folder 8.

42. "Transit Route 60 Miles Long Selected for L.A.," *Los Angeles Times,* July 3, 1975, A12.

43. Ray Hebert, "Region Informs U.S. of Transit Accord," *Los Angeles Times,* July 27, 1975, 3.

44. SCAG Staff Report, 1–1.

45. SCRTD, "Summary Report," 15–18.

46. SCRTD, 1974–75 Annual Report, 5.

47. Remy interview.

48. Letter from John Mansell, Long Beach City Manager, to the Long Beach Mayor and City Council, November 25, 1975, 1, in TBP, Box 1986, Folder 8.

49. Transcript of Meeting Regarding Decision Paper for Transit Development in Los Angeles, November 21, 1975, at 27, in TBP, Box 1986, Folder 9.

50. Ibid.

51. Ibid., 28–29.

52. Mansell letter, 3.

53. "A Program for Transportation Improvements in the Los Angeles Area," presented to William T. Coleman Jr., December 16, 1975, 4–5, in TBP, Box 1986, Folder 8.

54. Draft letter to Mark Pisano from Robert Patricelli, January 1977, in U.S. National Archives and Records Administration (NARA) Accession No. 408–81–7, DOT UMTA UOA-10 (hereafter referred to as DOT), Box 10, Folder "Los Angeles Jan.–Nov. 1977."

55. Letter to Tom Bradley from Baxter Ward, April 29, 1975, 1, in TBP, Box 4731, Folder 12.

56. "Program for Transportation Improvements in the Los Angeles Area," 5–6.

57. Ray Hebert, "Opposition Growing—Rail Rapid Transit: The Doubts Persist," Los Angeles Times, May 23, 1976, sec. 1, 1.

58. Memorandum to Tom Bradley from Norman Emerson, "Status of Sunset Coast Line Proposal and CRA Application for UMTA SLT/Urban Demonstration Funds," March 2, 1976, 2, in TBP, Box 2091, Folder 10.

59. Ibid., 1.

60. Ibid., 2.

61. News Release, Office of Mayor Bradley, "Los Angeles Transit Ideas Gain National Attention," March 29, 1976, 2, in TBP, Box 4730, Folder 13.

62. Ray Hebert, "RTD Gives Initial OK to Put Transit Proposal on Ballot," Los Angeles Times, March 27, 1976, 1.

63. "Committee for Rapid Transit—R & T," in TBP, Box 3894, Folder 2.

64. Schabarum profile, www.armchairgm.com/Pete_Schabarum (accessed 2008).

65. Anonymous interview by author.

66. Joe Mullich, "Turning Softball into Hardball Latest Form of Corporate Insanity," Business First, July 12, 1996; available at www.bizjournals.com/louisville/stories/1996/07/15/smallb3.html (accessed June 19, 2013).

67. Letter to Tom Bradley and City Council from Supervisor Peter F. Schabarum, February 19, 1976, 1–2, in TBP, Box 2091, Folder 10.

68. Letter to the People of Los Angeles County from Supervisor Schabarum, "The Sunset Coast Line: The Great Train Robbery," April 1976, 12, 13, in TBP, Box 3894, Folder 2.

69. Peter Gordon and R. D. Eckert, "Rail Rapid Transit for Southern California: An Expensive Mistake," 1–2, 4, in TBP, Box 3894, Folder 3.

70. Ibid., 1.

71. Ibid., 5–6.

72. Hebert, "Opposition Growing—Rail Rapid Transit: The Doubts Persist," sec. 1, 1.

73. "Ward Assails *Times'* Articles on Rapid Transit," *Los Angeles Times,* May 27, 1976, sec. 1, 1.

74. Ray Hebert, "Rail Transit for L.A. Dead, Ward Says," *Los Angeles Times,* June 10, 1976, sec. 1, 22.

75. "Majority in Poll Favor Transit Plan," *Los Angeles Times,* May 27, 1976, sec. 2, 1.

76. Hebert, "Rail Transit for L.A. Dead," 22.

77. Rich Connell, "I Have Deep Regret and I Groan . . . I Feel Anguish and Remorse," *Los Angeles Times,* January 27, 1988, , sec. 2, 3.

78. Remy interview.

79. Bradley, "Impossible Dream," 203.

80. Letter to Mayor Bradley from Secretary Coleman, December 22, 1976, 2–3, in TBP, Box 4730, Folder 2.

81. Ibid., 2.

82. Ray Hebert, "U.S. Concedes L.A. Transit Needs—But It's Too Late," *Los Angeles Times,* November 5, 1979, sec. 2, 1.

83. News Release, Office of Mayor Tom Bradley, "Los Angeles Receives Millions in Transit Monies, Mayor Says," December 22, 1976, 1, in TBP, Box 2091, Folder 13.

84. Coleman letter to Bradley, 3.

85. Michael Lewyn, "How City Hall Causes Sprawl: A Case Study," *Ecology Law Quarterly* 30 (2003): 189.

86. Altshuler and Luberoff, *Mega-Projects,* 196–197.

87. Ray Hebert, "U.S. Hardens Stand on L.A. Auto Woes," *Los Angeles Times,* May 22, 1977, D1.

88. William McPhillips, "Eight Called, Two Chosen for 'Carter Show,'" *Los Angeles Times,* May 19, 1977, SG1.

89. Kenneth Reich and Don Irwin, "Rail Transit in L.A. Unlikely, President Says," *Los Angeles Times,* May 18, 1977, A3.

90. Ray Hebert, "L.A. Rail Transit Not Ruled Out, Officials Claim," *Los Angeles Times,* May 19, 1977, sec. 1, 1.

91. Letter to Tom Bradley from Brock Adams, June 27, 1977, in DOT, Box 10, Folder "Los Angeles."

92. Memo to Acting Administrator from Dee V. Jacobs, May 20, 1977, in DOT, Box 10, Folder "Los Angeles."

93. News transcript, KNX Radio to RTD, Attn: Mike Barnes, March 15, 1979, 7:54 A.M., in DOT, Box 52, Folder "Los Angeles."

94. Ibid.

95. Memo to Richard Page from Dee V. Jacobs, April 12, 1979, in DOT, Box 52, Folder "Los Angeles."

96. Memo to Gary D. Gayton from Richard H. McManus, undated, in DOT, Box 52, Folder "Los Angeles."

97. Harre Demoro, "Baxter Ward's Choo-Choo," *MT,* September 1978, 87, in Kenneth Hahn Papers, Huntington Library, San Marino, California (hereafter cited as KHP), 3.5.1.3.

98. Mark Garrett, "The Struggle for Transit Justice: Race, Space, and Social Equity in Los Angeles," Ph.D. diss., UCLA, 2006, 453.

99. Memo to Lillian Liburdi from Dee Jacobs, August 27, 1979, in DOT, Box 52, Folder "Los Angeles."

100. Sharon Rosenhause, "Supervisors Back Subway Plan," *Los Angeles Times,* August 15, 1979, sec. 2, 1.

101. Edelman interview.

102. Letter to Lillian Liburdi from Dee Jacobs, August 27, 1979, in DOT, Box 52, Folder "Los Angeles."

103. Hebert, "U.S. Concedes L.A. Transit Needs," 1.

104. Memo to Neil Goldschmidt from Norman Emerson, September 26, 1979, 3, in DOT, Box 52, Folder "Los Angeles."

105. Hebert, "U.S. Concedes L.A. Transit Needs," 1.

106. Ibid.

107. Ibid.

108. "Carter Signs Compromise Oil Windfall Profits Bill," *Los Angeles Times,* April 2, 1980, A2.

109. Sharon Rosenhause, "Funds Granted for L.A. Subway," *Los Angeles Times,* June 5, 1980, B1.

110. Ibid.

CHAPTER TWO

1. John Stodder, "Mas Fukai, R.I.P.," http://johnstodderinexile.wordpress.com/2006/03/07/mas-fukai-rip/ (accessed December 5, 2012).

2. Letter to Pete Schabarum from Kenneth Hahn, August 19, 1980, in KHP 3.5.3.60.

3. "A Survey of Registered Voters in Los Angeles County and Their Attitudes toward Public Transportation Issues," Opinion Research of California, July 26, 1978, 1.1, in KHP 3.5.1.3.

4. Letter to Schabarum from Hahn, August 19, 1980.

5. Ibid.

6. Letter to Governor Edmund G. Brown Jr. from Walter M. Ingalls, August 26, 1976, 1–2, in Ed Edelman Papers, Huntington Library, San Marino, California (hereafter cited as EEP), Box 596, Folder 4.

7. State Senate Committee on Public Utilities, Transportation, and Environment (PUT&E), "Background on AB 1237 (Ingalls)," June 2, 1977, in TBP, Box 3093, Folder 7.

8. California Public Utilities Code, secs. 130254 and 130258.

9. Interview with Marv Holen by author, September 27, 2005, Los Angeles.

10. Letter to Governor Edmund G. Brown Jr. from Walter M. Ingalls, August 26, 1976, 1, in EEP, Box 596, Folder 4.

11. Ray Hebert, "New Agencies to Face Task of Unifying Jumbled Transit Plans," *Los Angeles Times,* December 27, 1976, at C1.

12. Letter to Brown from Ingalls, 1–2.

13. Mark Garrett, "The Struggle for Transit Justice: Race, Space and Social Equity in Los Angeles," Ph.D. diss., UCLA, 2006, 441.

14. Letter to Pete Schabarum from Walter Ingalls, September 26, 1980, in KHP 3.5.3.58.

15. Letter to Jerry Premo from Kenneth Hahn, October 6, 1978, in EEP, Box 596, Folder 1.

16. Letter to Supervisors from Kenneth Hahn, July 13, 1979, in EEP, Box 586, Folder 1.

17. LACTC Special Meeting, Minutes, August 20, 1980, 5, in KHP 6.1.4.2.7.

18. Ray Hebert, "Another Bus Fare Increase Likely Soon, Officials Say," *Los Angeles Times,* January 10, 1980, D8.

19. Sharon Rosenhause, "Hearings on Transit Sales Tax Will Begin," *Los Angeles Times,* July 21, 1980, B3.

20. David Holley, "Glendale, Burbank Rap Transit Sales Tax," *Los Angeles Times,* August 3, 1980, GB1.

21. Letter to Pete Schabarum from Kenneth Hahn, August 19, 1980, 1, in KHP 3.5.3.60.

22. "Proposition A by Kenneth Hahn," December 1990, 1, in KHP 6.1.4.2.20.

23. Remy interview.

24. Interview with Robert Geoghegan by author, August 30, 2005, Santa Monica.

25. Interview with Robert Geoghegan by author, October 19, 2012, by phone.

26. Lettergram to Ed Edelman from Bob Geoghegan, August 4, 1980, 1, in EEP, Box 601, Folder 1.

27. Geoghegan interview, Oct. 19, 2012.

28. Geoghegan interview, Aug. 30, 2005.

29. Geoghegan interview, Oct. 19, 2012.

30. LACTC Special Meeting, Minutes, August 20, 1980, 4, in KHP 6.1.4.2.7.

31. See Felicity Barringer, "The Water Fight That Inspired 'Chinatown,'" *New York Times,* "Green Blog," April 25, 2012; available at http://green.blogs.nytimes.com/2012/04/25/the-water-fight-that-inspired-chinatown/ (accessed December 5, 2012).

32. LACTC Special Meeting minutes, 4.

33. Ibid., 10–11.

34. Ibid., 12.

35. Ibid., 13. According to Geoghegan (Aug. 30, 2005, interview), the LACTC had small-city members like Russ because "they represented cities with wholly independent transit systems to keep the LACTC independent from the RTD."

36. Ibid., 14.

37. Ibid., 15–17.

38. Ibid., 12.

39. Geoghegan interview, Oct. 19, 2012.

40. LACTC Special Meeting minutes, 17.

41. Remy interview.

42. Ibid.

43. Geoghegan interview, Aug. 30, 2005.

44. LACTC Special Meeting minutes, 8.

45. Ibid., 25.

46. Ibid., 26.

47. Wendell Cox, "Present at the Creation: The Los Angeles Rail System," www.publicpurpose.com/ut-larail80.htm (accessed November 8, 2012).

48. Ibid.

49. LACTC Special Meeting minutes, 24.

50. Cox, "Present at the Creation."

51. LACTC Special Meeting minutes, 24.

52. Cox, "Present at the Creation."

53. Ibid.

54. LACTC Special Meeting minutes, 40.

55. Ibid., 44.

56. Ibid., 42.

57. "Proposition A by Kenneth Hahn," 3.

58. Kenneth Hahn, Notes for interview with staff, in KHP 6.1.4.2.9.

59. Telegram to Kenneth Hahn from Dan Wolf, September 22, 1980, 1, in KHP 6.1.4.2.5.

60. Bill Boyarsky, "Bradley Criticized on Tax Hikes for Transit," *Los Angeles Times,* September 9, 1980, 1.

61. Hahn campaign materials, Kenneth Hahn office list, in KHP 6.1.4.2.3.

62. Hahn campaign materials, Newspaper advertisement clipping, in KHP 6.1.4.2.5.

63. Letter to Kenneth Hahn from Bob Bush, "Prop. A Activities," September 19, 1980, 1, in KHP 6.1.4.2.3.

64. Hahn Proposition A campaign materials, in KHP 6.1.4.2.5.

65. Hahn campaign materials, "Groups Supporting Proposition A" memo, 1, in KHP 6.1.4.2.5.

66. Hahn campaign materials, LATAX, Letter to the editor, in KHP 6.1.4.2.5.

67. Hahn campaign materials, "Reduce Bus Fares Now," 3, in KHP 6.1.4.2.3.

68. Letter to Hahn from Bush, 1.

69. Letter to Publishers and Editors in Los Angeles County from Kenneth Hahn, October 21, 1980, 1–2, in KHP 6.1.4.2.3.

70. Letter to Anthony Day from Kenneth Hahn, September 23, 1980, in KHP 6.1.4.2.3.

71. Letter to Tom Johnson from Kenneth Hahn, October 14, 1980, in KHP 6.1.4.2.3.

72. Letter to Franklin Murphy from Kenneth Hahn, October 28, 1980, in KHP 6.1.4.2.3.

73. Editorial, "Transit: Yes on A," *Los Angeles Times,* October 26, 1980, sec. 7, 4.

74. Editorial, "This May Be the Most Important Question You Can Answer," *Los Angeles Herald-Examiner,* October 21, 1980, A14.

75. Editorial, "Vote Yes on Rapid Transit," *Coast Media Newspapers,* October 23, 1980, in KHP 6.1.4.2.5.

76. Hahn campaign materials, in KHP 6.1.4.2.3.

77. Letter to registered voters of Los Angeles County from Kenneth Hahn, October 29, 1980, 1, in KHP 6.1.4.2.3.

78. Proposition A text, 1980, in KHP 6.1.4.2.3.

79. The San Fernando Valley ended up supporting the proposition by 63.5 percent approval, larger even than the approval within the city of Los Angeles, which tallied 61 percent support. The high approval percentage is remarkable given the suburban nature of the valley. See Los Angeles City Council Resolution draft, November 18, 1980, in TBP, Box 1738, Folder 3.

80. Ibid.

81. Cecilia Rasmussen, "A Subway Saga," *Los Angeles Times,* January 31, 1993, B1.

82. The 1976 *Los Angeles Times* poll showed that only four in ten residents thought they would use a comprehensive rail system ("Majority in Poll Favor Transit Plan," *Los Angeles Times,* May 27, 1976, sec. 2, 1).

83. Hahn notes for interview with staff.

84. Editorial, "Two for Supervisor," *Los Angeles Times,* October 26, 1980, sec. 7, in KHP 6.1.4.2.3.

CHAPTER THREE

1. Los Angeles City Council Resolution draft, November 18, 1980, in TBP, Box 1738, Folder 3.

2. Ray Hebert, "Los Angeles: Two Systems Going, One on Hold," *Mass Transit,* January/February 1986, 14.

3. Letter to Russell Rubley from Kenneth Hahn, October 13, 1981, in KHP 3.5.1.11.

4. Interview with Thomas Rubin by author, November 18, 2008, Los Angeles.

5. Ibid.

6. Letter to Russell Rubley from Ken Hahn, October 7, 1981, in KHP 3.5.1.11.

7. Letter to Thomas Larwin from Ken Hahn, September 30, 1981, in KHP 3.5.1.11.

8. Letter to the Editor from Ken Hahn, *Los Angeles Times,* October 7, 1981, in KHP 3.5.1.11.

9. Letter to Rubley from Hahn, October 7, 1981, 2.

10. Ibid.

11. Jonathan Richmond, *Transport of Delight: The Mythical Conception of Rail Transit in Los Angeles* (Akron, Ohio: University of Akron Press, 2005), 196.

12. Ken Hahn press release, December 15, 1980, in KHP 5.1.4.14.

13. Ray Hebert, "Prop A from Bleak to Bright in L.A.," *Mass Transit,* September 1982, 38, in TBP, Box 697, Folder 6.

14. *Los Angeles County Transportation Commission (LACTC) v. George U. Richmond,* 31 Cal. 3d 197 (1982), 200.

15. Letter to Ed Edelman from Bob Geoghegan, December 15, 1980, in EEP, Box 593, Folder 3.

16. Letter to Rose Bird from Ken Hahn, July 8, 1981, in KHP 3.5.3.12.

17. Leo C. Wolinksy, "Decision May Be Near on County Rail System," *Los Angeles Times,* March 22, 1982, C1.

18. Ibid.

19. Letter to Edelman from Geoghegan, December 15, 1980.

20. Los Angeles County Transportation Commission, Minutes from December 16, 1981, meeting, 2; available at http://boardarchives.metro.net/PredecessorAgencies/LACTC%20Box%2001/LACTC00107.pdf (accessed June 16, 2013).

21. Los Angeles County Transportation Commission, Minutes from March 24, 1982, meeting, 2; available at http://boardarchives.metro.net/PredecessorAgencies/LACTC%20Box%2001/LACTC00275.pdf (accessed June 16, 2013).

22. Wolinksy, "Decision May Be Near on County Rail System," C1.

23. Ibid., sec. 2, 1.

24. Ibid., C1.

25. Holen interview.

26. Lettergram to Ed Edelman from Bob Geoghegan, March 23, 1982, in EEP, Box 628, Folder 4.

27. Ken Hahn, press release, November 17, 1980, in KHP 6.1.4.2.9.

28. Letter to Edelman from Geoghegan, December 15, 1980.

29. Lettergram to Edelman from Geoghegan, March 23, 1982.

30. Wolinksy, "Decision May Be Near on County Rail System," sec. 2, 1.

31. Letter to Edelman from Geoghegan, December 15, 1980.

32. Letter to Anthony Day from Ed Edelman, October 19, 1981, in EEP, Box 628, Folder 4.

33. Wolinksy, "Decision May Be Near on County Rail System," C1 and sec. 2, 1.

34. Lettergram to Edelman from Geoghegan, March 23, 1982, 2.

35. Ibid.

36. Wolinksy, "Decision May Be Near on County Rail System," sec. 2, 1.

37. LACTC, Transcript of commission meeting, March 24, 1982, 8–9; available at http://boardarchives.metro.net/PredecessorAgencies/LACTC%20Box%2001/LACTC00275.pdf (accessed December 21, 2012).

38. Interview with Richard Stanger by author, November 16, 2012, by telephone.

39. Leo C. Wolinksy, "Planning of Streetcar Line to Start," *Los Angeles Times,* March 25, 1982, sec. 2, 1.

40. Los Angeles Transportation Commission minutes, March 24, 1982, 2.

41. Wolinksy, "Planning of Streetcar Line to Start," sec. 2, 1.

42. *LACTC v. George U. Richmond,* 200.

43. The controversial 1982 decision relied on a narrow interpretation of Proposition 13 in order to exempt the LACTC from its requirements. The California Supreme Court at the time was notable for its left-leaning decisions, and the justices were unwilling to interpret broadly the intent of the decidedly antigovernment and antitax Proposition 13. In 1996, in response to the *Richmond* decision, the same antitax groups behind Proposition 13 got the voters to approve Proposition 218 to close the loophole they believed the California Supreme Court created with this decision. Prior to that vote, in 1995, the state Supreme Court had essentially overruled the *Richmond* decision, which meant future sales tax measures would require two-thirds majorities. See John S. Throckmorton, "What Is a Property-Related Fee?" *Hastings Law Journal* 48 (1997): 1059.

44. Letter to Rose Bird from Kenneth Hahn, May 13, 1982, in KHP 3.5.1.10.

45. LACTC News, June 25, 1982, 1, in TBP, Box 1740, Folder 1.

46. Letter to James Foy from Kenneth Hahn, May 14, 1982, in KHP 3.5.1.10.

47. Wolinksy, "Planning of Streetcar Line to Start," sec. 2, 8.

48. Letter to Ed Edelman from Robert Geoghegan, June 27, 1984, in EEP, Box 628, Folder 2.

49. Letter to Ernie Kell from Kenneth Hahn, September 20, 1984, 1, in KHP 6.1.4.2.7.

50. Letter to Kenneth Hahn from Ernie Kell, September 26, 1984, in KHP 3.5.1.14.

51. The LACTC's Richard Stanger believed that the initial estimates were unduly low because they budgeted for the most inexpensive system possible on the corridor. "The idea at the time was that Prop A was questionable—it had just barely passed and it was unclear whether the Supreme Court would approve it," Stanger said. The only funds assured to the LACTC for rail came from a relatively small portion of the state gas tax. "So the initial directive to the consultant was that we've got to make this project really as inexpensive as we can, because if Prop A doesn't go through, we're still committed to building this thing" (Stanger interview).

52. Letter to Kell from Hahn, September 20, 1984.

53. Letter to Edelman from Geoghegan, June 27, 1984.

54. City of Long Beach news release, March 18, 1985, in EEP, Box 628, Folder 1.

55. Los Angeles County Transportation Commission news release, March 27, 1985, in KHP 3.5.1.15.

56. Letter to Kenneth Hahn from Jacki Bacharach, May 22, 1985, in KHP 3.5.1.15.

57. Victor Merina, "County Approves LA–Long Beach Light Rail System," *Los Angeles Times,* March 28, 1985, sec. 2, 1.

58. LACTC, "Long Beach–Los Angeles Rail Transit Groundbreaking," October 31, 1985, in TBP, Box 696, Folder 2.

59. Jonathan Richmond, "Light Rail: The Dream vs. Reality," *Long Beach Press-Telegram,* January 24, 1986, in TBP, Collection 293, Box 696, Folder 1.

60. Rich Connell, "Question of Ridership: Light Rails—Visionary or a Step Back?" *Los Angeles Times,* October 20, 1985, A1.

61. Interview with Jeff Gates by author, February 23, 2008, by telephone.

62. Jeff Gates, "Essay 1983," at www.outtacontext.com/iop/essay-1983.html (accessed June 19, 2013).

63. Joseph DiMento, Jace Baker, Robert Detlefson, Dru Van Hengel, Dean Hestermann, and Brenda Nordenstam, "Court Intervention, the Consent Decree, and the Century Freeway," Working Paper, University of California Transportation Center, University of California, Berkeley, September 1991, II-16; available at www.uctc.net/papers/381.pdf (accessed June 19, 2013).

64. Ibid.

65. Ibid., 16–22.

66. Hebert, "Los Angeles: Two Systems Going, One on Hold," 18.

67. DiMento et al., "Court Intervention, the Consent Decree, and the Century Freeway," II-23.

68. Gates interview.

69. Ibid.

70. The LACTC's Richard Stanger noted that "in theory" you can replace a busway with rail, but in practice "no one has ever done it" (Stanger interview).

71. Letter to Kenneth Hahn from E. A. Center, March 14, 1983; Letter to Kenneth Hahn from George Barratt, March 3, 1983; both in KHP 3.5.20.2.

72. Letter to Ed Edelman from Charles K. Armstrong, June 6, 1984, in EEP, Box 615, Folder 7.

73. Letter to Carl H. Schiermeyer from Kenneth Hahn, January 14, 1983, in KHP 3.5.1.20.2.

74. Letter to Kenneth Hahn from Mervyn Dymally, March 25, 1983, in KHP 3.5.20.2.

75. Letter to Robert Geoghegan from Glenn Anderson, May 26, 1984, in EEP, Box 615, Folder 7.

76. Lettergram to Ed Edelman from Robert Geoghegan, October 28, 1983, in EEP, Box 594, Folder 4.

77. Los Angeles Transportation Commission, Minutes from June 13, 1984, meeting, 4; available at http://boardarchives.metro.net/PredecessorAgencies/LACTC%20Box%2001/LACTC00193.pdf (accessed June 19, 2013).

78. Ibid., 5.

79. Ibid.

80. Stanger interview.

81. Los Angeles Transportation Commission minutes, June 13, 1984, 25.

82. Hebert, "Los Angeles: Two Systems Going, One on Hold," 18.

83. Stanger interview.

84. Geoghegan interview, Aug. 30, 2005.

85. Ibid.

86. Remy interview.

87. Stanger interview.

88. Ibid.

89. Ibid.

90. Remy interview.

91. Interview with Jacki Bacharach by author, March 13, 2009, Los Angeles.

92. Geoghegan interview, Aug. 30, 2005.

93. Los Angeles Transportation Commission, Minutes from December 17, 1986, meeting, 8; available at http://boardarchives.metro.net/PredecessorAgencies /LACTC%20Box%2001/LACTC00231.pdf (accessed June 19, 2013).

94. Geoghegan interview, Aug. 30, 2005.

95. Remy interview.

96. Rail Construction Corporation, LACTC, "The Metro Green Line," 1992, in TBP, Box 84, Folder 7.

97. Calvin S. Hamilton, "What Can We Learn from Los Angeles?" *Journal of the American Planning Association,* December 1986, 500.

98. Calvin S. Hamilton, "Seven Decades of Planning and Development in the Los Angeles Region," interviewed by Edward A. Holden, Oral History Collection, Dept. of Special Collections, University Library, University of California, Los Angeles, 1995, 131.

99. Letter to Bill Boyarsky, *Los Angeles Times,* from Peter Broy, Senior City Planner, August 18, 1982, 1, in TBP, Box 3072, Folder 3.

100. Department of City Planning, Los Angeles, "Concept Los Angeles: The Concept for the Los Angeles General Plan," January 1970, 13; available at: www. planetizen.com/files/los-angeles-centers-plan.pdf (accessed June 6, 2013).

101. Holen interview.

102. Janet Clayton, "Bradley Calls for a '2-Way' Start on Metro Rail Project," *Los Angeles Times,* August 20, 1983, sec. 2, 5.

103. Interview with Mike Woo by author, November 5, 2007, West Hollywood.

104. Interview with Dave Roberti by author, November 20, 2008, Los Angeles.

105. Woo interview.

106. Ibid.

107. Ray Hebert, "U.S. Concedes L.A. Transit Needs—But It's Too Late," *Los Angeles Times,* November 5, 1979, sec. 2, 1.

108. For example, when plans came up to design a station at Fairfax and Wilshire below the Page Museum at the La Brea Tar Pits, Holen got a commitment from UMTA for $10 million to make the proposed subway station into a paleontological exhibit. Holen believed the exhibit would be "like the Louvre" in Paris. "I was so excited," he recalled at the prospect of the exhibit (Holen interview).

109. Letter to Richard Page from Jack Gilstrap, November 17, 1978, in DOT, Box 52, Folder "Los Angeles."

110. Ibid.

111. Roberti interview.

112. Memo to Neil Goldschmidt from Norman Emerson, September 26, 1979, in DOT, Box 52, Folder "Los Angeles."

113. Ibid.

114. Ray Hebert, "Rapid Transit District Gets Unwelcome County Partner," Los Angeles Times, May 5, 1980, C1.

115. RTD Draft Alternatives Analysis (1980), in Mark Garrett, "The Struggle for Transit Justice: Race, Space, and Social Equity in Los Angeles," Ph.D. diss., UCLA, 2006, 456.

116. "RTD Panel Urges Subway along Wilshire Route," Los Angeles Times, September 21, 1979, sec. 2, 4.

117. Hamilton, "Seven Decades of Planning and Development in the Los Angeles Region," 162.

118. William B. Fulton, The Reluctant Metropolis: The Politics of Urban Growth in Los Angeles (Baltimore: Johns Hopkins University Press, 2001), 51–55.

119. Interview with Zev Yaroslavsky by author, November 19, 2008, Los Angeles.

120. Fulton, Reluctant Metropolis, 65.

CHAPTER FOUR

1. Ita Hernandez, "Fairfax Disaster Recalls Heyday of Los Angeles Oil Drilling Boom," Los Angeles Times, March 26, 1985, sec. 1, 3.

2. Douglas H. Hamilton and Richard L. Meehan, "Explosion and Other Gas Ventings at the Fairfax District, Los Angeles," Paper presented at Meeting of the Pacific Section Convention American Association Petroleum Geologists and Western Regional Meeting of the Society of Petroleum Engineers, Westin Hotel, Long Beach, California; June 20, 2000; abstract available at www.stanford.edu/~meehan /class/ce2942000/press.htm (accessed June 16, 2013).

3. "Los Angeles," in The 1911 Classic Encyclopedia, www.1911encyclopedia.org /Los_Angeles (accessed June 19, 2013).

4. Ry B. Stammer, "Oil Fields Could Spell Trouble," Los Angeles Times, April 2, 1985, sec. 2, 1.

5. Los Angeles City Task Force, "Methane Gas Explosion and Fire in the Fairfax Area," May 31, 1985, 2–3, in TBP, Box 672, Folder 5.

6. Ibid.

7. Richart Fausset, "Experts Dig Into Subway Project," Los Angeles Times, October 15, 2005, B12.

8. Ita Hernandez, "'It Was Like a Cyclone,' Woman Says of Hellish Scene in Midst of Blast," Los Angeles Times, March 27, 1985, sec. 1, 26.

9. Ve Harvey, "Gas Explosion Shatters Fairfax Store; 23 Hurt," Los Angeles Times, March 25, 1985, , sec. 1, 1.

10. Hernandez, "'It Was Like a Cyclone,'" sec. 1, 26.

11. Ibid.

12. Harvey, "Gas Explosion Shatters Fairfax Store," sec. 1, 1.

13. Hernandez, "'It Was Like a Cyclone,'" sec. 1, 26.

14. George Ramos and Steve Harvey, "Gas Explosion Shatters Fairfax Store; 23 Hurt," *Los Angeles Times,* March 25, 1985, A1.

15. George Ramos, "'4-Day Vacation' Ends in Fairfax Blast Area," *Los Angeles Times,* March 29, 1985, sec. 1, 1.

16. Josh Getlin, "What Makes Henry Tick? Private, Persistent, and Powerful, Rep. Waxman Was Networking Long before the Strategy Became Chic," *Los Angeles Times,* April 25, 1990.

17. William B. Fulton, *The Reluctant Metropolis: The Politics of Urban Growth in Los Angeles* (Baltimore: Johns Hopkins University Press, 2001), 46.

18. Rich Connell, "Metro Rail Supporters Try to Heal Rift," *Los Angeles Times,* August 28, 1985, at B-1.

19. Dufty interview.

20. Waxman interview.

21. Remy interview.

22. Eric Berkowitz, "The Subway Mayor: How a Bus-Only Politician—and a Car-Obsessed City—Are Learning to Love the Underground," *Los Angeles Weekly,* August 18, 2005; available at www.laweekly.com/news/features/the-subway-mayor/349/?page=1 (accessed June 19, 2013).

23. Waxman interview.

24. Ibid.

25. Remy interview.

26. Quoted in Mathis Chazanov, "Methane Gas Pockets May Kill Metro Rail—Waxman," *Los Angeles Times,* June 15, 1985, B2.

27. Victor Merina, "Residents Swipe at Subway Corridor Development Plan," *Los Angeles Times,* August 2, 1985, B2.

28. Roberti interview.

29. Interview with George Takei by author, June 16, 2009, Los Angeles.

30. Letter to Kenneth Hahn from Burke Roche, July 29, 1982, in KHP 3.5.1.20.3.

31. Woo interview.

32. Takei interview.

33. Roberti interview.

34. Bill Boyarsky, "A Subway for the City," *Los Angeles Times,* August 15, 1982, sec. 4, 2.

35. Letter to Bill Boyarsky from Peter Broy, August 18, 1982, 2, in TBP, Box 3072, Folder 3.

36. Memo to Kenneth Hahn from Burke Roche, November 24, 1982, in KHP 3.5.1.20.3.

37. "Mapping L.A.: Central L.A.–Fairfax," *Los Angeles Times* website, citing U.S. Census, Southern California Association of Governments, and Los Angeles

Department of City Planning data; available at: http://projects.latimes.com /mapping-la/neighborhoods/neighborhood/fairfax/ (accessed November 14, 2012).

38. Yaroslavsky interview.

39. Remy interview.

40. Yaroslavsky interview.

41. Waxman interview.

42. Alan Altshuler and David Luberoff, *Mega-Projects: The Changing Politics of Urban Public Investment* (Washington, D.C.: Brookings Institution Press, 2003), 202.

43. Yaroslavsky interview.

44. Chazanov, "Methane Gas Pockets May Kill Metro Rail," B2.

45. Interview with Ronald Lofy by author, November 19, 2008, by telephone.

46. Chazanov, "Methane Gas Pockets May Kill Metro Rail," B2.

47. Letter to Henry Waxman from Byron Ishkanian, June 26, 1985, 1, in EEP, Box 614, Folder 6.

48. Letter to Henry Waxman from James E. Crawley, June 28, 1985, in EEP, Box 614, Folder 6.

49. Roberti interview.

50. Los Angeles City Task Force, "Methane Gas Explosion and Fire in the Fairfax Area," May 31, 1985, in TBP, Box 672, Folder 5.

51. Letter to Henry Waxman from John Dyer, August 23, 1985, in EEP, Box 614, Folder 6.

52. Rich Connell, "Waxman Demands Metro Rail Avoid Methane Zone," *Los Angeles Times,* August 27, 1985, B1.

53. Waxman interview.

54. Ibid.

55. Janet Clayton, "L.A. Subway Cost Estimate Revised Upward $1 Billion," *Los Angeles Times,* April 8, 1983, B1.

56. Janet Clayton, "L.A. Battles for a Share of Transit Funds," *Los Angeles Times,* March 20, 1983, SD3.

57. "$2.35 Billion Houston Rail System Loses," *Los Angeles Times,* June 12, 1983, A13.

58. Mark Garrett, "The Struggle for Transit Justice: Race, Space, and Social Equity in Los Angeles," Ph.D. diss., UCLA, 2006, 494.

59. Cecilia Rasmussen, "A Subway Saga," *Los Angeles Times,* January 31, 1993, B1.

60. Ray Hebert, "Los Angeles: Two Systems Going, One on Hold," *Mass Transit,* January/February 1986, 22.

61. William Trombley and Bill Boyarsky, "U.S. Lacks Funds for Metro Rail," *Los Angeles Times,* February 24, 1984, sec. 1, 1.

62. Garrett, "Struggle for Transit Justice," 516.

63. Zachary M. Schrag, *The Great Society Subway: A History of the Washington Metro* (Baltimore: Johns Hopkins University Press, 2006), 171–79.

64. "A History of BART: History and Facts," www.bart.gov/about/history /index.aspx (accessed November 15, 2012).

65. Dufty interview.

66. Garrett, "Struggle for Transit Justice," 517.

67. "Metro Rail Bill Requires Work to Start at Both Ends of the Line," *Los Angeles Times,* July 9, 1984, C5.

68. Lettergram to Ed Edelman from Robert Geoghegan, January 25, 1985, in EEP, Box 607, Folder 1.

69. Editorial, "Signal to Washington," *Los Angeles Times,* September 13, 1984, sec. 2, 4.

70. Peggy Pagano and Victor Merina, "U.S. Won't Budge on Metro Rail Cuts," *Los Angeles Times,* February 16, 1985, sec. 2, 1.

71. Press release, Ed Edelman, December 20, 1984, in EEP, Box 607, Folder 3.

72. Karen Tumulty, "Stockman Calls L.A. Metro Rail 'Foolish' Waste," *Los Angeles Times,* April 16, 1985, sec. 2, 1.

73. Pagano and Merina, "U.S. Won't Budge on Metro Rail Cuts," sec. 2, 1.

74. Op-Ed article by Henry Waxman, "The Subway Congressman," *L.A. Weekly,* September 23–29, 2005; available at http://waxman.house.gov/sites /waxman.house.gov/files/The_Subway_Congressman.pdf (accessed June 7, 2013).

75. Henry Weinstein, "Funds Announced for People Mover," *Los Angeles Times,* October 8, 1980, E1.

76. Interview with James Seeley by author, December 18, 2008, Washington, D.C.

77. Paul Houston, "Verbal Brawl Erupts over Metro Rail," *Los Angeles Times,* May 2, 1985, B3.

78. Lettergram to Ed Edelman from Robert Geoghegan, July 18, 1985, in EEP, Box 614, Folder 3.

79. Victor Merina, "Start-Up Funds for Metro Rail Gain in House," *Los Angeles Times,* July 19, 1985, B1.

80. Seeley interview.

81. Connell, "Metro Rail Supporters Try to Heal Rift," B1.

82. Remy interview.

83. Dufty interview.

84. Geoghegan interview, Aug. 30, 2005.

85. Berkowitz, "The Subway Mayor."

86. Rich Connell, "House Compromise Clears Way for Metro Rail Funds," *Los Angeles Times,* September 12, 1985, B1.

87. Merina, "Start-Up Funds for Metro Rail Gain in House," B1.

88. Rich Connell, "House Debate on Metro Rail Funds Stalls," *Los Angeles Times,* November 15, 1985, B1.

89. Rich Connell and Victor Merina, "Reagan Signs Bill Containing First Metro Rail Funds," *Los Angeles Times,* December 20, 1985, B2.

90. Rasmussen, "A Subway Saga," B1.

91. Connell and Merina, "Reagan Signs Bill Containing First Metro Rail Funds," Los Angeles Times, December 20, 1985, B2.

92. Ibid.

93. Letter to Kenneth Hahn from Burke Roche, July 9, 1986, in KHP 3.5.1.16.

94. See Brian D. Taylor, Eugene J. Kim, and John E. Gahbauer, "The Thin Red Line: A Case Study of Political Influence on Transportation Planning Practice," *Journal of Planning Education and Research,* 2009, 177. They described the Wilshire corridor as one of the most transit-friendly corridors in the West based on its level of development.

95. Edelman interview.

96. Geoghegan interview, Aug. 30, 2005.

97. Henry A. Waxman, "Why Metro Rail Is Still Unsafe," *Los Angeles Times,* June 1, 1987; available at www.house.gov/waxman/issues/issues_other_metro_rail_press_metro_unsafe_6_1_87.htm (accessed 2008).

98. Berkowitz, "The Subway Mayor."

99. Ibid.

100. D. J. Waldie, "Go West, Young Subway Rider," *Los Angeles Times,* December 5, 2008, B11.

101. Seeley interview.

102. Roberti interview.

103. Dufty interview.

104. Roberti interview.

105. Stanger interview.

106. Takei interview.

107. Roberti interview.

108. Taxpayers Watchdog news release, September 5, 1986, in KHP 3.5.1.16.

109. Tom Bradley, Press release, July 11, 1986, in KHP 3.5.1.16.

110. Rich Connell, "Metro Rail Start Feted in $90,000 Ceremony," *Los Angeles Times,* September 30, 1986, B2.

CHAPTER FIVE

1. Rich Connell, "Metro Rail's Big Day Arrives," *Los Angeles Times,* September 29, 1986, A1.

2. Ted Rohrlich, "Tunnel Project Metro Rail Digs," *Los Angeles Times,* March 22, 1987, A1.

3. Ibid.

4. James Smith, "The Thames Tunnel," in Horace Smith, Esq., ed. *Memoirs, Letters, and Comic Miscellanies in Prose and Verse of the Late James Smith,* vol. 2 (London: Henry Colburn, 1840), 185.

5. Rohrlich, "Tunnel Project Metro Rail Digs," A1.

6. Ted Rohrlich, "Metro Rail Tunneling Connects Past, Future," *Los Angeles Times,* December 14, 1987, A1.

7. Rohrlich, "Tunnel Project Metro Rail Digs," A1.

8. Ibid.

9. Ibid.

10. Rich Connell, "The Road to Mass Transit," *Los Angeles Times,* November 9, 1987, 1.

11. Rohrlich, "Tunnel Project Metro Rail Digs," A1.

12. Ibid.

13. Ibid.

14. Interview with James Okazaki by author, January 26, 2009, Venice, California.

15. Rohrlich, "Tunnel Project Metro Rail Digs," A1.

16. Okazaki interview.

17. Rohrlich, "Tunnel Project Metro Rail Digs," A1.

18. Ibid.

19. Ibid.

20. Ibid.

21. Interview with Ed McSpedon by author, March 14, 2009, Los Angeles.

22. Okazaki interview.

23. McSpedon interview.

24. Ibid.

25. Ibid.

26. Bob Pool, "MTA Tracks Down Artists to Beautify Rail Routes," *Los Angeles Times,* November 27, 1994, B1.

27. McSpedon interview.

28. Ibid.

29. Ibid.

30. Nora Zamichow, "Century Freeway Opening Is a Road Rally," *Los Angeles Times,* October 15, 1993, at A1.

31. McSpedon interview.

32. Ibid.

33. Ibid.

34. Ibid.

35. Ibid.

36. Ibid.

37. Stanger interview.

38. Okazaki interview.

39. McSpedon interview.

40. Scott Harris and Rich Connell, "400-Ton Bridge Being Constructed for Rail Line Falls," *Los Angeles Times,* March 29, 1989, 1.

41. McSpedon interview.

42. Ibid.

43. Stanger interview.

44. Okazaki interview.

45. Dean Murphy and Ronald B. Taylor, "Riders Get First Look at Blue Line Light Rail Transit," *Los Angeles Times,* July 15, 1990, A1.

46. Lettergram to Ed Edelman from Elizabeth W., July 16, 1990, in EEP, Box 599, Folder 8.

47. Interview with Neil Peterson by author, December 5, 2012, by telephone.

48. Murphy and Taylor, "Riders Get First Look at Blue Line Light Rail Transit," A1.

49. McSpedon interview.

50. Ibid.

51. Ibid.

52. Eric Malnic, "Fire under Freeway Subway Tunnel Caves In, Jams Downtown Traffic," *Los Angeles Times,* July 13, 1990, pt. P.

53. McSpedon interview.

54. Malnic, "Fire under Freeway Subway Tunnel Caves In."

55. McSpedon interview.

56. Rich Connell, "Lagging Metro Rail Work Could Delay 1993 Opening," *Los Angeles Times,* March 30, 1988, 1.

57. Kevin Roderick, "RTD Chief Concedes Need, Vows Fix-It Plan," *Los Angeles Times,* January 9, 1987, B2.

58. Connell, "Lagging Metro Rail Work Could Delay 1993 Opening," 1.

59. McSpedon interview.

60. Interview with Jeff Rabin by author, August 27, 2009, San Francisco.

61. Ibid.

62. Ibid.

63. David Willman, "Tunnel Walls Thinner Than Designed Red Line," *Los Angeles Times,* August 19, 1993, A1.

64. Letter to Frederico Peña from John Duncan, September 1, 1993, in NARA, Admin Policy & Planning File, Finding Aid UD-04W, Entry #1 (hereafter referred to as NARA), Box 14, Folder "September."

65. Letter to Franklin White from Gordon Linton, September 15, 1993, in NARA, Box 8, Folder "September."

66. Letter to Frederico Peña from John Walsh and Bob D'Amato, October 26, 1993, in NARA, Box 15, Folder "October."

67. Rabin interview.

68. Ibid.; Murphy and Taylor, "Riders Get First Look at Blue Line Light Rail Transit," A1.

69. Letter to Peña from Walsh and D'Amato.

70. Ibid.

71. David Willman, "Waxman Calls for U.S. Probe of Subway Transportation," *Los Angeles Times,* September 20, 1994, pt. B.

72. *Tutor-Saliba-Perini, J.V. v. The Los Angeles County Metropolitan Transportation Authority* (Jan. 25, 2005, B143430) [unpublished]; excerpt available at www. horvitzlevy.com/news/news.cfm?type=Recent%20Win&id=84 (accessed June 19, 2013).

73. Neil Peterson, Memo to Planning and Mobility Improvement Committee, March 11, 1992, 2, in TBP, Box 78, Folder 3.

74. Woo interview.

75. Dufty interview.

76. Letter to Tom Bradley from Warren B. Meyers, July 23, 1987, in TBP, Box 791, Folder 3.

77. Letter to Christine E. Reed from U.S. Congress Metro Rail Task Force, February 23, 1989, in EEP, Box 607, Folder 4.

78. Lettergram to Ed Edelman from Richard Cox, March 28, 1989, in EEP, Box 592, Folder 7.

79. Ibid.

80. Letter to Reed from U.S. Congress Metro Rail Task Force.

81. Edward J. Boyer, "U.S. Officials Release Funds for 2nd Leg of Metro Rail Line," *Los Angeles Times,* March 27, 1990, sec. 2, 1.

82. Rabin interview.

83. David Willman, "Gas Leaks in Subway Prompt New Questions," *Los Angeles Times,* May 23, 1994, A1.

84. Letter to MTA Board Members from Franklin White, July 22, 1994, in EEP, Box 591, Folder 8.

85. Deborah Schoch, "Soil Settling, Leaks Force Closure of Boulevard Transportation," *Los Angeles Times,* August 21, 1994, 1.

86. David Willman, "Waxman Calls for U.S. Probe of Subway Transportation," *Los Angeles Times,* September 20, 1994, pt. B.

87. Letter to Leo Wolinski from Edward McSpedon, September 22, 1994, in EEP, Box 591, Folder 8.

88. Richard Simon, "Report Blames Contractors for Tunnel Collapse," *Los Angeles Times,* October 20, 1995, A1.

89. J. Michael Kennedy, "Street Vanishes in Subway Sinkhole," *Los Angeles Times,* June 23, 1995, A1.

90. Ibid.

91. Ibid.

92. Simon, "Report Blames Contractors for Tunnel Collapse," A1.

93. Rabin interview.

94. Ibid.

95. LACTC News Release, "City To Celebrate L.A.'s 1st Modern Subway," January 25, 1993, in TBP, Box 26, Folder 9.

96. Nora Zamichow, "52,800 Ride the Rails of History as Subway Rolls," *Los Angeles Times,* January 31, 1993, pt. A.

CHAPTER SIX

1. LACTC Meeting Minutes, May 10, 1989, 2–3; available at http://boardarchives.metro.net/PredecessorAgencies/LACTC%20Box%2001/LACTC00158.pdf (accessed June 19, 2013).

2. Letter to David Roberti from Ed Edelman, April 10, 1990, in EEP, Box 626, Folder 9.

3. Lettergram to Ed Edelman from Robert Geoghegan, July 18, 1990, in EEP, Box 600, Folder 1.

4. Letter to Tom Bradley from Tom Houston, June 28, 1990, in TBP, Box 2588, Folder 11.

5. Mark Garrett, "The Struggle for Transit Justice: Race, Space and Social Equity in Los Angeles," Ph.D. diss., UCLA, 2006, 533.

6. Letter to Bradley from Houston, June 28, 1990.

7. Thomas K. Houston biography, at www.carlsmithla.com/Bio/ThomasHouston.asp?view=Expanded (accessed 2008).

8. Letter to Bradley from Houston, June 28, 1990, 3.

9. Rich Connell, "Sales Tax Hike OK'd for November Vote Transit," *Los Angeles Times,* August 9, 1990, B1.

10. Joint LACTC/RTD Meeting Minutes, August 8, 1990, 3–4; available at http://boardarchives.metro.net/PredecessorAgencies/LACTC%20Box%2001/LACTC00178.pdf (accessed June 19, 2013).

11. LACTC, Fact Sheet, "Proposition C: Transportation Congestion Relief," October 9, 1990, 1, in TBP, Box 2588, Folder 2.

12. Los Angeles County Transportation Commission Ordinance, chap. 3–10, sec. 3–10–040, 1990.

13. LACTC, Fact Sheet, "Proposition C," 7.

14. Tom Chorneau, "L.A. County Votes to Purchase Rail Lines," *Los Angeles Daily News,* October 25, 1990, N4.

15. Elaine Woo, "Deal Hailed as Key to Regional Rail System Commuter," *Los Angeles Times,* October 13, 1990, 1.

16. Ibid.

17. Bill Boyarsky, "How to Win by Simply Staying Quiet," *Los Angeles Times,* December 5, 1990, pt. B.

18. Ronald B. Taylor, "Transit Sales Tax Hike in Uphill Fight Despite Major Railroad Gifts," *Los Angeles Times,* November 2, 1990, B3.

19. Ibid.

20. Ronald B. Taylor, "Transit Plans Get Tax Boost from Voters," *Los Angeles Times,* November 8, 1990, B3.

21. Garrett, "Struggle for Transit Justice," 533–34.

22. Editorial, "Rail Way: Transit without Tears," *Los Angeles Times,* October 16, 1990, pt. B.

23. Remy interview.

24. Peterson interview.

25. Stanger interview.

26. Taylor, "Transit Plans Get Tax Boost from Voters."

27. Peterson interview.

28. Neil Peterson, Linda Bohlinger, Steve Gleason, and Manuel Padron & Associates, "Los Angeles County Transportation Commission 30-Year Integrated Transportation Plan," Los Angeles County Transportation Commission, April 1992, 37 and 60; available at www.scribd.com/doc/8223505/1992-Long-

Range-Plan-Los-Angeles-County-Transportation-Commission (accessed June 10, 2013).

29. Ibid., 42.

30. Lettergram to Ed Edelman from Richard Callahan, March 16, 1990, in EEP, Box 592, Folder 7.

31. Memo to Planning and Programming Committee from Judith A. Wilson, May 26, 1993, 2, in TBP, Box 62, Folder 11; Letter to Board of Airport Commissioners from William M. Schoenfeld, September 12, 1991, 1, in TBP, Box 4423, Folder 4.

32. Lettergram to Edelman from Callahan, March 16, 1990.

33. Wilson memo to Planning and Programming Committee, May 26, 1993, 2.

34. Schoenfeld letter to Board of Airport Commissioners, 2.

35. Minutes of LAX Interagency Transit Study Technical Task Force, September 17, 1991, 9, in TBP, Box 86, Folder 2.

36. Schoenfeld letter to Board of Airport Commissioners, 2.

37. Draft letter to Robert Cashin from William Schoenfeld, March 8, 1991, 1, in TBP, Box 293, Folder 2.

38. Letter to Bobbi Alward from Howard S. Yoshioka, May 14, 1991, in TBP, Box 86, Folder 2.

39. LAX Interagency Transit Study Technical Task Force minutes, September 17, 1991, 10.

40. Draft letter to Cashin from Schoenfeld, 1.

41. "We had been planning all along on a joint-use station in Lot C where our people mover, along with the possibility of a maglev system from Palmdale would interface with the Green Line," William Schoenfeld of the Los Angeles Department of Airports wrote the LACTC in response to an alignment plan that had a terminus south of Lot C. "We are therefore concerned that your station has moved south, some distance from Lot C where we will still have to build a station for our system," he wrote (ibid.).

42. A task force to address the dispute over station locations included the City of Los Angeles's Office of the Mayor, Galanter, Supervisor Dana, the FAA, the Department of Airport's Transportation and Planning Division, the RTD, and the LACTC. See Wilson memo to Planning and Programming Committee, May 26, 1993, 2.

43. The delay intensified a dispute among local elected officials about the best route for the light rail extension after it served LAX. Following the airport station, LACTC staff planned to route the Green Line extension north to the business and residential community of Westchester. The route would then continue to Marina Del Rey, a municipally financed minicity of multistory apartment buildings, restaurants, and private boat berths, mostly built during the 1980s on top of one of Southern California's last coastal wetlands. Los Angeles county supervisor Deane Dana, who represented the Marina, pushed hard for the rail link, but City Councilwoman Ruth Galanter was not supportive. As Galanter recalled, "Dana was looking to bring shoppers and hotel visitors to the Marina. But he was not particularly interested in what happened to the rail line after it went to the Marina." Galanter instead wanted

the extension to travel north along Sepulveda Boulevard to Westwood and UCLA, therefore bypassing the Marina. "If you're going to invest the gazillions it takes to build a rail line, it makes much more sense to get it up Westchester to UCLA, and then if technologically possible to take it to the San Fernando Valley." Otherwise, Galanter feared, airport communities in her district like Westchester would be isolated from the major employment centers of Westwood and the San Fernando Valley. The impasse with the FAA provided Galanter an opportunity to kill the light rail extension to the Marina. Instead, she proposed simply extending an airport people mover all the way to the existing Green Line station at Aviation Boulevard. See LAX Interagency Transit Study Technical Task Force minutes, September 17, 1991, 4–5. (Galanter was not enamored of a possible route up Lincoln Boulevard. "Every election somebody proposes light rail on Lincoln Boulevard," she remarked, "But I say, how many lanes of traffic are you willing to give up? And if it will go up above, the posts have to go somewhere" [Interview with Ruth Galanter by author, December 3, 2008, Los Angeles].) She then suggested a future extension that would take the Green Line from LAX toward the Interstate 405 freeway and eventually to Westwood. See Inter-Department Correspondence to Tom Conner from James M. Okazaki, November 21, 1991, 1, in TBP, Box 86, Folder 3. Her allies from the local business and labor community agreed. For example, the Westchester/LAX Chamber of Commerce (see Letter to Phil Depoian from Bill Gemmill, December 16, 1991, in TBP, Box 4424, Folder 1) and the El Segundo Employers Association (see Letter to Phil Depoian from Donald H. Camph, December 16, 1991, in TBP, Box 4424, Folder 1) both supported the people mover option. "To date," Galanter informed the LACTC, "my constituents in both the business and residential communities have conveyed to me strong support for the [people mover] alternative." She suggested that stopping the Green Line at Aviation might be "all the more compelling given recent revelations of yet more enormous cost overruns, most recently near $300 million" (Letter to the Los Angeles County Transportation Commission from Ruth Galanter, December 16, 1991, 2, in TBP, Box 86, Folder 3). Galanter's opposition to light rail service to the Marina complicated the efforts to implement the North Coast extension. Advocates for the line needed the support of the local city councilwoman and county supervisor who represented the area. But Supervisor Dana and Councilwoman Galanter had opposing views of how rail should interface with their communities beyond the airport. Without their agreement, LACTC leaders would have a more difficult time overcoming the objections of the FAA and airport officials to the proposed route.

44. Okazaki to Conner, Inter-Department Correspondence, November 21, 1991, 3.

45. Letter to LACTC Planning and Mobility Improvement Committee from Neil Peterson, March 11, 1992, 4; available at http://boardarchives.metro.net /Other/BOS/BOS_2_029.pdf (accessed June 10, 2013).

46. Galanter interview.

47. Peterson letter to LACTC Planning and Mobility Improvement Committee, March 11, 1992, 6.

48. Wilson memo to Planning and Programming Committee, May 26, 1993, 2–3.

49. Bacharach interview.

50. Galanter interview.

51. Christopher Reynolds, "Metro Rail's Green Line to LAX?" *Los Angeles Times,* July 24, 1994, pt. L.

52. Richard Simon, "Is New Green Line a Road to Nowhere?" *Los Angeles Times,* August 12, 1995, pt. A.

53. Stanger interview.

54. Metro Ridership Statistics, www.metro.net/news/pages/ridership-statistics/ (accessed May 16, 2010).

55. Bacharach interview.

56. Simon, "Is New Green Line a Road to Nowhere?"

57. Ibid.

58. Based on these and other similar factors, airport connections at John F. Kennedy International Airport in New York, Chicago O'Hare International Airport, and Hartsfield-Jackson Atlanta International Airport ranked well according to Mark William Peterson, "A New Procedure for Scoring Rail Transit Connections to U.S. Airports," thesis, Virginia Polytechnic Institute and State University, April 30, 2012, 73–76; available at http://scholar.lib.vt.edu/theses /available/etd-05142012–101644/unrestricted/Peterson_MW_T_2012.pdf (accessed November 13, 2012). Meanwhile, transportation expert and journalist Yonah Freemark contends that the most important factors for successful airport connections are one-seat service from several parts of the city and limited walking distance between airport stations and check-in counters. See Yonah Freemark, "The Airport-Transit Connection," November 24, 2008, www.thetransportpolitic.com/2008/11/24/the-airport-transit-connection/ (accessed November 13, 2012).

59. These barriers to a successful airport connection were not lost on local officials. "The systems that work well have the fewest impediments," noted Clifton A. Moore, executive director of the Los Angeles Department of Airports during the 1980s (quoted in Ray Hebert, "Litigation, Confusion, Road Paved with Good Intentions," *Los Angeles Times,* December 27, 1987).

60. Los Angeles Transportation Commission, "Rail Transit Implementation Strategy, Stage 2," January 1984, in Jacki Bacharach Collection, Dorothy Peyton Gray Transportation Library and Archives, Los Angeles, Folder "LACTC Correspondence 1982–1985."

61. LACTC Meeting Minutes, November 18, 1987, 2; available at http:// boardarchives.metro.net/PredecessorAgencies/LACTC%20Box%2001 /LACTC00085.pdf (accessed June 19, 2013).

62. Geoghegan interview, August 30, 2005.

63. Letter to Tom Bradley from Rabbi Chaim Schnur, Agudath Israel of California, October 18, 1988, in TBP, Box 2603, Folder 15.

64. Letter to Tom Bradley from Zev Yaroslavsky, February 9, 1987, in EEP, Box 627, Folder 6.

65. Letter from Bruce V. Barnum to Tom Bradley/Ray Remy, November 14, 1987, in TBP, Box 695, Folder 5.

66. Stacey Shaw, "Light Rail Plan Put Housewife on Activist Track," *Los Angeles Daily News*, November 22, 1987, 4, in TBP, Box 2603, Folder 15.

67. Bacharach interview.

68. LACTC Meeting Minutes, November 18, 1987, 5–6.

69. Vote discussed in lettergram to Ed Edelman from Bob Geoghegan, February 19, 1988, 2, in EEP, Box 593, Folder 1.

70. Some local officials believed Bacharach terminated the process too quickly, perhaps to favor rail for her constituents (a charge Bacharach vehemently denied). Bob Geoghegan believed that Edelman and Bradley were on the verge of reaching a compromise with Valley residents along Chandler Boulevard. But he recalled Bacharach's efforts to stop further discussion after one particularly tense meeting. "The LACTC had a big meeting in the San Fernando Valley. Antonovich, Ed, Bradley, Remy, and all the elected representatives were there, and they all supported [the rail extension]," he said. "Bobbi Feidler, who wasn't still elected at that point, stood up and said, 'You can't do this.' Bacharach said, 'I'm not going to support anything in the Valley until the Valley gets its act together.' That stopped the compromise. The rail line could've worked out and been running" (Geoghegan interview, August 30, 2005).

71. LACTC Meeting Minutes, March 8, 1989, 2–3; available at http:// boardarchives.metro.net/PredecessorAgencies/LACTC%20Box%2001/LACTC 00154.pdf (accessed June 19, 2013).

72. LACTC, "San Fernando Valley Rail Transit Project, Burbank Branch," n.d., fig. 1, in TBP, Box 2604, Folder 2.

73. James Quinn and Mark Gladstone, "Governor Vetoes Bill Requiring Rail Line to Be Underground," *Los Angeles Times*, July 4, 1990, 3.

74. Executive Summary, Final Environmental Impact Report for the San Fernando Valley East-West Transit Corridor Project; Bus Rapid Transit (BRT) on former Burbank/Chandler Southern Pacific (MTA) Railroad Right-of-Way, State Clearinghouse Number 1995101050, Los Angeles County Metropolitan Transportation Authority, February 2002, S-7; available at libraryarchives.metro.net/DPGTL /eirs/SFV_EastWest/images/executive_summary.pdf (accessed June 10, 2013).

75. Letter to LACTC members and alternates from Neil Peterson, March 1, 1989, 3, in TBP, Box 2603, Folder 17.

76. LACTC Meeting Minutes, March 28, 1990, 10; available at http://boardarchives.metro.net/PredecessorAgencies/LACTC%20Box%2001/LACTC00172.pdf (accessed June 19, 2013).

77. James Quinn, "Tax Increase May Help Metro Rail Reach Van Nuys by 2000, Planners Say," *Los Angeles Times*, December 6, 1990, B3.

78. James Quinn, "Proponents of Metro Rail Subway Play Down Delay," *Los Angeles Times*, May 17, 1991, B3.

79. Hugo Martin, "Riordan Seeks to Kill Valley Subway," *Los Angeles Times*, December 20, 1995, B1.

80. According to Bob Geoghegan in Supervisor Edelman's office, Los Angeles county supervisor "Mike Antonovich came back from a trip to Asia, where he went a lot and met his wife, and came back fascinated with the monorail. So he starts a campaign for a monorail line along the 134 freeway." Antonovich's proposed monorail would travel along a single elevated beam in the middle of, or next to, the freeway, following the same east-west direction as the Burbank route. The monorail would cost less than the subway, and because it was along a freeway, it avoided residential neighborhoods (although homeowners groups along the monorail route in Sherman Oaks criticized the idea). Antonovich had convinced the county to place an advisory referendum on the June 1990 ballot. The measure asked Valley voters to choose among four rail transit options, including the monorail. Antonovich enlisted the support of major real estate developers who hoped the cheaper monorail could eventually be extended to their developments in the far northern reaches of the county. These backers spent $40,000 for radio advertising to support their choice, and they enlisted former Apollo astronaut Edwin "Buzz" Aldrin in their radio ads. When the results came in, the Monorail was the preference of 48 percent of the voters, while 21 percent favored a light rail line and only 10 percent favored the LACTC-favored subway extension. Emboldened, Antonovich used his position as chair of the LACTC to approve further study of the monorail plan, including its costs and benefits. The plan attracted political support as a low-cost alternative to the expensive subway. An LACTC study showed the monorail option to be $440 million to $1 billion cheaper than the subway, leading many LACTC members to find the monorail option too appealing to reject. In December 1992, the LACTC conditionally approved on a six-to-three vote an elevated monorail for the Valley. Most members publicly cited the cost factor, as well as concern that the problems plaguing the current subway construction would continue with a Valley extension. But less than two years later, in 1994, the devastating Northridge Earthquake struck Los Angeles, collapsing freeways and homes. Just as suddenly, the cost equations on the monorail changed. In response to the quake, stricter construction standards meant that the monorail option would not in fact represent a huge cost savings over the subway option. In October 1994, transit officials reaffirmed support for the subway route, abandoning the monorail plan.

81. Interview with Darrell Clarke by author, May 3, 2011, Santa Monica.

82. Los Angeles Transportation Commission, "Rail Transit Implementation Strategy, Stage 1," May 1983, 13, in Jacki Bacharach Collection, Dorothy Peyton Gray Transportation Library and Archives, Folder "LACTC Correspondence 1982–1985."

83. Los Angeles Transportation Commission, "Rail Transit Implementation Strategy, Stage 2."

84. Stanger interview.

85. Letter to Ed Edelman from Mike Roos, February 12, 1990, in EEP, Box 600, Folder 1.

86. Letter to Ed Edelman from Diane Watson, July 19, 1991, in EEP, Box 599, Folder 8.

87. LACTC Meeting Minutes, May 10, 1989, 3; available at http://boardar-chives.metro.net/PredecessorAgencies/LACTC%20Box%2001/LACTC00158.pdf. On Reed, see Louise Yarnall, "S.M. May Get on Light Rail Line," *Santa Monica Outlook*, September 9, 1991, A3, in TBP, Box 2032, Folder 52.

88. Culver City Resolution No. 89-R 075, June 26, 1989, in TBP, Box 2603, Folder 8. The quotation is from a letter to Tom Bradley from Jozelle Smith, July 7, 1989, in TBP, Box 2603, Folder 8.

89. Memo to Planning and Mobility Improvement Committee of the LACTC from Neil Peterson, January 13, 1993, 2–3, in TBP, Box 77, Folder 6.

90. Lettergram to Ed Edelman from Rich Callahan, September 15, 1989, in EEP, Box 599, Folder 8.

91. West of Westwood Homeowners flyer, 1989, in EEP, Box 599, Folder 8.

92. Galanter interview.

93. Stanger interview.

94. Peterson memo to Planning and Mobility Improvement Committee, January 13, 1993, 3.

95. Yarnall, "S.M. May Get on Light Rail Line," A3.

96. Louise Yarnall, "S.M. Light Rail Gets Mixed Reviews," *Santa Monica Outlook*, September 14, 1991, A3, in TBP, Box 2032, Folder 52.

97. Yarnall, "S.M. May Get on Light Rail Line," A3.

98. Galanter interview.

99. Peterson memo to Planning and Mobility Improvement Committee, January 13, 1993, 3.

100. LACTC Meeting Minutes, March 28, 1990, 5.

101. Without the connector, travelers from Long Beach to Pasadena would have to transfer from the Long Beach line to the heavy rail Red Line subway, since the incompatible rail formats prevented sharing of the same tracks. After just a few stops on the subway, the passengers would have to transfer again to the light rail Pasadena line, this time via a lengthy walk through Union Station to an aboveground plat-form. Overall, the transfers would add significant delays and inconvenience. As a result, the incompatibility of the Red Line heavy rail and the light rail technologies was a major source of consternation for LACTC critics like former Supervisor Baxter Ward. Appearing at a 1988 LACTC meeting, he warned commissioners that they were legally liable for approving light rail over heavy rail in contradiction to what he believed Proposition A intended (see Lettergram to Ed Edelman from Bob Geoghegan, April 28, 1988, in EEP, Box 592, Folder 7). As a result of the RTD deci-sion to build the Red Line as heavy rail and the LACTC decision to build the Blue Line as light rail, a separate light rail connector was now needed to connect the Blue Line to the Pasadena line. This connector would essentially duplicate the Red Line route from 7th and Flower to Union Station, although it would travel a different route through downtown Los Angeles.

102. Los Angeles Transportation Commission, "Rail Transit Implementation Strategy, Stage 2," 4.

103. Ibid., 14.

104. Remy interview.

105. Bill Boyarsky, "Satisfying 2 Powerful Politicians a Tough Challenge for MTA Chief," *Los Angeles Times,* February 23, 1996, B1.

106. Councilman Richard Alatorre, Metropolitan Transportation Authority, "Mission Statement 1993," in TBP, Box 65, Folder 3.

107. Berkley Hudson, "Getting Back on Track Transit," *Los Angeles Times,* August 29, 1993, J1.

108. Remy interview.

109. Doug Smith, "Study Could Shift Mass Transit Funds to San Gabriel Valley," *Los Angeles Times,* November 26, 1987, 3.

110. See LACTC, "L.A. Rail 2000: A Blueprint for Action," November 1988, 2, in EEP, Box 593, Folder 1. See also LACTC Meeting Minutes, March 28, 1990, 11.

111. LACTC Meeting Minutes, March 28, 1990, 11.

112. Peterson interview.

113. MTA Planning and Programming Committee Meeting Minutes, Attachment B, September 9, 1993, 10; available at http://boardarchives.metro.net /Items/1993/09_September/items_h_0313.pdf (accessed June 19, 2013).

114. LACTC Meeting Minutes, January 27, 1993, 24–26; available at http:// boardarchives.metro.net/PredecessorAgencies/LACTC%20Box%2001 /LACTC%2093%20Jan.pdf (accessed June 19, 2013).

115. Nora Zamichow, "County Clears Way for Light-Rail Line," *Los Angeles Times,* January 28, 1993, 4.

CHAPTER SEVEN

1. LACTC Meeting Minutes, December 18, 1991, 11–13; available at http:// boardarchives.metro.net/PredecessorAgencies/LACTC%20Box%2001 /LACTC00015.pdf (accessed June 19, 2013). The history of Sumitomo can be found at http://en.wikipedia.org/wiki/Sumitomo (accessed June 19, 2013).

2. John Greenwald, "The Wreck of Morrison Knudsen," *Time,* April 3, 1995.

3. LACTC, "Metro Green Line: Summary of Automation and Vehicle Procurement Actions," draft, January 1992, 1, 3–4, in TBP, Box 83, Folder 7.

4. Rail Construction Corporation, "The Metro Green Line, Comparison Sumitomo and Morrison-Knudsen," n.d., in TBP, Box 84, Folder 7.

5. LACTC Meeting Minutes, December 18, 1991, 11.

6. Rail Construction Corporation, "Metro Green Line."

7. Dufty interview.

8. Richard Reeves, "Buy American, or Maybe Japanese," *Los Angeles Times,* December 29, 1991, M5.

9. Bill Boyarsky, "Governor No and Selling of Rail Cars," *Los Angeles Times,* December 18, 1991, B2.

10. Draft letter to the *Los Angeles Times* from Ray Grabinsky, December 31, 1991, in TBP, Box 4013, Folder 9.

11. Letter to Tom Bradley from Willie L. Brown, January 3, 1992, in TBP, Box 84, Folder 2.

12. Handwritten comments on a letter to Edmund D. Edelman from Willie L. Brown, January 3, 1992, in EEP, Box 606, Folder 1.

13. Citizens for Public Transportation in the Public Interest statement, January 14, 1992, 1, in TBP, Box 84, Folder 2.

14. Letter to Ray Grabinski from Julian Dixon, Edward Roybal, Glenn Anderson, Carlos Moorhead, Jerry Lewis, Howard Berman, Mel Levine, Mervin Dymally, and Matthew Martinez, January 7, 1992, 2, in TBP, Box 84, Folder 1.

15. Letter to Tom Bradley from Bill Chandler, January 16, 1992, 1, in TBP, Box 954, Folder 6.

16. Zev Yaroslavsky, Press release, January 6, 1992, in EEP, Box 606, Folder 1.

17. Letter to Ed Edelman from Phil [no last name given], January 6, 1992, in EEP, Box 606, Folder 1.

18. Mark Stein, "Transit Panel Cancels Pact with Sumitomo Green Line," *Los Angeles Times,* January 23, 1992, A1.

19. Bacharach interview.

20. Letter to Edelman from Phil, January 6, 1992.

21. Metro news release, January 17, 1992, in TBP, Box 82, Folder 6.

22. Editorial, "The Subway That Ate L.A.," *Wall Street Journal,* April 13, 1992, A16.

23. Letter to Ray Grabinski from Julian Dixon, Edward Roybal, Glenn Anderson, Carlos Moorhead, Jerry Lewis, Howard Berman, Mel Levine, Mervin Dymally, and Matthew Martinez, January 7, 1992, 2, in TBP, Box 84, Folder 1.

24. Bill Boyarsky, "Green Line Rhetoric and the Japanese," *Los Angeles Times,* January 22, 1992, B2.

25. Letter to Neil Peterson from Koichi Narikawa, January 21, 1992, in TBP, Box 83, Folder 3.

26. Mark Stein, "County to Buy 15 Rail Cars from Sumitomo," *Los Angeles Times,* October 6, 1992, A1.

27. Nora Zamichow, "German-U.S. Team to Build Green Line Cars," *Los Angeles Times,* July 29, 1993, B1.

28. "Construction," *Los Angeles Times,* August 27, 1996, D2.

29. Memo to LACTC Commissioners from Neil Peterson, March 5, 1992, 1–2, in TBP, Box 68, Folder 6.

30. Jane Fritsch, "Cash-Rich Transit Agency Spends Freely on Itself," *Los Angeles Times,* March 10, 1992, A1.

31. Ibid.

32. Jane Fritsch, "U.S. Opens Inquiries on Spending for Los Angeles Rail System," *New York Times,* September 17, 1992, A1.

33. Los Angeles County Board of Supervisors Motion, Kenneth Hahn, December 6, 1983, in KHP 3.5.1.15, Box 229.

34. Bill Boyarsky, "Bradley Says He's Opposed to Transit Merger Plan," *Los Angeles Times,* February 12, 1987, B2.

35. "The State: Deukmejian's Veto Saves RTD," *Los Angeles Times,* September 30, 1987, B1.

36. Boyarsky, "Bradley Says He's Opposed to Transit Merger Plan," B2; Letter to Governor George Deukmejian from Kenneth Hahn, September 18, 1987, in KHP 3.5.1.19, Box 229.

37. Rich Connell, "RTD Stripped of Power on Future Metro Rail Work," *Los Angeles Times,* September 29, 1988, sec. 2, 2.

38. SCRTD Resolution, September 9, 1988, in TBP, Box 2660, Folder 3.

39. Letter to Alan Pegg from Paul Taylor, October 11, 1988, 2–3, in TBP, Box 2660, Folder 4.

40. Connell, "RTD Stripped of Power," sec. 2, 2.

41. Letter to Alan Pegg from Paul Taylor, October 11, 1988, in TBP, Box 2660, Folder 4.

42. Bacharach interview.

43. LACTC Meeting Minutes, September 28, 1988, 8; available at http://boardarchives.metro.net/PredecessorAgencies/LACTC%20Box%2001/LACTC00206.pdf (accessed June 19, 2013).

44. Pete Schabarum, Draft letter, November 29, 1988, in TBP, Box 2660, Folder 3.

45. Ibid., 3–4.

46. LACTC Meeting Minutes, December 9, 1988, 2–3; available at http://boardarchives.metro.net/PredecessorAgencies/LACTC%20Box%2001/LACTC00211.pdf (accessed June 19, 2013).

47. MTA, "Proposed Interim Delegation of Authority and Interim Committee Structures," February 2, 1993, 1; available at http://boardarchives.metro.net/Items/1993/02_February/items_0350.pdf (accessed June 19, 2013).

48. Franklin White, Draft CEO's Message, FY 93–94 Budget, May 21, 1993, 1, in TBP, Box 66, Folder 2.

49. Ibid.

50. Editorial, "Let's Be Clear, the Merger Is Here," *Los Angeles Times,* March 8, 1993, pt. B.

51. Letter to Tom Bradley from Pat Russell, January 7, 1993, in TBP, Box 2185, Folder 7.

52. Nora Zamichow, "New York Official to Head Huge L.A. Transit Agency," *Los Angeles Times,* February 5, 1993, pt. A.

53. Anonymous interview.

54. That roof soon became literal: the MTA needed to find a building for its headquarters. As an example of the past rivalry between agencies, the RTD had selected a site for a new headquarters above Union Station, while the LACTC decided to build one a mile away at 7th Street and Bixel in the Central City West district. The LACTC choice was less attractive politically because the agency had negotiated exclusively with developers led by Ray Watt, a longtime supporter of Mayor Bradley, raising charges of undue influence. The site was also across the freeway from the nearest subway station, resulting in poor symbolism. (See Brad Berton,

"LACTC Ignores Critics and Sticks with Decision on Headquarters Site," *Los Angeles Business Journal,* March 1, 1993, 3.) Franklin White therefore decided to locate MTA headquarters at the RTD building site (see Memo to Ad Hoc Committee from Franklin E. White, April 9, 1993, 1–2, in TBP, Box 61, Folder 14), in a building that one critic called the "Taj Mahal" due to its opulent features.

55. LACTC Meeting Minutes, September 28, 1988, 8; available at http://board-archives.metro.net/PredecessorAgencies/LACTC%20Box%2001/LACTC00206.pdf (accessed June 19, 2013).

56. Councilman Richard Alatorre, Mission Statement 1993, Metropolitan Transportation Authority, in TBP, Box 65, Folder 3.

57. MTA Board Meeting Minutes, June 23, 1993, 19; available at http://boardar-chives.metro.net/Minutes/1994/minutes_0280.pdf (accessed June 19, 2013).

58. Mark Garrett, "The Struggle for Transit Justice: Race, Space, and Social Equity in Los Angeles," Ph.D. diss., UCLA, 2006, 605.

59. White, Draft CEO's Message, May 21, 1993, 4.

60. Garrett, "Struggle for Transit Justice," 611.

61. White, Draft CEO's Message, May 21, 1993, 6.

62. MTA Board Meeting Minutes, August 25, 1993, 2; available at http://boardarchives.metro.net/Minutes/1993/00363.pdf (accessed June 19, 2013).

63. Garrett, "Struggle for Transit Justice," 613–16.

64. Ibid., 708, 618–19.

65. Nora Zamichow, "MTA, in Budget Compromise, OKs Design Funds for Pasadena Rail Line," *Los Angeles Times,* August 26, 1993, B1.

66. Los Angeles County Metropolitan Transportation Authority Budget Resolution, Adopted August 25, 1993, 2; available at http://boardarchives.metro.net/Minutes/1993/00363.pdf (accessed June 19, 2013).

67. Zamichow, "MTA, in Budget Compromise, OKs Design Funds," B1.

68. Ibid.

69. Neil Peterson, Linda Bohlinger, Steve Gleason, and Manuel Padron & Associates, "Los Angeles County Transportation Commission 30-Year Integrated Transportation Plan," April 1992, 60; available at www.scribd.com/doc/8223505/1992-Long-Range-Plan-Los-Angeles-County-Transportation-Commission (accessed June 10, 2013).

70. Garrett, "Struggle for Transit Justice," 687.

71. Eric Lichtblau and Richard Simon, "MTA Scuttles Rail Projects in Drastic Retrenchment," *Los Angeles Times,* February 2, 1995, pt. A.

72. MTA Board Meeting Minutes, August 24, 1994, 13; available at http://boardarchives.metro.net/Minutes/1994/minutes_0372.pdf (accessed June 19, 2013).

73. Federal Transit Administration Project Management Oversight, August 1994, 3, in EEP, Box 591, Folder 8.

74. Los Angeles County Metropolitan Transportation Authority, Resolution, November 3, 1994, in EEP, Box 591, Folder 8.

75. Bill Boyarsky, "MTA's Countdown to TV Earthquake," *Los Angeles Times,* December 15, 1995, pt. B.

76. Richard Simon and Eric Lichtblau, "White, Embattled Head of Transit Agency, Is Fired," *Los Angeles Times,* December 21, 1995, A1.

77. James E. Moore II and Thomas A. Rubin, "Admit Rail Plan Is Dead and Move On," *Los Angeles Times,* December 13, 1996, B9.

78. Richard Markman and Jon D. Simon, "Future of Subway Project Questioned by MTA Officials," *Los Angeles Times,* December 10, 1996, A1.

79. Scott Harris, "Prop. A as Exorcist for MTA's Evil Ways," *Los Angeles Times,* November 1, 1998, pt. B.

80. Rabin interview.

81. David Willman, "Dana Colleagues Call for Contract-Voting Reform," *Los Angeles Times,* December 17, 1992, B1.

82. David Willman, "Bill Targets Conflicts in Voting on MTA Bids," *Los Angeles Times,* September 11, 1993, B3.

83. Rabin interview.

CHAPTER EIGHT

1. Mark Garrett, "The Struggle for Transit Justice: Race, Space, and Social Equity in Los Angeles," Ph.D. diss., UCLA, 2006, 625–26.

2. Ryan Snyder and Antonio Villaraigosa, "Perspectives on Public Transit," *Los Angeles Times,* November 27, 1992, B5.

3. Garrett, "Struggle for Transit Justice," 638–41.

4. Nora Zamichow and Henry Chu, "Judge Blocks Bus Fare Hike, Sets Review," *Los Angeles Times,* September 2, 1994, pt. A.

5. MTA Board Meeting Minutes, July 13, 1994, 3–4; available at http://boardarchives.metro.net/Minutes/1994/minutes_0373.pdf (accessed June 19, 2013).

6. Ibid., 7.

7. Eric Mann, "The Trains Are the Robbers Buses," *Los Angeles Times,* July 20, 1994, B7.

8. Eric Mann, "Veterans of the Civil Rights Movement," August 25, 2004, www.crmvet.org/vet/manne.htm (accessed June 19, 2013).

9. Garrett, "Struggle for Transit Justice," 663.

10. Interview with Manuel Criollo by author, June 30, 2009, Los Angeles.

11. Garrett, "Struggle for Transit Justice," 655 and 663.

12. Criollo interview.

13. Ibid.

14. Garrett, "Struggle for Transit Justice," 655.

15. Mann, "The Trains Are the Robbers Buses," B7.

16. Garrett, "Struggle for Transit Justice," 665.

17. Criollo interview.

18. Rubin interview.

19. Ibid.

20. Interview with Robert Garcia by author, February 19, 2010, by telephone.

21. Ibid.

22. Ibid.

23. Richard Simon, "County to Pay $6.3 Million in Voting Rights Lawsuit Settlement," *Los Angeles Times,* May 3, 1991, B3.

24. Criollo interview.

25. Garcia interview.

26. Garrett, "Struggle for Transit Justice," 668.

27. Ibid., 669.

28. Ibid., 631.

29. Plaintiffs Revised Statement of Contentions of Fact and Law, *Labor /Community Strategy Center et al. vs. Los Angeles County Metropolitan Transportation Authority,* United States District Court, October 24, 1996, 85.

30. MTA, Los Angeles County Transit Total Expenditures By Mode, n.d., 800159; Testimony of Thomas Rubin, 14 (citation from Plaintiffs Revised Statement, 15).

31. Plaintiffs Revised Statement, 19.

32. Ibid., 19, 15.

33. Ibid., 18.

34. Ibid., 27.

35. Ibid., 14.

36. Ibid., 16.

37. MTA, "Status Report on MTA Bus System," July 2, 1993, with attached report entitled "Status Report on MTA Bus System, Phase I—June 1993," July 1993 (M514364), M514360 at M514374–75 (citation at Plaintiffs Revised Statement, 16).

38. Dufty interview.

39. McCone Commission, "Violence in the City: An End or a Beginning?," December 1965; available at www.usc.edu/libraries/archives/cityinstress/mccone /contents.html (accessed June 19, 2013).

40. California African American Museum, History Council Invitation, 2008, at www.eighthandwall.org/pdfs/041708_hatter.pdf (accessed 2008). For more information on Judge Hatter, see his biography at www.jtbf.org/index.php?src=dir ectory&view=biographies&srctype=detail&refno=75 (accessed June 11, 2013).

41. Lisa Trei, "Black Judges Speak Out on Racism, Sexism They Face," *Stanford Report,* February 27, 2002; available at http://news.stanford.edu/news/2002 /february27/judges-227.html (accessed June 19, 2013).

42. Garcia interview.

43. Henry Chu, "Judge Blocks Bus Fare Hike, Sets Review," *Los Angeles Times,* September 2, 1994, 1.

44. Garcia interview.

45. Chu, "Judge Blocks Bus Fare Hike," 1.

46. Garcia interview.

47. Garrett, "Struggle for Transit Justice," 683.

48. Eric Berkowitz, "The Subway Mayor: How a Bus-Only Politician—and a Car-Obsessed City—Are Learning to Love the Underground," *Los Angeles Weekly,*

August 18, 2005; available at www.laweekly.com/news/features/the-subway-mayor/349/?page=1 (accessed June 19, 2013).

49. Chu, "Judge Blocks Bus Fare Hike," 1.

50. Garcia interview.

51. Ibid.

52. Garrett, "Struggle for Transit Justice," 681–82.

53. Ibid., 703.

54. Rubin interview.

55. Consent Decree, *Labor/Community Strategy Center et al. v. Los Angeles County Metropolitan Transportation Authority,* October 31, 1996, 3; available at http://oldbru.thestrategycenter.org/engli/pdf%20files/Consent%20Decree%20 pdfs/Consent%20Decree%20Documents/consent-decree-10–96.pdf (accessed June 17, 2013).

56. Ibid., 8.

57. Ibid., 3.

58. Ibid., 4.

59. Berkowitz, "Subway Mayor."

60. Briefing by MTA Management, County Counsel, and Outside Counsel, "Consent Decree," prepared for Mayor's Office by City of Los Angeles Department of Transportation, August 2001, 3–1 to 3–3, in Papers of Mayor James Hahn, Los Angeles City Archive, Box 642188, UBN 0000000007, Folder "Department of Transportation Briefing Papers, 2001."

61. Ibid.

62. Rubin interview.

63. Garcia interview.

64. Richard Simon, "Settlement of Bus Suit Approved," *Los Angeles Times,* October 29, 1996, B1.

65. Garcia interview.

66. Berkowitz, "Subway Mayor."

67. Briefing by MTA Management et al., "Consent Decree," 3–1 to 3–3.

68. Berkowitz, "Subway Mayor."

69. Rubin interview.

70. Briefing by MTA Management et al., "Consent Decree," 3–1 to 3–3.

71. Berkowitz, "Subway Mayor."

72. Ibid.

73. Garrett, "Struggle for Transit Justice," 764–65.

74. Jeffrey L. Rabin, "MTA Told to Buy 532 Buses to Ease Crowding Transit," *Los Angeles Times,* March 9, 1999, A1.

75. Garrett, "Struggle for Transit Justice," 771–72.

76. Sharon Bernstein, "MTA Ordered to Expand Its Fleet of Rapid Buses," *Los Angeles Times,* April 15, 2005, B3.

77. Dan Weikel, "MTA to Buy 200 New Buses; Riders Want More," *Los Angeles Times,* September 23, 2005, B8.

78. Berkowitz, "Subway Mayor."

79. James Moore and Tom Rubin, "The MTA's Train Wreck" (op-ed), *Los Angeles Times,* January 13, 2008, M5.

80. Berkowitz, "Subway Mayor."

81. Criollo interview.

82. Jean Guccione, "Court Oversight of Buses Lifted," *Los Angeles Times,* October 26, 2006, B1.

83. Consent Decree, *Labor/Community Strategy Center et al. v. MTA,* 11, 12.

84. Guccione, "Court Oversight of Buses Lifted."

85. Criollo interview.

86. Rong-Gong Lin II and Jeffrey L. Rabin, "MTA Approves Steep Hikes for Bus, Rail Fares," *Los Angeles Times,* May 25, 2007, A1.

87. Roger Snoble, "Is 86 Cents a Ride Really Too Much?" (op-ed), *Los Angeles Times,* April 27, 2007, A33.

88. Tiffany Hsu, "Coalition Sues in Bid to Block MTA Fare Hikes," *Los Angeles Times,* June 27, 2001, B2.

89. *Alexander v. Sandoval,* 532 U.S. 275 (2001).

90. Rong-Gong Lin II, "Judge Refuses to Bar MTA Rate Hikes," *Los Angeles Times,* June 28, 2007, B11.

91. Steve Hymon, "Bus Riders Union Loses Court Ruling," *Los Angeles Times,* August 26, 2008, B4.

CHAPTER NINE

1. Jeffrey L. Rabin, "MTA Borrowing Puts the Agency $7 Billion in Debt," *Los Angeles Times,* June 21, 1998, A1.

2. Rabin interview.

3. Richard Simon, "U.S. Orders Third MTA Fiscal Plan," *Los Angeles Times,* August 2, 1997, B1.

4. Jon D. Markman, "White House Cuts Subway Fund Request," *Los Angeles Times,* February 7, 1997, B1

5. Jon D. Markman and Jeffrey L. Rabin, "MTA Board Divided by Regional Rift Over Funds," *Los Angeles Times,* February 20, 1997, B1.

6. MTA Board Meeting Minutes, February 19, 1997, 3; available at http://boardarchives.metro.net/Minutes/1997/Minutes_D_0015.pdf (accessed June 12, 2013).

7. Richard Simon, "U.S. Orders Third MTA Fiscal Plan," *Los Angeles Times,* August 2, 1997, B1.

8. Mark Garrett, "The Struggle for Transit Justice: Race, Space and Social Equity in Los Angeles," Ph.D. diss., UCLA, 2006, 743.

9. Ibid., 744–47.

10. Ibid., 748–51.

11. MTA Board Minutes, January 14, 1998, 4; available at http://boardarchives.metro.net/Minutes/1998/Minutes_SBM_19980114.pdf (accessed June 17, 2013).

12. Garrett, "Struggle for Transit Justice," 751–52.

13. Los Angeles Eastside Corridor Final SEIS/SEIR, November 2, 2001, S-8; available at www.metro.net/projects_studies/eastside/images/Executive%20 Summary.pdf (accessed June 17, 2013).

14. Jeffrey L. Rabin and Richard Simon, "U.S. Agency Approves MTA's Recovery Plan," *Los Angeles Times,* July 3, 1998, A1.

15. Garrett, "Struggle for Transit Justice," 758.

16. Jeffrey L. Rabin and Richard Simon, "Backing for Anti-Subway Measure Equally Strong in All Areas of City," *Los Angeles Times,* November 5, 1998, pt. B.

17. Garrett, "Struggle for Transit Justice," 762.

18. Yaroslavsky interview.

19. Ibid.

20. Rabin interview.

21. Yaroslavsky interview.

22. Anonymous interview with the author.

23. Jeffrey L. Rabin and Jon D. Markman, "L.A. Residents Divided on Subway Completion," *Los Angeles Times,* February 7, 1997, pt. B.

24. Garrett, "Struggle for Transit Justice," 762.

25. Rabin and Simon, "Backing for Anti-Subway Measure Equally Strong"; Rabin interview.

26. Rabin interview.

27. Rabin and Simon, "Backing for Anti-Subway Measure Equally Strong."

28. Yaroslavsky interview.

29. Richard Simon and Jon D. Markman, "Future of Wilshire May Ride on Subway Extension," *Los Angeles Times,* July 12, 1996, A1.

30. Jeffrey L. Rabin, "Hollywood Subway Line Opens Today," *Los Angeles Times,* June 12, 1999, B1.

31. John L. Mitchell, "Metro Rail's Hollywood Connection Gets Thumbs Up from Commuters," *Los Angeles Times,* June 13, 1999, B3.

32. Jeffrey L. Rabin, "Subway's Arrival in Valley Ends a Long, Costly Journey," *Los Angeles Times,* June 18, 2000, pt. A.

33. Jeffrey L. Rabin, "Riordan Ready to Leave MTA Driver's Seat," *Los Angeles Times,* June 28, 1999, B1.

34. Jim Newton and Beth Shuster, "Tom Bradley: 1917–1998, Mayor Who Reshaped L.A. Dies," *Los Angeles Times,* September 30, 1998, A1.

35. Garrett, "Struggle for Transit Justice," 760–61.

36. MTA Ridership Statistics, www.metro.net/news/pages/ridership-statistics (accessed June 19, 2013).

37. Kurt Streeter, "Gold Line Railway on Track for Summer Start," *Los Angeles Times,* March 31, 2003, B1.

38. Terry Pristin, "Trading the Car for the Train," *New York Times,* November 2, 2005.

39. Kurt Streeter, "MTA's New Leader Says He's Ready for Challenge," *Los Angeles Times,* September 30, 2001, B4.

40. Interview with Roger Snoble by author, November 21, 2008, Los Angeles.

41. Ibid.

42. Kurt Streeter, "MTA OKs Budget to Expand Rail and Avoid Fare Increase," *Los Angeles Times,* May 24, 2002, B3.

43. Garrett, "Struggle for Transit Justice," 778.

44. Los Angeles Eastside Corridor Final SEIS/SEIR, November 2, 2001, S-8, -2, -15.

45. Snoble interview.

46. Ibid.

47. Kurt Streeter and Caitlin Liu, "Los Angeles Eastside Rail Line Gets Green Light from MTA," *Los Angeles Times,* March 1, 2002, B4.

48. Garrett, "Struggle for Transit Justice," 803.

49. Ari B. Bloomekatz and Hector Becerra, "After Decades of Waiting, Their Trains Have Arrived," *Los Angeles Times,* November 16, 2009, A1.

50. MTA Ridership Statistics, www.metro.net/news/pages/ridership-statistics (accessed June 19, 2013).

51. Clarke interview.

52. Ibid.

53. Ibid.

54. Kurt Streeter, "Transit Nerds Making Themselves Heard," *Los Angeles Times,* November 12, 2002, B1.

55. Clarke interview.

56. Ibid.

57. Douglas P. Shuit, "MTA OKs Downtown-Westside Light Rail," *Los Angeles Times,* June 29, 2001, B4.

58. Streeter, "Transit Nerds Making Themselves Heard."

59. Clarke interview.

60. Shuit, "MTA OKs Downtown-Westside Light Rail."

61. Los Angeles Mid-City/Westside Transit Corridor Final SEIS/SEIR, October 2005, 8; available at http://libraryarchives.metro.net/DPGTL/eirs/Expo /ExpositionPhaseOneFEIR.htm (accessed June 17, 2013).

62. Kurt Streeter, "MTA Scales Back Projects," Los Angeles Times, December 5, 2003, B4.

63. Caitlin Liu, "MTA to Borrow $1.1 Billion to Speed Up Delayed Projects," *Los Angeles Times,* September 24, 2004, 4.

64. SB 504 (Kuehl, Chapter 7, Statutes of 2003); available at leginfo.ca.gov /pub/03–04/bill/sen/sb_0501–0550/sb_504_bill_20031011_chaptered.pdf (accessed June 12, 2013).

65. Los Angeles Mid-City/Westside Transit Corridor Final SEIS/SEIR, October 2005, 3.

66. Editorial, "Westward Ho," *Los Angeles Times,* December 4, 2004, B20.

67. Martha Groves, "MTA's Plan for Westside Transit Line Detours South," *Los Angeles Times,* October 8, 2005, A1.

68. Ibid.

69. Notes by the author, Expo Groundbreaking Ceremony, Los Angeles, September 29, 2006.

70. Interview with Ken Alpern by author, September 29, 2006, Los Angeles.

71. Expo Groundbreaking Ceremony notes.

72. Gene Maddaus, "L.A.'s Light-Rail Fiasco," *Los Angeles Weekly,* December 2, 2010.

73. Rubin interview.

74. Maddaus, "L.A.'s Light-Rail Fiasco."

75. Clarke interview.

76. Maddaus, "L.A.'s Light-Rail Fiasco."

77. Clarke interview.

78. Ibid.

79. Ibid.

80. Neal R. Peirce, "Curitiba's World-Class Congestion Cure," *Washington Post Writers Group,* March 20, 2000; available at lightrailnow.org/facts/fa_cur01.htm (accessed June 12, 2013).

81. Ibid.

82. Yaroslavsky interview.

83. Jeffrey L. Rabin, "Voters Force a Detour for MTA Subway Builders," *Los Angeles Times,* November 27, 1998, B1.

84. Garrett, "Struggle for Transit Justice," 802.

85. Caitlin Liu, "Road Is Paved for Valley Busway's Opening Day," *Los Angeles Times,* October 26, 2005, B2.

86. Yaroslavsky interview.

CHAPTER TEN

1. Criollo interview.

2. Sharon Bernstein and Caitlin Liu, "Cars Jam Road to Victory," *Los Angeles Times,* February 19, 2005, B14.

3. Ibid., B1.

4. Ibid., B14.

5. Ibid.

6. Steve Hymon, "Cliches Are as Persistent as the Crises at King/Drew," *Los Angeles Times,* October 16, 2006, B2.

7. Eric Berkowitz, "The Subway Mayor: How a Bus-Only Politician—and a Car-Obsessed City—Are Learning to Love the Underground," *Los Angeles Weekly,* August 18, 2005; available at www.laweekly.com/news/features/the-subway-mayor/349/?page=1 (accessed June 19, 2013).

8. Starting in 1991, Beverly Hills leaders tried to convince Waxman to change his mind, with no luck. Beverly Hills mayor Allan Alexander gathered representatives from various civic and cultural institutions to get the subway extended down Wilshire (Letter to Ed Edelman from Phil [no last name given], February 26, 1992, in EEP, Box 593, Folder 5), and Vicki Reynolds, who became the new mayor of Beverly Hills in 1992, also supported Metro Rail service down Wilshire and began

calling local politicians to expand the coalition to persuade Congressman Waxman to change his mind. She advocated a subway route that would dip south of Fairfax and then rejoin Wilshire Boulevard at Curson. Although Curson lay within Waxman's methane zone, it avoided the heart of the Jewish community on Wilshire that resisted the subway. As a staffer of Supervisor Edelman described, "A Curson tie in would bypass the core of the Fairfax community whose opposition to a subway may underlie [Waxman's] position" against tunneling in the area (Lettergram to Ed Edelman from Phil [no last name given], May 7, 1991, in EEP, Box 606, Folder 1).

Local leaders then met with Waxman on Valentine's Day 1992, including former mayor and now Beverly Hills city council member Allan Alexander, top officials from local urban planning and architecture groups, the chairman of the board of the Los Angeles County Museum of Art, and the president of the American Jewish Committee in Los Angeles (Agenda, Meeting with Henry Waxman, February 14, 1992, 1, in TBP, Box 78, Folder 3). But Waxman refused to budge, reiterating that his only concern was methane and its effect on public safety. Later that year, when the LACTC showed inclinations to extend the subway west, both Waxman and Congressman Dixon inserted language into the federal subway funding bill that required the LACTC to adopt a subway extension south of the methane zone from Wilshire and Western or else risk delaying the entire funding package for MOS-3 (Memo to Planning and Mobility Improvement Committee from Neil Peterson, March 11, 1992, 2, in TBP, Box 78, Folder 3.). The LACTC had no choice but to follow suit (LACTC Meeting Minutes, March 25, 1992, 11; available at http://boardarchives.metro.net/PredecessorAgencies/LACTC%20Box%2001/LACTC00311.pdf [accessed June 19, 2013]), and an unperturbed Waxman was pilloried in the press. The *Los Angeles Times* ran a story quoting extensively from some of the original delegation to Waxman's office, including Maguire and Beverly Hills city councilman Allan Alexander (Mark A. Stein, "Group Attacks Diversion of Subway Route," *Los Angeles Times,* April 1, 1992, B1). Next to the story was a science piece on construction experts' unanimous conclusion that tunneling under Wilshire would be safe (Thomas Maugh, "Gas Explosions in Tunnels Easily Avoided, Experts Say," *Los Angeles Times,* April 1, 1992, B1). And an editorial on KNX 1070 Newsradio blasted Waxman for forcing a less practical subway extension. "So why are we about to spend more to attract fewer riders?" the station asked its listeners. It then answered its own question: "Because a stubborn congressman won't budge from an outmoded, ill-founded decision" (KNX Editorial, April 7, 1992, in TBP, Box 78, Folder 3.)

9. Snoble interview.

10. Berkowitz, "Subway Mayor."

11. Caitlin Lu and Jessica Garrison, "Council Backs Expansion of the Red Line," *Los Angeles Times,* September 29, 2004, B3.

12. Martha Groves, "Waxman Rethinks Tunneling Ban," *Los Angeles Times,* November 29, 2005, B1.

13. Victor Merina, "Residents Swipe at Subway Corridor Development Plan," *Los Angeles Times,* August 2, 1985, B2.

14. Berkowitz, "Subway Mayor."

15. Martha Groves, "In a Reversal, Waxman Backs Westside Subway," *Los Angeles Times,* December 17, 2005, B1.

16. Berkowitz, "Subway Mayor."

17. Richard Fausset, "Experts Dig into Subway Project," *Los Angeles Times,* October 15, 2005, B1.

18. Richard Fausset, "Building Subway beneath Wilshire Deemed Safe," *Los Angeles Times,* October 28, 2005, B4.

19. Waxman interview.

20. Snoble interview.

21. Groves, "In a Reversal, Waxman Backs Westside Subway," B1.

22. Waxman interview.

23. "House Lifts Obstacles to Westside Subway," *Los Angeles Times,* February 8, 2007, B1.

24. Office of Congressman Henry Waxman, "Issues and Legislation: Metro Rail," www.house.gov/waxman/issues/issues_other_metro_rail.htm (accessed 2009).

25. Yaroslavsky interview.

26. Noam N. Levey, "Subway Tunnel Ban May Be Lifted," *Los Angeles Times,* September 19, 2006, B1.

27. Jeffrey L. Rabin and Howard Blume, "Cost of Building Expo Line Rises 23%," *Los Angeles Times,* November 2, 2007, B1.

28. Jeffrey L. Rabin and Rong-Gong Lin II, "MTA Rail Projects May Not Get There Despite Fare Hike," *Los Angeles Times,* May 26, 2007, A1.

29. Jean Guccione, "MTA Budget Boosts Services," *Los Angeles Times,* May 26, 2006, B4.

30. Interview with Terry O'Day by author, December 4, 2008, Santa Monica.

31. Interview with Denny Zane by author, December 11, 2008, by phone.

32. O'Day interview.

33. Transit planners had been discussing the light rail line down Crenshaw Boulevard ever since the 1992 riots, which took place in the heart of that corridor. By 2008, MTA staff began seriously examining either a light rail or busway down Crenshaw. The line would travel from the Crenshaw station on the Expo line and head down Crenshaw Boulevard to the Green Line. The MTA considered bus rapid transit for the route. This option was much cheaper than light rail. But given that MTA studies determined that ridership would be high, the agency's 2008 plan assumed that it would build light rail (MTA, Draft 2008 Long Range Transportation Plan, 26; final version available at www.metro.net/projects/reports [accessed June 17, 2013]). The agency earmarked $955 million in funding for the project (Gene Maddaus, "Crenshaw Rail Plans Back on Track?," *Daily Breeze,* October 8, 2007, A1). One of the critical benefits to the Crenshaw line was that it finally offered planners a way to reach LAX by rail. The LAX component helped Crenshaw line boosters assemble critical political support. Supervisor Yvonne Brathwaite Burke had worked for over a decade on the MTA board to get the line

built. With the LAX connection, city council members from the area were now supportive as well. Councilmen Bill Rosendahl, occupying former councilwoman Ruth Galanter's seat, and Bernard Parks had already been clamoring to get a LAX extension of the Green Line ("Councilmen Seek Rail Line Extension to LAX," *Los Angeles Times,* July 6, 2006, B4). Under Rosendahl's leadership, the city council set aside $250,000 for the MTA to study the line. The project even had Supervisor Antonovich's support. His office publicly blamed airport officials for trying to protect their parking revenue by opposing the extension (Jean Guccione, "Proposed Rail Line Would Go to LAX," *Los Angeles Times,* October 23, 2006, B1).

34. MTA, Draft 2008 Long Range Transportation Plan, 26.

35. Steve Hymon, "Gold Line Extension Plays Cruel Joke on Riders," *Los Angeles Times,* October 1, 2007, B2.

36. Noam N. Levey, "Competing Maps for L.A. Transit," *Los Angeles Times,* September 13, 2006, B3.

37. Richard Simon, "Golden State Has Its Hand Out for Long Green," *Los Angeles Times,* December 10, 2003, A20.

38. Caitlin Liu and Kurt Streeter, "MTA Rolls Out Name Change for New Valley Bus Corridor," *Los Angeles Times,* January 23, 2004, B4.

39. Caitlin Liu, "Gold Line Extension Switches to Fast Track," *Los Angeles Times,* August 22, 2005, B1.

40. Ibid.

41. Caitlin Liu, "Gov.'s Plan Targets Southland Traffic Hot Spots," *Los Angeles Times,* February 13, 2006, B2.

42. Steve Hymon, "Panning for Gold Line Funding," *Los Angeles Times,* June 18, 2008, B3.

43. Kurt Streeter, "Gold Line So Far Has Few Takers," *Los Angeles Times,* March 8, 2004, B3.

44. Steve Hymon and Dan Weikel, "MTA Seeks Sales Tax Hike," *Los Angeles Times,* July 25, 2008, A1.

45. Ibid.

46. Hymon, "Panning for Gold Line Funding," B3.

47. Snoble interview.

48. Letter to David Dreier from Roger Snoble, August 21, 2008, http://latimes-blogs.latimes.com/bottleneck/2008/08/snoble-fires-ba.html (accessed September 2008).

49. Letter to Roger Snoble from Michael Antonovich, August 29, 2008, http://latimesblogs.latimes.com/bottleneck/2008/08/antonovich-to-s.html (accessed September 2008).

50. Steve Hymon and Garrett Therolf, "L.A. County Sales Tax Hike for Transit Hits Roadblock," *Los Angeles Times,* August 6, 2008, A1.

51. "Public Transit Ego Trips," *Los Angeles Times,* August 6, 2008, A20.

52. Steve Hymon and Garrett Therolf, "L.A. County Supervisor Says He Will Vote to Put MTA Sales Tax Hike on November Ballot," *Los Angeles Times,* August 8, 2008, B3.

53. O'Day interview.

54. Hymon and Therolf, "L.A. County Supervisor Says He Will Vote to Put MTA Sales Tax Hike on November Ballot."

55. Tim Rutten, "Transit Held Hostage," *Los Angeles Times,* August 13, 2008, A17.

56. Zane interview.

57. Steve Hymon, "Middle Ground Found in Debate on Sales Tax Hike," *Los Angeles Times,* August 14, 2008, B3.

58. Zane interview.

59. Steve Hymon, "Sales Tax Hike Could Fund Subway to Sea," *Los Angeles Times,* January 11, 2008, B1.

60. Valley Industry and Commerce Association, ballot support website, www.vica.com/documents/Nov.%20Ballot%20positions (accessed 2008); Steve Hymon, "Auto Club Supports Measure R," *Los Angeles Times,* Bottleneck Blog, September 3, 2008, http://latimesblogs.latimes.com/bottleneck/2008/09/auto-club-suppo.html (accessed September 2008).

61. Phil Willon, "Mayor Villaraigosa Urges Business Leaders to Support Half-Cent Sales Tax," *Los Angeles Times,* September 6, 2008.

62. Zane interview.

63. Ibid.

64. "Villaraigosa Fails SoCal on Transportation Measure," *Pasadena Star News,* August 30, 2008; available at www.pasadenastarnews.com/ci_10345932 (accessed June 17, 2013).

65. Zane interview.

66. O'Day interview.

67. Zane interview.

68. David Zahniser, Steve Hymon, and Martha Groves, "Close Vote on Transit Sales-Tax Hike," *Los Angeles Times,* November 5, 2008, A22.

69. MTA, Sales Tax Measure, Attachment 2, July 29, 2008, 2; available at www.metro.net/board/Items/2008/07_July/20080724RBMItem36Rev.pdf (accessed June 17, 2013).

70. Ibid.

71. Rich Connell, Steve Hymon, and Eric Bailey, "Challenges Accelerate for Transit," *Los Angeles Times,* November 6, 2008, A1.

72. Patrick McGreevy and Martha Groves, "More than 60% of Eligible California Voters Went to Polls," *Los Angeles Times,* December 3, 2008, A3.

73. O'Day interview.

74. Yaroslavsky interview.

75. "Interest in New Urbanism is strongest among those over age 60 and those under age 40." See Gregg Logan, Stephanie Siejka, and Shyam Kannan, "The Market for Smart Growth," 5; available at www.epa.gov/smartgrowth/pdf/logan.pdf (accessed November 21, 2012).

76. Connell, Hymon, and Bailey, "Challenges Accelerate for Transit," A1.

1. Dean Murphy and Ronald B. Taylor, "Riders Get First Look at Blue Line Light Rail Transit," *Los Angeles Times,* July 15, 1990, A1.

2. Pine Avenue in the middle of the Blue Line transit mall has seen a resurgence since the 1980s, following the introduction of rail service. See Nancy Wride, "Long Beach Sees Successes, Growing Pains," *Los Angeles Times,* September 28, 2006, B2.

3. Terry Pristin, "Trading the Car for the Train," *New York Times,* November 2, 2005.

4. Erick Guerra and Robert Cervero, "Transit and the 'D' Word," *ACCESS: The Magazine of UCTC [University of California Transportation Center],* no. 40 (Spring 2012): 4–5; available at www.uctc.net/access/40/access40.pdf (accessed June 19, 2013).

5. Move L.A., "Accomplishments of 2011," December 2011, www.movela.org /PDF/2011Accomplishments.pdf (accessed January 2012).

6. Los Angeles County Metropolitan Transportation Authority, "Crenshaw /LAX Transit Corridor," www.metro.net/projects/crenshaw_corridor (accessed December 20, 2012).

7. Gene Maddaus, "Crenshaw Rail Plans Back on Track?" *Daily Breeze,* October 8, 2007, A1.

8. Jean Guccione, "Proposed Rail Line Would Go to LAX," *Los Angeles Times,* October 23, 2006, B1.

9. County of Los Angeles Registrar-Recorder, "Los Angeles County Measure J," 2012, available at http://rrccmain.co.la.ca.us/0012_CountyMeasure_Frame.htm (accessed December 20, 2012).

10. Move L.A., "Accomplishments of 2011."

11. Stanger interview.

12. These restrictions typically involve local zoning codes that restrict the size of buildings, number of stories, types of uses allowed, and distance from sidewalks, to name just a few. In desirable areas where outspoken neighbors form community groups to oppose development, these codes effectively prohibit urban-style projects. Melvin Webber, for example, describes the Rockridge neighborhood in Oakland restricting development around its BART station in *The BART Experience: What Have We Learned?,* Monograph No. 26, Institute of Urban and Regional Development and Institute of Transportation Studies, University of California, Berkeley, October 1976, 15. Statutes and regulations also drive up the costs of these developments sometimes beyond profitability, such as requirements for expensive environmental review and excessive parking requirements. For example, Sacramento's zoning code requires that beauty shops provide one parking space per 250 gross square feet; banks, one space per 400 gross square feet; bowling alleys, six spaces per lane (Sacramento City Code 17.64.020: Parking requirement by land use type).

13. Scott L. Bottles, *Los Angeles and the Automobile: The Making of the Modern City* (Berkeley: University of California Press, 1987), 253.

14. For example, a U.S. Environmental Protection Agency (EPA) survey of residential building permit data in the fifty largest metropolitan areas between 1990 and 2009 showed a substantial increase in the share of new construction built in central cities and older suburbs, including a particularly dramatic rise during the 2005–2009 years covering the real estate downturn compared to 2000–2004. Over half of all new homes in Los Angeles were built in previously developed areas (although these numbers do not include neighboring counties within the metropolitan sphere), while the core areas of the Los Angeles metropolitan region experienced an increase from 23 to 34 percent of the overall share of residential building permits. See U.S. EPA, "Residential Construction Trends in America's Metropolitan Regions," January 2010, 1 and 10, and December 2012, iii–iv; available at epa.gov/smartgrowth /construction_trends.htm (accessed June 17, 2013). Studies from the Urban Land Institute and other scholars documented similar trends. See Christopher B. Leinberger, *The Option of Urbanism: Investing in a New American Dream* (Washington, D.C.: Island Press, 2009); and Urban Land Institute/PricewaterhouseCoopers, "Best Bets: 2007—Emerging Trends in Real Estate 2007," www.uli.org/wp-content /uploads/ULI-Documents/EmergingTrendsUs2007.pdf (accessed June 17, 2013).

BIBLIOGRAPHY

PRIMARY SOURCES

Manuscript Collections

Jacki Bacharach Collection, Dorothy Peyton Gray Transportation Library and Archives, Los Angeles.

Tom Bradley Papers (TBP), University of California, Los Angeles, Department of Special Collections, University Library, Los Angeles.

Ed Edelman Papers (EEP), Huntington Library, San Marino, California.

Kenneth Hahn Papers (KHP), Huntington Library, San Marino, California.

James Hahn Papers, Los Angeles City Archive, Los Angeles.

U.S. Department of Transportation (DOT), Urban Mass Transportation Authority, National Archives and Records Administration II (NARA), College Park, Maryland.

Interviews

Ken Alpern, September 29, 2006, Los Angeles.

Jacki Bacharach, March 13, 2009, Los Angeles.

Darrell Clarke, May 3, 2011, Santa Monica.

Manuel Criollo, June 30, 2009, Los Angeles.

Bevan Dufty, December 17, 2012, San Francisco.

Ed Edelman, December 9, 2004, Los Angeles.

Ruth Galanter, December 3, 2008, Los Angeles.

Robert Garcia, February 19, 2010, phone interview.

Jeff Gates, February 23, 2008, phone interview.

Robert Geoghegan, August 30, 2005, Santa Monica; and October 19, 2012, phone interview.

Marv Holen, September 27, 2005, Los Angeles.

Con Howe, May 2, 2011, Los Angeles (background; not quoted in book).

Ronald J. Lofy, November 19, 2008, phone interview.
Ed McSpedon, March 14, 2009, Los Angeles.
Terry O'Day, December 4, 2008, Santa Monica, California.
James Okazaki, January 26, 2008, Los Angeles.
Neil Peterson, December 5, 2012, phone interview.
Jeffrey Rabin, August 27, 2009, San Francisco.
Ray Remy, February 3, 2006, South Pasadena.
David Roberti, November 20, 2008, Los Angeles.
Thomas Rubin, November 18, 2008, Los Angeles.
Zachary Schrag, December 18, 2008, Arlington, Va. (background; not quoted in book).
James Seeley, December 18, 2008, Washington, D.C.
Roger Snoble, November 21, 2008, Los Angeles.
Richard Stanger, November 16, 2012, phone interview.
George Takei, June 16, 2009, Los Angeles.
Henry Waxman, April 13, 2009, phone interview.
Mike Woo, November 5, 2007, West Hollywood.
Zev Yaroslavsky, November 19, 2008, Los Angeles.
Denny Zane, December 11, 2008, phone interview.

SECONDARY SOURCES

Altshuler, Alan, and David Luberoff. *Mega-Projects: The Changing Politics of Urban Public Investment.* Washington, D.C.: Brookings Institution Press, 2003.
Beebe, Rose Marie, and Robert M. Senkewicz, eds. *Lands of Promise and Despair: Chronicles of Early California, 1535–1846.* Berkeley, Ca.: Heyday Books, 2001.
Bottles, Scott L. *Los Angeles and the Automobile: The Making of the Modern City.* Berkeley: University of California Press, 1987.
Bradley, Thomas. "The Impossible Dream: Oral History Transcript." Oral History Collection, Dept. of Special Collections, University Library, University of California, Los Angeles, 1984 (interviewed by Bernard Galm, 1978 and 1979). Available at http://archive.org/details/impossibledreamoooobrad.
Brown, Marilyn A., Frank Southworth, and Andrea Sarzynski. "Shrinking the Carbon Footprint of Metropolitan America." Brookings Institution, May 29, 2008. Available at www.brookings.edu/research/reports/2008/05/carbon-footprint-sarzynski.
Calthorpe, Peter. *The Next American Metropolis: Ecology, Community, and the American Dream.* New York: Princeton Architectural Press, 1993.
Cervero, Robert. *The Transit Metropolis: A Global Inquiry.* Washington, D.C.: Island Press, 1998.
Divall, Colin, and Winstan Bond, eds. *Suburbanizing the Masses: Public Transport and Urban Development in Historical Perspective.* Aldershot, Hants., Eng., and Burlington, Vt.: Ashgate Publishing, 2003.

Fogelson, Robert M. *The Fragmented Metropolis: Los Angeles, 1850–1930*. Berkeley: University of California Press, 1993.

Fulton, William. *The Reluctant Metropolis: The Politics of Urban Growth in Los Angeles*. Baltimore: Johns Hopkins University Press, 2001.

Garrett, Mark. "The Struggle for Transit Justice: Race, Space, and Social Equity in Los Angeles." Ph.D. diss., University of California, Los Angeles, 2006.

Guerra, Erick, and Robert Cervero. "Transit and the 'D' Word." *ACCESS: The Magazine of UCTC [University of California Transportation Center]*, no. 40 (Spring 2012). Available at www.uctc.net/access/40/access40_transitanddensity.shtml.

Holcombe, Randall G., and Samuel R. Staley, eds. *Smarter Growth: Market-Based Strategies for Land Use Planning in the 21st Century*. Westport, Conn.: Greenwood Press, 2001.

Lund, Hollie M., Robert Cervero, and Richard W. Wilson. "Travel Characteristics of Transit-Oriented Development in California." CalTrans Transportation Grant, January 2004. Available at www.bart.gov/docs/planning/travel_of_tod.pdf.

Meyer, John R., John F. Kain, and Martin Wohl. *The Urban Transportation Problem*. Cambridge, Mass.: Harvard University Press, 1965.

Pushkarev, Boris, and Jeffrey Zupan. *Urban Rail in America: An Exploration of Criteria for Fixed-Guideway Transit*. Washington, D.C.: Urban Mass Transportation Administration, U.S. Department of Transportation, 1980.

Richmond, Jonathan. *Transport of Delight: The Mythical Conception of Rail Transit in Los Angeles*. Akron, Ohio: University of Akron Press, 2005.

Schneider, Jack. "Escape from Los Angeles: White Flight from Los Angeles and Its Schools, 1960–1980." *Journal of Urban History* 34 (2008). Available at http://juh.sagepub.com/cgi/content/abstract/34/6/995.

Schrag, Zachary M. *The Great Society Subway: A History of the Washington Metro*. Baltimore: Johns Hopkins University Press, 2006.

Schrank, David, Tim Lomax, and Shawn Turner. "2012 Urban Mobility Report, Texas Transportation Institute." Texas Transportation Institute, Texas A&M University, Dec. 2012.

Smith, James. *Memoirs, Letters, and Comic Miscellanies in Prose and Verse of the Late James Smith*. Vol. 2. Edited by Horace Smith, Esq. London: Henry Colburn Publisher, 1840.

Stone, Clarence N. *Regime Politics: Governing Atlanta, 1946–1988*. Lawrence: University Press of Kansas, 1989.

Taylor, Brian D., Eugene J. Kim, and John E. Gahbauer. "The Thin Red Line: A Case Study of Political Influence on Transportation Planning Practice." *Journal of Planning Education and Research* 29, no. 2 (2009).

Wachs, Martin. "Autos, Transit, and the Sprawl of Los Angeles: The 1920s." *Journal of the American Planning Association* 50 (1984): 297–310, 1984. Available at www.tandfonline.com/doi/abs/10.1080/01944368408976597.

———. "Learning from Los Angeles: Transport, Urban Form, and Air Quality." Seventh Smeed Memorial Lecture at University College, London; Working

Paper No. 166, University of California Transportation Center, May 1993. Available at www.uctc.net/papers/166.pdf.

Webber, Melvin M. "The BART Experience: What Have We Learned?" Institute of Urban and Regional Development and Institute of Transportation Studies, University of California, Berkeley, Monograph No. 26, October 1976. Available atwww.nationalaffairs.com/public_interest/detail/the-bart-experience-what-have-we-learned.

Zwerling, Stephen. *Mass Transit and the Politics of Technology: A Study of BART and the San Francisco Bay Area*. New York: Praeger, 1974.

INDEX

Page numbers in italics refer to illustrations.

Eight-Point Plan, MTA, 150
Ellickson, Robert, 26
El Monte, 31, 214
El Salvador, 19
El Segundo, 65, 67, 68, *69*, 132
Emerson, Norm, 17, 32
Engineering Management Consultants, 120
Environmental Defense, 63
Environmental Impact Statement (EIS), 85, 140, 163–64
environmental movement, 8, 15, 26, 55, 63, 159–60, 175, 180, 205–7, 213
Environmental Protection Agency (EPA), U.S., 276n14
environmental review, 141, 175, 186, 275n12; of Expo Line, 190, 193; of Green Line, 128, 131; mitigation of impacts identified in, 224–25; of San Fernando Valley routes, 134
Environment Now, 206, 207
Exposition (Expo) Line, 128, 137, 176, 186, 188–91, *192*, *219*, 225; advocates of, 138, 144, 189–91, 193, 196, 224; connection of Green Line to. *See* Crenshaw line; construction of, 191, 193–95, 206, 218; funding of, 207, 210, 211; homeowner opposition to, 138–41, 143, 152, 180, 188–89, 194–96; opening of, *196*, 218, 223; purchase of railroad right-of-way for, 122, 125, 139, 140, 188; ridership potential of, 55, 197; transit-oriented development projects along, 217
Exposition Park, 98

Fairfax, 79–83, *81*, 85–88, 93, 95, 96, 100, 107, 108, 135, 218, 271n8
Fasana, John, 190, 210–11
Fast-Track Anti-Gridlock Transit Improvement Proposition. *See* Proposition C
Federal Aviation Administration (FAA), 131, 254n42, 255n43
Federal Bureau of Investigation (FBI), 149, 180
Federal Transit Administration (FTA), 117, 119, 152, 154, 155, 177–79, 182, 186, 211–12
Feinstein, Dianne, 205
Ferraro, John, 88
Feuer, Mike, 207, 212–13

Fiedler, Bobbi, 92, 93, 257n70
Fine, Julie, 135
Firestone Boulevard corridor, 55, 58
Fogelson, Robert M., 231n25
Ford, Gerald, 19, 70, 169
Foshay Learning Center (Los Angeles), 194
Freemark, Yonah, 256n58
freeways, 23, 26–27, 39, 40, 47, 134, 136, 137. *See also* Century Freeway; clogged. *See* traffic congestion
Friends4Expo, 190–91, 193, 196, 224
Fritsch, Jane, 148–49
Fukai, Mas, 148
Fulton, William, 6, 232n28

Gahbauer, John, 230n11
Galanter, Ruth, 131, 140–41, 254n41, 254–55n43, 273n33
Garcia, Robert, 162–63, 165–67, 170, 171
Gardena, 40
gasoline shortages, 46
gas tax, 14–16, 19–20, 21, 23, 52, 75–76, 123, 191, 242n51
Gates, Jeff, 64
Gehry, Frank, 107
General Accounting Office, 149, 155
General Motors, 159
gentrification, 1, 10, 80, 84, 86
Geoghegan, Bob, 39–43, 54, 55, 65–68, 70, 91, 94, 238n35, 257n70, 258n80
Georgia, 28, 29. *See also* Atlanta
Germany, 52, 148
gerrymandering, 82
Getty Oil, 45
Gianturco, Adriana, 64
Gilmore, Arthur Fremont, 79
Gilstrap, Jack, 20
Glendale, 38
Goldberg, Jackie, 120
Gold Line, *xviii–xix*, 179, 183, *184*, 195, 217, 224. *See also* Pasadena line; connector between Blue Line and, 199, *220*, 220; extensions of, *22*, 185, *187*, 187–88, 193, 194, 207–11, 224. *See also* Eastside, light rail line to
Goldschmidt, Neil, 56
Gordon, Peter, 3, 25–26, 61, 167
Grabinsky, Ray, 124, 146, 147

National Association for the Advancement of Colored People (NAACP), 55, 174, 175; Legal Defense Fund (LDF), 162–63, 165–68, 170

National Association of Realtors, 232n34

National Environmental Policy Act (NEPA; 1970), 63–64

Natural Resources Defense Council (NRDC), 175

Neusom, Tom, 56

New Deal, 5, 14

Newman, Randy, 121

New York City, 29, 30, 32, 118; John F. Kennedy International Airport, 256n58

New York Times, 116, 185

New York Transportation Commission, 151

Nicaragua, 19

NIMBY (Not In My Backyard), 10, 95–96

Nixon, Richard M., 15

North Hollywood, subway to, 74–75, 77, 127, 134, 152, 176, 178. *See also* Red Line; Burbank links to, 125, 136; construction of station for, 91; opening of, 182; opposition to light rail as alternative to, 136–37; tunnel under Santa Monica mountains for, 75, 98

Northridge Earthquake, 137, 258n80

Norwalk, 66, *69*, 132, 208

Oakland, 189, 275n12

Oakland–San Francisco Bay Bridge, 145

Obama, Barack, 205

Occidental Petroleum, 45

O'Connor, Pam, 190, 191, *196*, 207

O'Day, Terry, 206, 207, 212, 214, 216

oil fields, 79, 84. *See also* methane gas

Okazaki, James, 110, 111, 131

Olympic Games, 59, 109, 112

Orange County, 17, 23, 36, 66, 132

Orange Line, 197, *198*, *199*, 199, 221

Oropeza, Jenny, 212–13

Owens Valley Aqueduct, 40, 112

Pacific Electric light rail system, *7*, 26, 34, 35, 111, 187; nostalgia for, 8, 19, 23, 27; Red Cars, 6, 51–53, 55, 109, 112, 189; right-of-way of, 59, 234n36; Santa Monica Air Line, 138; Yellow Cars, 6, 96, 112

Page, Richard, 30

Page Museum, 75, 244n108

Palm Springs, 149

Palos Verdes, 68, 135, 136

Paramount, 125

Park Mile Plan, 84

Parks, Bernard, 273n33

Parsons Brinckerhoff Quade & Douglas, Inc., 55, 58

Parsons-Dillingham, 117

Pasadena line, 154, 159, 176, 178, 191, 227, 259n101. *See also* Gold Line; completion of, 199; extension of, 186, 190; funding shortfalls for, 152–54, 157, 177; Metro Blue Line Construction Authority (PMBLCA) for, 183, 185; politically powerful backers of, 182–83; Proposition C and funding of, 124, 125, 127, 128, 136, 141–44

Pasadena Star News, 214

Passenger Rail and Clean Air Bond Act (1990). *See* Proposition 108

patronage, 143. *See also* ridership; potential, 21, 55, 67–68, 70, 142; systemwide decline in, 165

Patsaouras, Nick, *99*, 112, 150, 172

Peña, Federico, 117, 152, 155

Peterson, Mark William, 256n58

Peterson, Neil, 112, 122–24, 126, 127, 136, 143, 147–49

Pico Rivera, 215

Pico–San Vicente subway extension, 189

Pierce, Ted, 66

Plotkin, Diana, 84, 203

Polanco, Richard, 183

population density. *See* density

Post Office, U.S., 68

Proctor, Richard, 87

Proposition 5 (1974), 19

Proposition 13 (1978), 38, 53, 58, 128, 214, 242n43

Proposition 108 (1990), 123, 125

Proposition 111 (1990), 123

Proposition 116 (1990), 125

Proposition 209 (1996), 166

Proposition A (1974), 16–18

Proposition A (1980), 122–26, 150, 153, 164, 179, 210; campaign for, 44–47, 123, 126;

and Century Freeway corridor, 64–67. *See also* Green Line; legal challenge to, 53–54, 58–59, 242n51; map produced for, *48*, 133; passage of, 47–51, 61, 89, 138, 142, 215; selection of routes for funding with, 55–58, 64, 112

Proposition A (1998), 179–81, 185, 189, 204, 206, 259n101

Proposition C (1990), 122–29, 137, 191, 206, 210; Pasadena line and, 141, 143–44; passage of, 126–28, 133, 136, 140, 143, 145, 215; for purchase of rights-of-way, 122–26, 160

Proposition U (1988), 78

Pulitzer Prize, 116

Purple Line, *219*

Pushkarev, Boris, 230n11

Rabin, Jeff, 115–16, 119, 121, 155–56, 177, 180, 181

racism, 10, 84–85, 160, 165, 170–75

Rail Implementation Strategy, 142

Ramirez, Marcos Pacheco, 111

Rancho Park, 139–41, 189

Reagan, Ronald, 89–93, 118–19, 142

recessions, 126, 128, 131, 145, 146, 154, 215–16, 224

Red Line, 121, 148, 182, 193, 197, 199; construction of, 122, 149, 164; extensions of, 179, 181, 186; federal funding of, 154, 168, 209; Pasadena line connector to, 142, 259n101

Redondo Beach, 186

Reed, Christine, 124, 139

Reluctant Metropolis, The (Fulton), 6

Remy, Ray, 45, 57, 83, 86; as Bradley's chief of staff, 14, 20, 82, 126, 142; on LACTC, 39–42, 56, 67–68, 70, 123, 143, 257n70

Republican Party, 91–93, 116, 119, 142, 147, 153, 209

Reseda, 135

Reynolds, Vicki, 270n8

Rhine, William, 115

Rice, Constance, 162, 163, 165, 166

Richardson, Harry W., 26–27, 167

Richmond, Jonathan, 61, 229n8

Richmond, Rick, 44

ridership, 3–5, 29, 49, 89, 138, 213, 220. *See also* patronage; BART, 231n16; Blue Line, 217; bus, 17, 94, 158, 163–65, 168–74; Crenshaw line, 221, 272n33; Expo line, 195; Gold Line, 142, 183, 188, 195, 210; Green Line, 66–68, 132–33, 136; Orange line, 197; planning process and increases in, 224–26; in rail decision-making process, 50, 55, 70, 91, 139; of Tijuana Trolley, 52

Ridley-Thomas, Mark, *196*

rights-of-way, 6, 19, 37, 134, 164; for bus rapid transit, 4, 197, *199*; for light rail, 23, 58. *See also specific corridors and lines;* purchase of, 52–53, 122–26, 139, 143, 160, 234n36

Riordan, Richard, 153–55, 162, 171–72, 178, 182, 190, 197, 201

Riverside County, 36

Robbins, Alan, 91, 136, 150

Roberti, David, 74–76, 83, 85, 87, 96, 98, 118

Rockwell International, 65

Roos, Mike, 139

Rose Bowl, 141, 183

Rosendahl, Bill, 273n33

Ross Dress-for-Less department store, explosion at, 79–80, *81*, 205

Roybal-Allard, Lucille, 177, 186

Rubin, Tom, 51, 52, 153, 154, 161–62, 166, 168, 170, 171, 173, 194

Rubley, Russell, 41, 42

Russ, Ed, 40, 42, 238n35

Russell, Pat, 42, 58, 151

Sacramento, 275n12

sales tax revenues, 131, 153, 177, 179, 187; ballot initiatives for funding transit with, 19–20, 34–44. *See also* Measure R, *specific propositions*

Salt Lake Oil Field, 79

San Bernardino, 36, 125, 140, 143

Sanchez, Rose, 80

San Diego, 51–52, 234; Freeway, 70

San Fernando Valley, 18, 47, 73, 91, 124, 141, 144, 160, 218, 240n79, 255n43; bus rapid transit line in. *See* Orange Line; homeowner opposition in, 133–37, 139, 143, 152, 257n70; MTA prioritization of rail line to, 154, 186; Orthodox Jewish